HERMENEUTICS AND PRAXIS

REVISIONS
A Series of Books on Ethics

General Editors:
Stanley Hauerwas and Alasdair MacIntyre

Hermeneutics and Praxis

ROBERT HOLLINGER, editor

UNIVERSITY OF NOTRE DAME PRESS
NOTRE DAME, INDIANA 46556

Library of Congress Cataloging in Publication Data

Main entry under title:

Hermeneutics and praxis.

    1. Heidegger, Martin, 1889-1976 — Addresses, essays,
lectures. 2. Gadamer, Hans Georg, 1900-   — Addresses,
essays, lectures. 3. Rorty, Richard — Addresses, essays,
lectures. 4. Hermeneutics — Addresses, essays, lectures.
5. Pragmatism — Addresses, essays, lectures. I. Hollinger,
Robert.
B3279.H49H385   1985   121'.68   85-40599
ISBN 0-268-01080-3
ISBN 0-268-01081-1 (pbk.)

Manufactured in the United States of America

CONTENTS

PART IV: HERMENEUTICS AND PRAGMATISM:
CONFRONTATION, CONVERGENCE, AND CRITIQUE

ACKNOWLEDGMENTS

I would like to thank Professors Alasdair MacIntyre and Stanley Hauerwas, the editors of the University of Notre Dame Press's Revisions Series, for their willingness to publish this collection. I would also like to thank Mr. James Langford, the director of the University of Notre Dame Press, for his cooperation and advice. Professor MacIntyre was very helpful in providing sound editorial advice from the beginning; I am especially indebted to him for his generosity and assistance. Mr. Joseph Wilder of Notre Dame Press has been of great help in preparing the manuscript for publication. My department secretary, Edna Wiser, prepared part of the typescript for Mr. Wilder's task of getting the typescript ready for the printers.

Thanks are due to the authors of the papers reprinted here, and to the journals and editors who gave us permission to reprint.

To I.P.R. Associates for "The Happening of Tradition," *Man and World*, vol. 2, no. 3 (1969); to the editor and publisher of the *Journal of the British Society of Phenomenology* for "Hermeneutics and Truth," first published in that journal, vol. 15, no. 1 (1984); to the editor and publisher of the *Review of Metaphysics* for "Philosophy in the Conversation of Mankind," "Holism and Hermeneutics," "From Hermeneutics to *Praxis*," and "The Thought of Being and the Conversation of Mankind," published respectively in nos. 132, 133, 140, 143; to the editors and publishers of *Neue Hefte für Philosophie* for "Epistemological Behaviorism and the De-Transcendentalization of Analytic Philosophy," first published in vol. 9 (1978); to the Philosophy of Science Association for "Reason, Social Practice and Scientific Realism," first published in *The Philosophy of Science*, vol. 48 (1981); to the editor and publisher of *American Philosophical Quarterly* for "Freedom and Constraint by Norms" and "The Rational Governance of Practice," first published respectively in vol. 16 (1979) and vol. 18 (1981); to the editor and publisher of *Philosophy of the Social Sciences* for "On Gadamer's Hermeneutics," first published in vol. 9 (1979); and to the editors and publisher of the *Journal of Philosophy* for "Postmodernist Bourgeois Liberalism" and "Moral Arguments and Social Contexts," both first published in vol. 10 (1983).

INTRODUCTION:
HERMENEUTICS AND PRAGMATISM

This collection of essays focuses on the work of three important philosophers: Martin Heidegger, Hans-Georg Gadamer, and Richard Rorty. I take Heidegger and Gadamer to be the foremost proponents of a style of thought called 'hermeneutics', and Rorty as the defender of at least one tendency in 'pragmatism'. Both movements predate the authors just mentioned; but they have given these styles of thought an importance and currency that warrants attention to their writings.

With the exception of two essays by Rorty, all the other essays are by expositors and critics concerned with the same themes and tendencies within either hermeneutics and pragmatism, or some combination of these. The writings of Heidegger and Gadamer are of course less accessible than those of Rorty, and what has been provided here is important secondary material which will allow the reader to supplement a reading of the original texts and to relate them to Rorty's preoccupations. I have thought it undesirable to include in this collection any essays that have already been anthologized elsewhere or otherwise included in book-length works.

The fruitfulness of comparative and contrastive studies of these two styles of thought, as worked out by Heidegger, Rorty, and Gadamer — including possible syntheses of compatible lines of development — has been one criterion of selection. Otherwise I have selected essays that provide an overall access into the thought of each author, or essays which can be seen as developing one or another line of thought found in their works, so as to allow the reader to explore the ramifications of the most important recent hermeneutical and pragmatist thinking.

In this introduction I want to provide a background for approaching the essays, and thus also the work of Heidegger, Gadamer, and Rorty. Since no brief introduction can do this successfully without severely limiting its field of vision, the remarks that follow will zero in on two sets of themes that set the tone of both styles of thought and provide the basis for comparisons and contrasts between them. The first set of themes, largely critical, has to do with the analysis of certain elements in the philosophical tradition, which center around the role of philosophy and science in Western Culture. The second set of themes, which seeks to provide a non- or anti-philosophical model of culture and community, will be brought out in terms of the related notions of traditions, practices, historicity, and conversation.

THE PHILOSOPHICAL TRADITION AND WESTERN CULTURE

Ever since Socrates, philosophers have aspired to ground culture and everything that transpires within it by appeal to ahistorical, or at least universal and necessary, definitions, criteria, or theories. Ideals of knowledge, truth, rationality, morals, politics, beauty, and human nature are largely motivated by this aspiration. A conceptual net which incorporates fundamental and incontrovertible truths in these areas in a comprehensive system is needed. It would allow human beings to comprehend the world and our place in it, and thereby promote the most satisfying lives for ourselves. In short, philosophy is by-and-large utopian in its aspiration.

Modern philosophy, whose archetypal figures are Descartes and Kant, seeks to provide necessary and universal criteria for discovering truth and universal moral principles. This gives rise to the Enlightenment ideal of the moral and epistemological unity of humankind which was to provide us with the tools for "relieving man's estate" (Bacon) without (theoretical) limit. This led to the notion of a scientific culture, in which everything was either grounded in scientific doctrine or method, or committed to the flames as sophistry and illusion, as Hume put it.

Broadly speaking, this has resulted in the twin crises of modern Western civilization: scientism and nihilism, which are really two sides of the same coin. The followers of Descartes and Kantian epistemology came to advocate the view that only scientific methods and doctrines were of any cognitive or social value. Some results of these ideas are: 1) utilitarianism in morality; 2) technological or instrumental rationality, combined with subjectivism about goals and values in the social

and political realm; 3) the usurpation of all realms of private and public life by experts, e.g., in terms of technique, the latest scientific doctrine, cost-benefit analysis.

At the same time, thanks again to Descartes's influence, and to
the dialectic of Kant's practical philosophy in the nineteenth century,
everything not assimilable to what Heidegger called "the Age of World
as Picture"[1] became "merely" subjective, irrational, or non-rational,
"in here" as opposed to "out there." Thus many versions of romanticism, existentialism, analytic philosophy, as well as movements in literature and high culture, politics and morality, make everything not scientific matters of "mere" (subjective) opinion. This makes everything not
"scientific" subject to either power struggle or indeterminate debate,
and hence to a kind of skepticism, mixed with a kind of dogmatism.

"Objectivism" and "subjectivism" (and "absolutism" and "relativism") appear to contradict each other. But they share a common
assumption: "If God is dead, everything is permitted." Objectivism
believes that there must be either one set of objective (and/or absolute) truth, method, and values or else wholesale skepticism will result.
In practice, this leads to skepticism about existing practices, beliefs,
and values, usually combined with dogmatism about others (namely,
those of science). The nihilist believes the "God" (i.e., objective and
absolute truth and values) is dead; hence we appear to get wholesale
skepticism here. But many nihilists take the customs of their own society
or the personal preferences of individuals as an absolute given.

Both doctrines thus assume that our practices, beliefs, and values
must rule out all other logical possibilities to be rational. Otherwise
they are arbitrary and irrational. Our practices, beliefs, and values are,
for *both* views, either totally rational by some idealized Platonic standard; or else they are totally arbitrary and irrational. (Many scientific
realists today accept the former ideal.) There is no middle ground,
i.e., the recognition that many of our practices, beliefs, and values
are both contingent or historical and rational. I take it that Gadamer,
Heidegger, and Rorty (as well as Dewey and Wittgenstein) want to
work in this "middle ground".[2]

The oscillation between dogmatism and skepticism, bemoaned
by Kant, is thus no coincidence, for they are two sides of the same
coin, just as objectivism and subjectivism (absolutism and relativism)
are. The clearest example of this is the realist, who is often both an
objectivist or absolutist in principle and a skeptic in practice. Hence

the claim that "for all we know all or most of our beliefs might be false." Indeed, on Heidegger's analysis objectivism and absolutism (e.g., scientism) are forms of nihilism.

According to Heidegger, Western culture is pervaded by the will to power: the desire to dominate in order to remake the world to satisfy human (more specifically, Western) desires. Following Nietzsche in this respect, he believes that philosophy and modern science, which replaces philosophy by virtue of succeeding in practice at what philosophy has always advocated as an ideal—the control of the entire planet for human purposes—are essentially technological. Technological civilization is the culmination of the will to power and the culmination of scientism and nihilism as two manifestations of this will. Forms of inquiry and doctrines as various as Hegel's search for absolutely transparent knowledge of the whole, modern versions of scientific realism (e.g., Sellars's), the claim that human beings ought to control the course of evolution, and the beliefs of Dostoyevsky's Underground Man and his existentialist successors, are all manifestations of this same fundamental attitude.

Gadamer uses some of Heidegger's insights in the service of his own project: a systematic critique of the Enlightenment thesis that epistemological method is the road to truth and that everything not guaranteed by such method is mere prejudice and illusion. In other words, the Enlightenment project is the modern form of Platonism. Modern doctrines of objectivism, and their "subjectivist" and relativist counterparts, are equally mistaken. For Gadamer, counter-Enlightenment movements such as romanticism and the German Historical school (e.g., Dilthey) exemplify the dialectics between objectivism and subjectivism outlined above. So, despite his loyalty to the spirit of the counter-Enlightenment, the whole issue of what interpretation and tradition mean must be reworked.

Finally, Rorty's version of pragmatism shares with Heidegger and Gadamer a distrust for the search for philosophical principles to ground culture, our lives and practices, in ahistorical standards. Influenced by James and Dewey, Rorty rejects the belief in ahistorical standards that lie outside all our practices. We must seek for solidarity among ourselves by engaging in the Socratic conversation which makes us what we are and by preserving what's best in the liberal, democratic, Judeo-Christian tradition—without trying to give this tradition any philosophical grounding, but by adopting a more or less ethnocentric attitude toward it. Our social practices are the given within which we must talk and act and improve things as best we can.

There are, to be sure, radical differences among Heidegger, Gadamer, and Rorty on many key issues. These will be mentioned in the next section. But for now I want to mention another similarity: their belief in the finitude and historicity of human life and cultures, and in the rootedness of truth, knowledge, and morality in traditions and social practices. This leads to the notion of an aesthetic or post-Platonic or non-philosophic culture, which takes its bearings from those finite practices and traditions and not from some favored philosophical — i.e., utopian — ideal of how things should be with us. It is this general direction in their thought that needs to be brought out more fully if the positive doctrines of hermeneutics and pragmatism are to be understood and if we are to begin exploring the strengths and weaknesses, similarities and differences, of these two styles of thought.

TRADITIONS, PRACTICES, AND HISTORICITY

For both hermeneutics and pragmatism, the social practices and traditions of a specific historical or cultural world are the horizons of existence. There are no "free floating" universal truths, although the hope always exists that there will be some consensus among cultures about, say, moral ideals, e.g., through what Gadamer dubs "the fusion of horizons": the merging of different outlooks through dialogue and interpretation. But dialogue rests upon the willingness and ability of people in different traditions, or differing people within one tradition, to work toward mutual understanding and cooperation through continued dialogue. This gives rise to a communicative model of community, as shall be seen below. (The question of whether a universal notion of humanity is the ideal behind dialogue and community is an important one. Gadamer gives a more unambiguously affirmative answer to this question than either Rorty or Heidegger.)

To treat practices, traditions, and historicity as the horizons of existence is not to fall into gross subjectivism or relativism. It is to abandon the Platonic quest for a philosophical foundation for culture. But it is also to take seriously Heidegger's view that truth is the disclosure of events as these are encountered against the background of historically specific cultural horizons; a theme already found in early romantics and Herder. The most characteristic doctrines of Heidegger, Gadamer, and Rorty also seek to undercut the assumptions that give rise to the objectivism/subjectivism and absolutism/relativism disputes without falling into nihilism or back to some form of Platonism. To vary Neurath's famous metaphor, our culture and its practices are the vessel on which our earthly sojourn must be made. In Nietzsche's phrase, we must learn to be true to the earth, which means abandoning both Platonism and nihilism. Rather than some version of epistemological relativism, we get something closer to what may be dubbed ontological and cultural pluralism: the idea, as Hannah Arendt puts it, that "plurality is the law of the earth."[3] The appeal to practices, traditions, and historicity is to help stake out the middle ground mentioned earlier. The notions of conversation and interpretation form the basis for a culture and community that is neither Platonic (philosophically grounded) nor subject to continual nihilistic failure of nerve.

This approach makes all the more urgent such questions as how we can distinguish between vital and deformed traditions, and to what extent a dialogue can allow us to do so. The problem is addressed by Bernstein in the final essay, but it comes up throughout many of the articles reprinted here. The short answer is that only further efforts at dialogue about our common practices and history will allow us to advance. In this respect, hermeneutics and pragmatism, while open to a radical critique of our practices, are committed to a kind of immanent Hegelian critique since we cannot stand outside of our history or engage in the sort of wholesale critique of our traditions that philosophers from Socrates to Descartes to Habermas think both necessary and desirable. But, as Will and Brandom explicitly argue, the notion that practices are "rationally governed" and amenable to criticism is part of the outlook of both movements we are discussing.

The ontological force of the doctrine that traditions, social practices, and historicity are the horizons of human existence is sometimes expressed in terms of the contrasts between modern society, with its theoretical culture, and the culture which writers such as Heidegger, Rorty, and Nietzsche claim to see in pre-Socratic Athens. For Rorty, the Sophists were the first intellectual pragmatists. For Gadamer, Aristotle's "practical philosophy," with its emphasis on *praxis* and *phronesis*, is the precursor to modern hermeneutics. And for Heidegger, the Greeks had a pragmatic outlook on life, although it is hard to spell out just what he meant by this. Roughly, Heidegger, like Dewey,[4] thought that there were no sharp divisions for the Greeks among theory, practice, and making, or among *episteme*, *phronesis*, and *techne*. Phenomena were disclosed within a cultural matrix which made no sharp distinction between "subject" and "object," and the Greeks managed to sustain a harmony between the three main spheres of human life. It is only with the rise of philosophy, and later science, with the attempt to order all phenomena in a comprehensive, rational system that Western culture becomes dominated by the desire to control all phenomena, and to level all spheres of culture down to the categories of science. This idea, connected with what Heidegger calls "humanism," "subjectivism," or "nihilism" (all manifestations of the will to power) is a kind of *hubris* which seeks to escape historicity. Philosophy itself, one may say, is a form of the will to power. Here is one difference between Heidegger and Rorty, who defends the liberal humanist tradition against Heidegger and Nietzsche.[5]

Despite their insistence that philosophy is constitutive of Western thought, and despite the presence of a kind of surrogate for the Philosopher-Ruler in the aesthetic or non-philosophical model of culture (a great-souled political or intellectual leader or leaders), Heidegger and to a lesser extent Rorty (but more so Dewey) insist upon the need for a non-philosophical culture and life: Heidegger's idyllic attitude toward the Bavarian peasant—dare we see here the Vermont farmer Dewey knew?—is symbolic of this vision. Is this attempt to use philosophy to destroy philosophy a paradox or contradiction? To some extent this depends upon one's view of dialectical reasoning and the force of "deconstructionist" or "genealogical strategies."

But Heidegger does articulate a notion of truth in terms of the disclosure of phenomena within a cultural context; Gadamer sees truth as the phenomena that are revealed through, and appropriated by, language and tradition; and Rorty takes truth and knowledge to be the result of dialogue or inquiry with one's peers, at least in situations where an open society exists. Even here there are differences between pragmatism and hermeneutics, as can be seen from some of the readings in parts 2 and 4. Although both views see truth and knowledge as tied to traditions and social practices, they differ in terms of how tied we are to our past, to what degree scientific method, construed as Deweyan social intelligence, pushes us in the direction of changing our social practices in order to "cope" better with modern life, and to what extent tradition speaks to us with a univocal voice. Although the notion of phronesis as a kind of practical wisdom that allows traditions to be appropriated in novel and healthy ways is a common element in all three writers, Rorty conceives of culture as without any foundations or center, perhaps because of his greater loyalty to the pluralistic elements at least in our own American past. Gadamer, and surely Heidegger, still want to preserve the place the philosopher occupies in classical culture by a charismatic leader of some sort. Perhaps some divisions between hermeneutics and pragmatism are the result of the differences between European (especially German) experience and ideals and those of our own pluralistic and liberal heritage. However, it can be argued that Gadamer and even Heidegger are open to a form of pluralism, and that Rorty envisions a community with at least the shared ideal of promoting the good of the whole through dialogue.

CONVERSATION, COMMUNITY AND CULTURE

According to Gadamer, Rorty, and Heidegger human language is the vehicle through which traditions are carried on, however modified. The twin ideals of interpretation and dialogue thus play a major role in their works, as they do in major influences on them: Holderlin (on Heidegger), Oakeshott (on Rorty). One can conceive of Socratic dialogue as a model for this ideal, although the language of poets and not only the argumentative language of Socrates is part of the ideal. As Oakeshott puts it, a conversation may contain arguments, but is not reducible to arguments.[6]

The notions of culture and community embedded in this ideal can be seen in Dewey's search for the great community,[7] in Habermas's consensus theory of truth,[8] and in the otherwise diverse views of writers such as MacIntyre[9] and Hannah Arendt.[10] In contrast to the modern, utilitarian, instrumental notion of politics, which Rorty insists upon, the communicative ideal of culture harks back to what Arendt dubs classical politics. Politics was a shared public space in which citizens engaged in dialogue about (in MacIntyre's words) "the point and purposes of their traditions; in which the aim of politics was to interpret and appropriate shared cultural traditions." This ideal, which Charles Taylor labels "expressivism,"[11] hooks up with the ideals of Herder and finds expression in the connection between aesthetics and politics that Heidegger develops in his "Origins of the Work of Art."[12] Politics involves a dialogue about a culture's competing self-understandings, rooted in arguments about the meaning of a shared tradition. On this view, philosophy becomes what Oakeshott calls the abbreviation of a tradition, which provides the occasion for immanent critique and discussion of a common heritage. But, as Bernstein and Dreyfus (among others) insist, if we live in a time when our traditions have become deformed or corrupted or at best latent, we have a real problem. If the traditions of modern science have come to dominate and foreclose the possibility of other traditions, we must begin with a radical critique and reconstitution of the traditions from our own past. It is only by doing so that we can prepare for a non-technological culture. Here again Rorty is both less radical in the extent to which he feels the need for this and more sanguine about the dominant traditions of liberal-democratic, Judeo-Christian origin. In any case, he is to some extent less explicitly concerned to extend the conversation of the West to these basic issues than either Gadamer, Heidegger, or, for that matter, Habermas. Put in other words, he is convinced that the liberal version of society and Socratic conversation, without the philosophical underpinnings, represents the greatest achievement of our civilization. This loyalty is also connected to his stress on instrumental politics as a form of coping—i.e., of getting what we want, of humanism, of "solidarity" as opposed to "objectivity." From Heidegger's point of view, this decidedly un-Greek version of pragmatism is of a piece with the will to power and technological civilization. Rorty tries to turn a necessity into a virtue by maintaining that pragmatism, like Marxism and other forms of humanism, requires us to use technology to make good on the promise of this part of our heritage. He thus opposes the interpretation of Christianity, liberal democracy, and scientific civilization one finds in Heidegger and Nietzsche. Yet this reading of modern liberalism is but one of two competing stories about our heritage; in the end, Rorty cannot dismiss the story told by Nietzsche and Heidegger. Nor, I suspect, would he wish to, if only to sustain the conversation of the West. (Gadamer perhaps stands midway between Rorty and Heidegger here, since his views are much more congenial to democracy than Heidegger's, yet much more committed to preserving other elements of our tradition than is Rorty.) So we wind up with what Rorty calls two competing interpretations of our culture which will guide the conversation of the West for the foreseeable future.

I'd like to elaborate on these two competing understandings of our culture by focusing on the major differences between Rorty, on the one hand, and Gadamer and Heidegger, on the other. (The essays

by Bernstein, Dreyfus, and Caputo should be consulted here for details.)
As a first approximation, Rorty sees himself, I believe, as what Mann-
heim, following Weber, called a "free floating intellectual." Rorty tries
to distance himself from all traditions, including his own, thus placing
himself outside history in order to give a God's eye perspective on the
goings on. To turn liberal pluralistic society into a community, he can
only appeal to procedural norms, to what Weber called *Zweckration-
alitat*. There may be, on pragmatic grounds, motivation to scotch those
of our traditions which no longer help us "cope." Coupled with a
Weber-like decisionism about ultimate values, Rorty's ideals can either
not be defended by rational argument or leave us with what Weber
characterized as a set of incommensurable and irreconcilable ultimate
values and goals for cultural development. Gadamer, Heidegger, and
commentators such as Caputo and Bernstein object to this vision, for
a variety of reasons. In essence, they want to insist that we cannot escape
or throw off our past so easily, that we need some basis for deliberation about which elements of our shared culture need to be preserved
and revitalized. We need (to use Ricoeur's terms) a restoration of meaning as well as a hermeneutics of suspicion. Ironically, it is by emphasizing his version of historicism that leads Rorty to escape from the
historicity which says that we can only shape our future by modifying
our existing traditions. For Gadamer, our traditions are historically timeless but not atemporal: this is what Charles Guignon calls "transcendental historicism" in several important essays on Rorty, Heidegger,
and Gadamer.[13] Our shared past provides a kind of historical continuity
that gets us "beyond objectivism and relativism." It also moves Gadamer and Heidegger much closer to certain classical, even "Platonic,"
ideals of unity than Rorty's views allow. Whether this makes Rorty's
vision of culture more or less palatable is for the reader to judge.

Put in terms of the issue of pluralism, Heidegger and Gadamer
side with writers such as Herder, Scheler, and Arendt, who see pluralism as compatible with a certain kind of universal set of values or ideals:
the plurality shows how the same ideals can be manifested in a variety
of ways. (This amounts to the kind of "perspectivism" often associated
with Nietzsche and Husserl.) Rorty, who recently talks about "ethno-
centrism" as a way of steering between objectivism and nihilism, doesn't
seem to take this notion seriously. All we get are different and perhaps
incommensurable forms of life, loyalty to which is a matter of ethnocentric allegiance.

It is hoped that the readings in this volume will serve as a supplement to the writings of Gadamer, Rorty, and Heidegger, as well as a substantial continuation of the dialogue which is part of what we all are.

Robert Hollinger

NOTES

1. M. Heidegger, "The Age of the World as Picture," in *The Question Concerning Technology and Other Essays* (New York: Harper and Row, 1969).

2. R. Rorty, "Pragmatism, Relativism and Irrationalism" and "Philosophy and Pragmatism," in *Consequences of Pragmatism* (Minneapolis: University of Minnesota Press, 1981).

3. H. Arendt, *Life of the Mind* (New York: Harcourt, Brace and Jovanovich, 1979), vol. 1, p. 19.

4. J. Dewey, *Experience and Nature* (La Salle: Open Court Publishing Co., 1925), and *Quest for Certainty* (New York: G. P. Putnam's Sons, 1929).

5. R. Rorty, "Heidegger Against the Pragmatists," unpublished (German version in *Neue Hefte für Philosophie*, 1983). "Overcoming the Tradition," in *Consequences of Pragmatism*. Cf. M. Heidegger, "Letter on Humanism," in *Basic Writings* (New York: Harper and Row, 1977).

6. M. Oakeshott, "The Voice of Poetry in the Conversation of Mankind," in *Rationalism in Politics and Other Essays* (New York: Basic Books, 1962). Cf. M. Heidegger, "Holderlin and the Essence of Poetry," in *Existence and Being* (Chicago: Henry Regnery, 1949), and "What Are Poets For?" in M. Heidegger, *Poetry Language Thought* (New York: Harper and Row, 1971).

7. J. Dewey, *The Public and its Problems* (New York: Henry Holt and Co., 1927).

8. J. Habermas, *Communication and the Evolution of Society* (Boston: Beacon Press, 1980). *Theory of Communicative Action* (Boston: Beacon Press, 1983), vol. 1, *Reason and the Rationalization of Society*.

9. A. MacIntyre, *After Virtue*, 2d ed. (Notre Dame, Ind.: University of Notre Dame Press, 1984).

10. Arendt, *Life of the Mind*; *The Human Condition* (Chicago: University of Chicago Press, 1959). *See also*, R. Bernstein, *Beyond Objectivism and Relativism* (Philadelphia: University of Pennsylvania Press, 1984), and Ronald Beiner, *Political Judgement* (Chicago: University of Chicago Press, 1984).

11. Charles Taylor, *Hegel and Modern Society* (New York: Cambridge University Press, 1980), and "Philosophy of Social Science," in M. Richter, ed., *Political Theory and Political Education* (Princeton: Princeton Univer-

sity Press, 1979). *See also* C. Taylor, "Interpretation and the Science of Man," *Review of Metaphysics*, 1971.

12. Heidegger, *Poetry Language Thought*.

13. Charles Guignon, "The Twofold Task: Heidegger's Foundational Historicism in *Being and Time*," in *The Thought of Martin Heidegger*, Tulane Studies in Philosophy, Michael Zimmerman, ed. (New Orleans: Tulane University Press, 1984), vol. 32; and "Saving the Difference: Gadamer and Rorty," in *PSA* (1982), vol. 2, P. D. Asquith and T. Nickles, eds. (East Lansing: Philosophy of Science Association, 1983). I'd like to thank Guignon for letting me see a paper called "On Saving Heidegger from Rorty," and for discussing the issues raised in this Introduction with me. His comments, criticisms, and insights on the differences between Heidegger and Gadamer, on the one hand, and Rorty, on the other, were invaluable.

PART I

Traditions as the
Horizons of Existence

1. THE HAPPENING OF TRADITION: THE HERMENEUTICS OF GADAMER AND HEIDEGGER

Theodore Kisiel

From the exegesis of Biblical texts to the methodical interpretation of the human actions that constitute history, the hermeneutical in general pertains to the process of exposing hidden meanings. Uncovering the sense of classical texts, understanding a poem, performing one of Shakespeare's plays, interpreting the precedents of the law in a particular case, reading the historical signs of the times—all of these aporetic situations have come to be seen within the purview of a hermeneutic, whether as a science or the art of interpretation. At first, in the ancient philological tradition, hermeneutics was an occasional affair, to be evoked only when some inherent obscurity blocked textual understanding. Later, in the romantic period of the nineteenth century, Schleiermacher and Dilthey projected hermeneutics as the general method of the humanities, a movement which inspired, among other things, the *Verstehen* approach in psychology and sociology. But it was Heidegger who went even further and suggested that man's existence in the aporia of Being is hermeneutical through and through. Although his hermeneutic of existence is still linked with the phenomenological "method" of explicating the implicit structures of existence, this procedure itself is to be traced back and rooted in the more spontaneous process of human existence as a unique voyage of discovery which envelops all the minor revelations and major epiphanies of the meaning of existence. In Heidegger's terms, *Dasein*, human existence in its situation, stands in the "event of unconcealment," and accordingly understands. It is in this "event" then, that the heart of the matter of the hermeneutical is to be found.

In its concern for the interpretation of the texts of the great thinkers of the past, Heidegger's work still bears a manifest relation to the classical notion of hermeneutics. But its thrust toward a more comprehensive and radical hermeneutic which envelops the older conceptions can only be called a "hermeneutic of hermeneutics." Its radicality is one with that of phenomenology in its endeavor to be witness to the birth of meaning in experience, to find its way back to the nodal point where meaning first emerges into the open at the very origins of human experience. Here hermeneutic is precisely the phenomenology of the event of understanding traced back to its very incipience, which ultimately means back to the level of the non-understood, to that which can never be understood, the mysterious, the concealment of unconcealment. It is here that the hermeneutical, the process of the exposure of hidden meanings, finds its most radical problems.

And it is this level that prompts Heidegger to make the cryptic pronouncements which alienate so many of his readers. An antidote to this frustrating obfuscation is to be found in the work of Hans-Georg Gadamer, which locates itself between Heidegger's comprehensive and radical hermeneutic and the more customary problems of textual interpretation, thereby providing a specific context and concreteness to the profound and elusive issues involved here, like the filter glasses used to peer into white-hot furnaces. For Gadamer focuses on the "fact" that the actual situation in which human understanding takes place is always an understanding through *language* within a *tradition*, both of which have always been manifest considerations in hermeneutical thinking. Understanding as the linguistic happening of tradition thus provides a much more accessible entrance to the problems common to hermeneutic and phenomenology, e.g., the problem of *Sinngebung*. For it is readily apparent that it is the linguistic tradition which in some sense delivers meaning to human understanding. Just how this happens is the node of the following study, which eventually aims to set off the hermeneutic of Gadamer from that of the thinker who gives him his start, Martin Heidegger.[1]

One further series of remarks may help to indicate the relationships and differences between the comprehensive hermeneutic under study here and the older versions of hermeneutics. Consider the problem of the relation of text to context in interpretation, sometimes understood in terms of the "hermeneutical circle." In classical philological hermeneutics, the circle was the grammatical whole-part relationship. The word (or larger unit) is understood in the context of its sentence (or larger grammatical object), and the meaning of the sentence is in turn illuminated in terms of the functions of the individual words. In romantic hermeneutics, the subjectivity of the author (e.g. his "unconscious genius") became the prime concern, where the text is understood as a moment of his creative life, which in turn is illuminated by his individual works. The circle in the following study is between a living tradition and its interpretation, which itself is part as well as parcel of the tradition. The interpretation is therefore partial, i.e., finite, governed by the historical situation in which it takes place. For we interpret a tradition from within a tradition. Tradition provides the basis for interpretation and invites new interpretation, and this renovating interpretation keeps the tradition alive. The movement of interpretation is evoked by the movement of transmission, and the two together constitute the circular movement of the hermeneutical happening. The happening most basically is not an encounter between interpreter and author or with a text, but "between" human existence and the unique historical situation in which it is already involved, where the subject-object model is no longer really applicable. Both the "text" and the "author" of the earlier hermeneutical theories are drawn into the larger context of the historical movement into which they are spontaneously gathered and carried forth.

GADAMER: THE OCCURRENCE OF TRANSMISSION

The title of Gadamer's *magnum opus, Truth and Method: Fundamental Features of a Philosophical Hermeneutic,*[2] contains certain ironies which highlight some sources of the misunderstanding of his work. For his "hermeneutic" is not directed toward devising a "method" for the humanities, as Schleiermacher and Dilthey would have it. Although his hermeneutic is still a matter of understanding and interpretation, it is not concerned with the scientific control of understanding and interpretation so that the humanities may also arrive at intellectually respectable conclusions, but rather with what always actually *happens* in any genuine understanding at a level "beyond our willing and doing" (xiv), where "understanding is not so much a method . . . as a standing within a happening of tradition (*Überlieferungsgeschehen*)" (293). His aim is to describe the conditions that make understanding possible, a question that transcends methodological considerations. Here hermeneutic is a "theory of the actual experience that thinking is" (xxii), which is not intended to supersede methodological hermeneutics, but to explore dimensions which underlie the latter and to develop insights which might well aid them as well as correcting some of their possibly exaggerated claims, insofar as they neglect "how much happening is operative in all understanding" (xxvii). Once this is recognized, it follows that the most fundamental task of hermeneutic is not to develop a procedure of understanding, but to clarify the conditions under which understanding actually happens (279). It was Heidegger who pointed the way. In *Being and Time* the movement of understanding is conceived as the very way of *Dasein's* Being, thus giving the hermeneutic phenomenon a universality far exceeding its restriction to methodological and theoretical matters. Henceforth, the concept "hermeneutic" "designates the fundamental movement of *Dasein*, which constitutes its finitude and historicity and thus circumscribes the whole of its world experience" (xvi). Since human experience is hermeneutical through and through, its description along these lines constitutes an all-embracing and hence philosophical hermeneutic.[3] This broader conception of *Verstehen* broke through the methodic spirit of modern science to rejoin a longer tradition of theological and juridical hermeneutic concerned with the more practical problems of the preacher and the judge and dealing with modes of knowledge and truth not strictly scientific. Heidegger's deepening of the phenomenon of understanding thus indicated the possibility of its being extended to legitimizing the claims to truth of modes of knowledge which cannot be verified by the current methodological standards of science, e.g., the experiences of art, history and philosophy. Antedating the Cartesian conception of method is the old Greek idea that the "object" determines the method by which it is to be approached (PCH 14).[4] Pure method is never possible since it can never detach itself from its origins, which *per se* lie outside of method.

Taking his guiding clues from Heidegger's "hermeneutic of facticity," Gadamer aims in particular at exploring the movement of understanding in its concrete appropriation of possibility from the transmitted heritage of the past. It is this historical movement of understanding that he adopts as his central clue to the hermeneutic problem. "Understanding itself is not to be considered so much an action of subjectivity, but rather as entering into an occurrence of transmission (*Überlieferungsgeschehen*) in which past and present are constantly being mediated. This is what must gain acceptance in hermeneutic theory, which is too much dominated by the idea of procedure, method" (275). This means first of all that one must accept as basic the radical finitude and temporality of facticity, behind which one cannot go, which cannot be superseded by any formalized ego or absolute spirit or some similar entity lurking behind the scenes in previous hermeneutic theories.

More explicitly, the focus on facticity devolves into the task of grasping the full significance of what it means to belong to a tradition. And since we have been insurmountably pre-ceded, we belong to history much more than it belongs to us. "Long before we understand ourselves in retrospect we understand ourselves as a matter of course in the family, society and state in which we live. . . . Hence the individual's prejudgments much more than his judgments are the historical reality of his Being" (261). Even before they become a problem of knowledge, our "prejudices" are an ontological fact, the facticity of historically transmitted contents, on the basis of which we understand anything at all. The trick is to begin appropriately in knowledge where we have already been begun in Being. The epistemological problem for finite understanding is therefore not a matter of discarding prejudices in order to begin absolutely, but to determine what distinguishes the legitimate prejudices from the prejudices which obstruct understanding. It is not a matter of a rejection but of a cultivation of a tradition that still lives on in us, in such a way that it not only gives us access to the past, but also continually opens up new possibilities of meaning. This productivity of our "precedents" gives the hermeneutic circle a more positive and fruitful sense, provided that care is taken to avoid being misled by "fancies and popular conceptions" and to develop these presuppositions *aus den Sachen selbst* (SZ 153). The hermeneutic circle is not "vicious" because it is not a logical circle which posits formal axioms from which further propositions are deductively derived, but rather the intrinsically circular structure of a temporal existence whose future projects are necessarily determined and guided by past presuppositions. The anticipations of meaning which guide our understanding of a text, for example, are basically not the methodological positings of a formal subjectivity, but rather emerge from a spontaneous preunderstanding of the presuppositions of the text arising from the common affinity that we and it have with the tradition in which we find ourselves (277). And this common bond finds its ultimate common ground in its constant reference to "the things themselves."[5]

Hence hermeneutic has to start from the fact that to understand means to be related at once to a tradition out of which "the things" can speak to us, as well as to these "things" themselves, which necessarily comes to language through the tradition. And it will soon become apparent that it is language itself which is our most basic "prejudice." We move in a dimension of meaning in common with our ancestors precisely through the transmission, the "tradition" of language.

But our bond with the tradition is not so common that it is always self-evident to us. The hermeneutic consciousness begins only when the message transmitted by the tradition falls out of its customary familiarity and strikes us as problematic. The very sense and structure of hermeneutic historicity is this tension between familiarity and strangeness (279, PCH 80). Hermeneutic locates itself in the "between" of belonging to a tradition of facing an "object" uprooted from the customary and posing a question to us. Explicit understanding begins only when this challenging event *happens* to us, creating a distance between us, the interpreters, and the transmitted message. The distance is temporal and not spatial, and must first be stripped of all the privative connotations accruing from the latter. For it is the recoil of time that first opens up the issue in its appropriate light, in a way that suggests fruitful directions of interpretation. Hence it is not a distance to be surmounted and overcome, but one to be cultivated for its productive possibilities for understanding. Temporal distance is not an empty void, a "yawning abyss" (281), but a fullness of the continuity of transmitted articulations mediating present and past. It serves not only to filter out the sources of error that accrue from being too close to, for example, a mode of art or a historical event, but also to release new sources of understanding that manifest unsuspected relations of meaning. It thus permits prejudices that are of a particular nature to die away, and prejudgments that are more comprehensive in scope, which accomplish a true understanding, to come forth. It is temporal distance that serves to distinguish the true prejudgments from the false obstructive prejudices and hence is the condition for the resolution of the critical epistemological problem of hermeneutic (282, PCH 82). Here we have history at work, and it is not too much to speak of a genuine productivity of the historical process.

It does this by provoking my prejudices into consciousness and, by placing them under question, suspending their action as prejudices. But what holds my opinions under question is precisely the strange otherness of the challenging message. Hence what hermeneutic must consider as its "object" is not an object at all, but the relation between what is mine and what is other, between the present and the past, which initially bring each other into relief through contrast, and ultimately blend into each other through a mediation that expands one's horizons. For the fundamental thrust of the hermeneutic consciousness is benevolent and ecumenical. It is out to establish accord, which means the willingness to move beyond one's own horizons and the readiness to intensify and strengthen the arguments of the other. The hermeneutic experience begins by being negative, but in such a way that it is open to new experiences, i.e., to the "other," so that the other may have something to say to me (344).

Such a laying open and holding open of possibilities is the very essence of the question (283). Any experience worthy of the name is structured according to the probing logic of question and answer in its more intense forms. It is true that we may begin by posing an "academic question" with regard to the text, but the true hermeneutic experience does not begin until we are sufficiently open to permit the text to question us, i.e., to "unhinge" our prejudices and to suggest its own.[6] The dialectic of question and answer which now ensues leaves all pre-established methods behind. For one thing, all methodological presuppositions are held in suspense. For another, the questioning does not posit anything, but only probes the possibilities lying fallow in the hermeneutic situation and sprung open in the tension of the dialectic. The process can only be encouraged through what could at most be called a discipline, the discipline that constitutes any creative research (465). The logic of question and answer is a "logic" of discovery only in an extended sense at the level at which that "something" happens in which "things speak for themselves," in an experience which we undergo (er-fahren) rather than control. Understanding is an undergoing. Πάθει μάθος (339).

The dialectic of question and answer suggests the reciprocal relation of a conversation as a model for the hermeneutic phenomenon. To say that a text strikes us in the form of a question is to say that it speaks like a partner communicating to us in a dialogue. Of course, the relation between interpreter and text is not really a communion between two persons, not even that of reader and author (who at times is anonymous), an assumption that vitiates the validity of much of Schleiermacher's hermeneutic, but rather a communication in the common sphere of meaning, and only after the interpreter himself actually converts the written script into sense. But it is precisely this coming to language of a common subject matter that makes the hermeneutic relation akin to a conversation *between* persons, though it is not the "I-thou" relation, but the linguistic happening of the transmission of meaning that makes the tradition like a conversation. That there is a transpersonal dimension to a conversation is suggested by the "brainstorming" session which spontaneously wends its creative way to a new "breakthrough," and when done, none of the participants can really claim the discovery as exclusively his own. And even during the "groupthink," no one individual can claim to have guided the conversation, for the creative discourse simply "takes its course" and our task is to *let* that *happen.*[7] The more authentic a conversation, the less do the participants guide it (361). It rather guides us, through the common ground of *die Sache*, the subject matter of the interchange.

All this happens in the medium of language. Conversation is a linguistic process, language on the move. According to Heidegger, language is essentially language only as conversation, which in turn is one and the same as being historical (HD 36–37, US 152). Language as a stockpile of words to be used according to certain rules is only the obvious foreground of language viewed statically and objectively. Placing language back into the original movement of conversation emphasizes not only its eventful but also its creative character. But because language at its best is the invisible background within which the explicit concern is to achieve right understanding of the subject matter, its power to advance meaning and promulgate insight works behind the scenes. But it is operative when the partners in dialogue, in order to achieve accord over the subject matter, must work out a common language in a process which is more than a matter of "the sharpening of work tools" (360, 365). For the language thus established is intrinsically involved with the fulfillment rather than the propaedeutic of understanding. It is not even a matter of adapting to each other's viewpoint, for the creative conversation translates its participants into a new community in the subject matter through a language which is a possession of neither one but which rather lies between them. Language itself mediates accord at a level that transcends the individuals involved. One is almost tempted to summarize Gadamer's most original thesis simply by asserting that: the medium mediates.

In the hermeneutic conversation, the linguistic achievement of understanding occurs in the form of a mediation of the horizons of present and past. The hermeneutic process normally begins in the encounter of the interpreter in his present situation with a transmitted text that is written. In the form of writing all that is transmitted from the past is contemporaneous for every present. The literary tradition offers the opportunity of being here and there at the same time, providing a depth dimension to one's world and the possibility of widening one's own horizons. But to realize this, one must overcome the estrangement of a strange past and perhaps a foreign language, as focused by a script which is always self-estrangement. For with the written word language is alienated from its empirical execution. But detached from its author as well as from its intended reader, i.e., from all things psychological, it is virtually elevated into the sphere of meaning pure and simple. Speaking, of course, also participates in the "pure ideality of meaning" (370); but with writing the immediacy of all the emotional overtones of expression are left behind. A text demands first of all to be understood in terms of what is said, and not as an expression of an individual life. Detached from the contingency of its origin, what is put down in writing is freed for new relations of meaning exceeding those which may have been intended by the author. It enters into its *Sinnsgeschichte*. The apparent deficiency of the written word, the lack of such helpful factors as intonation and circumstance through which the spoken word really interprets itself, now appears as an ad vantage. Without these aids, the interpreter of the script must concentrate on the essential, namely, to give full weight to what the text means, to the point of strengthening the arguments in its favor in order to achieve accord in the topic at issue. *Die Sache* is the central concern of the hermeneutic consciousness. It is this common ground of being related to what is meant, to the subject matter about which language speaks, that ultimately makes interpretation possible. "Here the process of understanding moves entirely in the sphere of meaning which is mediated through the linguistic tradition" (368).

But preservation through the written word which permits the coexistence of past with present is only a precondition for the transmission of tradition, for it only transmits the object that provokes the hermeneutic consciousness. "The bearer of tradition is really not this handwriting as a piece of 'once upon a time,' but rather the continuity of recollection. Through this continuity the tradition becomes a part of my own world and thus enables that which it communicates to come to language immediately" (368). What "happens" in reading the transmitted texts is then basically a re-collection. That interpretation is an occurrence has already been emphasized. But what of the recurrence of recollection that takes place within it? Gadamer insists that the occurrence is quite current, that it cannot but be *au courant*. Seeking concurrence with the text concerning its subject matter, the reading nevertheless is not a simple "repetition of something past, but rather a participation in a present meaning" (370).[8] It is not a matter of going back to some original first, but it is also not simply placing the other under one's own measure. To strive for accord in the subject matter means to strive for a higher universality that transcends both my own partiality and the other's. Conscious of the productivity of history, interpretive understanding is suspended in the tension between the sameness of the transmitted text and the peculiar difference of the present hermeneutic situation. The central task of hermeneutic is really to appropriate this single and same message to the times, hence of mediating between present and past. It seeks to blend the two apparently distinct horizons of present and past in order to rejoin (recollect!) the higher universality of the single all-encompassing horizon at the depths of history, that of the *Sinnsgeschichte*, time itself. Interpretive understanding fulfills itself in the controlled execution of this amalgamation. It is the time-honored hermeneutic problem of application, which does not mean the employment of an abstract universal first understood in itself and then applied to a concrete case (323). Rather, the concretion of meaning derived from mediating the text to the hermeneutic situation in which one finds oneself is the universal that understanding seeks (375).

The mediation takes place in and through language. The task of application is to administer the translation that happens to the concepts of the past. Fusing the seemingly opposed backgrounds and prejudgments provides the horizon of interpretation within which the text again speaks to us. This consists of working out the common language which is the invisible background in which the subject matter reveals itself, now in this way, then in another way. The secret of the occurrence of transmission is thus intrinsically interwoven with the illusiveness of language, which of its nature tends to efface itself in favor of its subject matter.[9] Because language is first of all not an object but the element in which our understanding is lived, the continual "concept formation" which occurs historically on a pre-conceptual level has naturally been overlooked by many past students of the reality of language. For a word multiplies itself not only uniformly, as logic would have it, but also creatively, according to a varying context, in what might be called "the living metaphoric of language" (409).

How to describe this "inner dimension of multiplication" (434) which is the secret of the fruitfulness of linguistic transmission? Gadamer speaks of mirroring, hence of the "speculative" structure of language,[10] but not in the sense of a static duplication of a being or of a fixed pregiven order of Being, but more like a "mirror play," e.g., on a lake or a myriad gem. Each word mirrors the totality of meaning, as "through a glass darkly."

> Every word breaks forth as out of a medium and has a relation to a whole, through which it alone is word. Every word permits the reverberation of the whole of language to which it belongs and the appearance of the whole of the world view which lies at its basis. Every word thus also lets be, as the happening of its fulfilled moment, the co-presence of the unsaid, to which it relates itself in a responsive and suggestive way. The occasional character of human discourse is not an incidental imperfection of its power of expression — it is rather the logical expression of the living virtuality of discourse, which brings into play a totality of meaning without being able to say it totally. All human speaking is finite in such a way that an infinity of extractable and interpretable meaning is tied up in it. (434)

Because each word lets the whole of language appear as its suggestive unsaid, it has infinite possibilities of finding ever new answering "antiwords." The ensuing dialectic is an inexhaustible "play on words," a selfpropelled language game,[11] "the play of language itself, which speaks to us, strikes forth and draws back, questions and in the answer fulfills itself" (464). Just as conversation at its most spontaneous transcends the participants and moves where it will, so the speculative movement of language is not a methodic act of the subject but a doing of the subject matter which thinking undergoes. In the speculative happening, what is unsaid and to be said comes to language, incipiently if you want, whereas procedures designed to make methodically exact statements tend to obscure the meaning horizon of what is really to be said. To truly say what one means is to speak pregnantly, by holding together an infinity of the unsaid with what is said (444).

It is clear, then, that the word is not only a sign, if this means that the word is simply conventional, instrumental and univocal. We are moving in the realm of natural rather than scientific concept formation. How further to describe the relation between *Sprache* and *Sache* (*Sinn, Sein*)? Its speculative movement suggests that, more than just signifying, a word in some sense displays and reveals its subject matter. In fact, words have no *raison d'être* other than to reveal what they bring to language. On the other hand, what comes to language is not something that precedes language "but receives in the word the determination of itself" (450). For an experience is not first wordless and then subsumed under the generality of a word through naming. One seeks and finds just the right words to display one's experience, and without them the experience itself would not be possible. In this sense, the words are intimately involved in and really belong to their subject matter. The speculative relation between *Sprache* and *Sache* is such that the distinction between Being and its representation is not really a distinction at all. For it intrinsically belongs to Being to display itself in order to be understood, and reciprocally "whatever can be understood is language" (450). Hence Being is language, i.e., self-display, self-representation (*Sichdarstellen*) (461).

> Coming-to-language does not mean getting a second existence. As that which itself represents something, it belongs rather to its own Being. In all that is language, it is thus a matter of a speculative unity: a distinction in itself: to be and to represent itself, a distinction which nevertheless strictly is not really intended to be a distinction. (450)

In order to make itself understood, historical Being divides itself from itself (452), past from present, the said from the unsaid, horizon from horizon, only to recollect itself in its speculative unity. Being of necessity articulates itself.

The same holds for aesthetic Being. In the presentation of, for example, a musical work or a play, the reproduction does not become thematic as reproduction. Instead, through it and in it the work brings itself to representation. The work depends on the representation to display itself. The true experience of an artwork involves the nondistinction of the mediation from the work (114). The reproduction re-presents the work itself, no matter how far removed in time it originally may be, and in fact in such a way that the work undergoes an enhancement in Being (133). Yet it is the same work that remains and perdures in its varying interpretations through changes of time and circumstances. It is there in all of its changing aspects. All of these are contemporaneous with it (115).

HEIDEGGER: THE EVENT OF INCIPIENCE

To be one and the same and yet always different — the same paradox was exposed for the content of tradition in its speculative unity and movement (448). "A being which only is, in always being an other, is in a radical sense temporal" (118n). "It has its Being only in becoming and in recurrence" (117). How to comprehend the temporality of aesthetic Being, of historical Being, of Being as such? Gadamer refers explicitly to Heidegger at this point (118n), for the issue of Being "and" time is the driving motif of his precursor's thought. "Everything is haunted by the enigma of Being and . . . by that of movement" (SZ 392). Hence "the ontological enigma of the movement of happening in general" (SZ 389) is the heart of the matter for both philosophers.

But having accepted a starting point of radical finitude, Heidegger can no longer resort to the customary metaphysical strategies of characterizing the unity and continuity of this movement. Hence he refuses to resort to either the fixed and timeless universal of Platonism or the necessary law of dialectic of Hegel, but without being able to assert just how to think the continuity that pervades the epochal movement of the history of Being (ID 66). The metaphysical solutions distort the finite experience of history, out of which alone even the appropriate questions with regard to the unity and movement of history can be formulated.

In his historical situation, man is called upon to seek, in what has already been thought, the unthought that is to be thought as appropriate to his epoch. The discussion with the tradition thus involves a displacement. It is not a matter of understanding the Greeks, for example, better than they understood themselves, but to understand them differently (US 134, HW 197).[12] In his own place, each great thinker understands himself the best; but from another vantage point, something unthought can disclose itself in what he has thought. In the process of disclosing this new aspect of thought, some of what has already been thought sinks back into the unthought, and what is disclosed tends to conceal the undisclosed as such. Even the thinker's most pro-

found and unique thought, which plumbs most deeply into the unthought, can never be said. "It must remain unsaid, because the sayable
word receives its determination from the unsayable" (N II 484). What
he does say is thus surrounded by both the unsaid and the unsayable,
which both distinguish and unite him with other epochal positions.
Hence the unity and movement of the history of Being is intrinsically
involved with what Heidegger calls concealment, both of mystery and
errancy, or the "silent language of Being." "Without the erratic there
would be no relation from mission to mission, there would be no
history" (HW 311). And in the intermission, it is the mystery which
remains, never wholly revealing itself, yet from time to time ("when
the time is ripe") granting an opening to man. But what sort of a "pervasive sameness" is this? Certainly no stable ground upon which to
stand, but instead a lack of ground, an abyss (*Ab-grund*). No ultimate
grounding is possible, the mystery is inexhaustible and the process of
exploring it is endless.

At this point, the relevance of comparing the process to "play"
finds its place. Heidegger makes only a brief reference to this comparison, while Gadamer develops an entire phenomenology of play
to support it. Heidegger's most significant remark: "The 'because' disap-
pears in play. Play is without a 'why.' It plays because it plays" (SG
188). Play is "endless" in the twofold sense of being without an aim
in which it terminates, and thus in being an ongoing process which
continually renews itself in repetition. Yet the repetition is not uniform,
for any number of "chance" factors contribute to providing endless
variations on the theme of the play. But the most original meaning
of play is neither the object nor the subject of play, but the medial
meaning, the play as such, i.e., the spontaneous to-and-fro movement
accomplished by play. The heart of the matter in play is the to-and-
fro movement as such, which goes of itself, not only without aim or
purpose but also without effort. The players are drawn into the play
in such a way that they are unburdened, released from the strain of
taking the initiative, and "it takes over," as a pure self-display. But
even though "the play's the thing," it still needs the players as those
to whom it displays itself, who begin by playing only to become played
in the process. Beguiled by the fascination of its spontaneous movement, they accept the scope and bounds of the playing field and the
general movement of the game, as well as the risk and uncertainty
of success or failure, winning or losing (99-105).

The relation of all this to the linguistic play that takes place in the temporal playing field (*Zeit-Spiel-Raum*) of tradition has already been suggested in the above account of conversation. Gadamer applies it not only to the historical dis-course which takes its course but also to the artistic performance. In both cases, the performer is bound by his subject matter, and yet is free to create within those boundaries of his playing field. But does one really know these boundaries, when the subject matter is the mystery as such, which is ultimately the case in all of these examples? So the players can easily step out of bounds and commit any number of the errors which are part of the game. But according to Heidegger, the greatest error is the conservative approach to tradition, in which one restricts the field to overexplicit rules and systematic procedures and insists on adherence to these familiar rules and controllable tactics to the point of stifling the "spirit" of the game, which most fundamentally involves being faithful to inner limits which, because of the "proximity of the unsaid unsayable" (N II 484), the thinker himself does not know. The first thing to recognize is that the to-and-fro movement of tradition is essentially erratic and confused. But if we let the meanderings of history lead us where they will, there is the possibility of "a flash of light through the confusion of the erratic" (HW 312) into the mystery for those "knights errant" who persist in the search. "Once in a while (*je-weils*), when the "breaks of the game" permit, an exceptional breakthrough can take place which gives free access to hidden possibilities never yet explored."

Through the breaks of the game, times change, the scene shifts and a new variation of the theme of the game emerges, which in the West is "Being," according to Heidegger. And it is the oscillation between the erratic foreground and the mysterious background which articulates its history into epochs. There is a transmission from epoch to epoch, but one epoch cannot be derived from another after the fashion of a sequence of a consecutive process. Each epoch breaks on the scene abruptly, out of the depths of the perduring concealment. "The tradition does not run between the epochs like a connecting cord; rather its trans-mission (*Überlieferung*) each time comes out of the concealment of the e-mission (*Geschick*), just as different streamlets springing from a single source feed a stream which is everywhere and nowhere" (SG 154). But what more can be said of this perpetual pregnancy in the womb of time, which periodically delivers, "when the time is ripe," what is proper to each epoch? Can we speak of a "periodic law" that differentiates the epochs, sets limits and measures what is possible, hence allots and apportions proper concerns in their proper time? Heidegger at least speaks of a law, "the simplest and gentlest of all laws . . . not a law in the sense of a norm that hovers somewhere above us, not an ordinance which orders and regulates a process. The appropriating e-vent (*Ereignis*) is *the* law, insofar as it gathers mortals into the appropriation to their source and holds them there" (US 259). Persistently striving to purify his formulations of the contamination of objectifiable "ontic" representations of process, of "mechanisms," he nevertheless grapples with the issue of how the movement "makes way" (*be-wëgt*), how time "ripens," through attempted purifications of the formulation of its "what": "What does time temporalize? Answer: the con-temporaneous . . . " (US 213). How then to think of the unity of past, present and future, if not as a sequential span? The three dimensions of time are mutually implicated in a reciprocal play in which they pass into one another and at once hold each other apart, and hence yield an opening, a clearing, the playing field of time. All these metaphors are further re-duced to suggest a region which regions, a proximity which proximates, a situating of all situations which is the gathering place of every epochal *situs*, a "fourth dimension" which modulates the three dimensions of time through restraint as well as release, an ἐποχή or self-withholding that determines every epoch of the history of Being (N II 383, HW 311), a rest which is not a cessation of movement but the gathering of all movement (SG 144), "the play of the still" (US 214).

But why this final reduction? From the vantage of human contingency, it can be considered as the final seal on the radical finitude of the "logic" of happening, the insistence on a region which incubates the ultimate possibility of rupture and abrupt new start in an event of startling irruption "in which epochs spring up suddenly like shoots" (SG 154). Hence the transmission of tradition is ultimately not a smooth transition from old to new, but a deliverance of the unexpectedly new, which, even though preparation for it may be gradual, a matter of "waiting," "catches on" abruptly as from an abyss. Hence Heidegger finally takes *Überlieferung* to be the liberating release (SG 171) of the start of "in-cipience" (*An-fang*). "In-cipience is: tra-dition" (N II 29). "History is rare. There is history only whenever the essence of truth is incipiently decided" (HD 73).

To see how far Heidegger has travelled here, it is necessary only to recall his discussion of historicity and its happening in *Being and Time*. There, repetition emerged as that mode of individual *Dasein's* resolute decision which explicitly transmitted the heritage of the community in which it was implicated. *Dasein's* exposition of the implicit here bears the stamp of the circular structure of existence. But repetition not only appropriates what is implicitly transmitted, but also transmutes or "destroys" it. The communal heritage is thus reworked and developed in order to work out the possibilities of what has been which are relevant, timely, momentous (SZ 385-86).

AUSEINANDERSETZUNG

All this in *Being and Time* appears to resemble what Gadamer is trying is say about understanding as exposition and application. In fact, Gadamer recognizes that his conception of understanding as "the interplay of the movement of tradition and the movement of interpretation" (277) appears only as a "special case" (KS I 145) in *Being and Time*. For what now emerges as striking even in *Being and Time* are certain elements of Heidegger's analysis of historicity which do not find their correspondence in Gadamer's treatment. For its full structure is to be found in the "anticipatory-repetitive moment" (SZ 391), and it is the radical and *individualizing* Being-toward-the-end that anticipates death which is the basis in *Dasein* for the retrieve of the *communal* heritage. "Authentic Being toward death, i.e., the finitude of temporality, is the concealed ground for the historicity of *Dasein*. *Dasein* does not first become historical in repetition, but because it is historical as temporal, it can overtake itself in its history by repeating" (SZ 386). More basic than any possibility latent in the tradition is the possibility of the impossibility of existence, which in effect countermands or "destroys" all the possibilities which arise from the heritage. Heidegger's radical intentions are already evident in *Being and Time* in his continual gravitation toward the "extreme possibilities" (SZ 122, 182), e.g., Being-with as being alone, *das Man* and most important, authentic Being toward death. If "higher than actuality stands *possibility*" (SZ 38), what could be higher than the possibility of impossibility, a possibility which must be kept open as possibility if we are to speak at all of possibility, the possibility without which there would be no other possibilities? Just as later the untruth of mystery will become the "*Ur*-truth", so now the possibility of impossibility becomes the "*Ur*-possibility."

Co-original with possibility is facticity, and the same difference appears here in their starting points for a "hermeneutic of facticity." For Gadamer, facticity is held to man's belonging to a tradition. For Heidegger, it is more fundamentally a Being-thrown into Being in such a way that "the pure 'that it is' shows itself, but the whence and whither remain in darkness" (SZ 134), so that an abyss (*Ab-grund*) precedes the ground of facticity and its historical precedents. Here is our most basic precedent and an impossibility as such, for I can never precede my own ground in such a way as to overtake it from the ground up (SZ 284). All I can do is to affirm that "that's the way things are" and "that's how I am and have to be," and let them be accordingly, in their full uniqueness. And so the pure "there it is," the throw that gives (*es gibt*), is more fundamental than the thereness of our historical beginnings in a tradition and in a language. More basic than *Geschichte* is the *Geschick*.

Here we begin to perceive the full radicality of Heidegger's return to origins, in a phenomenological backtracking to the immediacy of experience which culminates in affirming its ineffability, in which all that can finally be said is that "there it is." Yet it is this very ineffability which "wants" thought, which calls out (in this sense "speaks") to be thought, hence draws thought in its very withdrawal (WD 85). Hence the "there it is" at once *gives* the very food for thought, provides the sustenance for thought throughout. Thought inevitably emerges from and directs itself toward the comprehensive immediacy of experience, which it cannot in principle ever attain in its full immediacy. Once again the extreme possibility, that of the "unavoidable unattainable" (VA 66) which lies at the heart of the matter of human experience, where "Being is the transcendent pure and simple" (SZ 38), so near and yet so far, nearest in immediacy, farthest in accessibility.

The reversal of the circle is now evident. Instead of the exposition of *Dasein* over its implications, it is the disposition of Being which now enables thought. Thought is now a possibility of Being's "want" before it is a possibility of *Dasein*. Instead of the anticipatory-repetitive moment, it is the rethinking that thinks ahead according to the bidding of Being, which comes unexpectedly and in its own good time, in whose aura thought can do nothing but wait. At this radical level of the incipience of human experience there is no repetition of a tradition but only a release into an inexhaustible domain beyond the horizon of tradition. "In this ever more incipient leaping of the leap there is no repetition and no recurrence. The leap is needed until the rethinking that thinks ahead into Being as Being has transmuted itself out of the truth of Being into another language" (SG 159). It is by plunging toward its experiential origins, living in this extremity, enduring the limits of finitude and waiting with patient tenacity that *Dasein* in its exception may catch some glimpse of the inexhaustible richness of immediacy which is capable of transmuting its existential movement. For the eternal pregnance of the immediate holds out the possibility of the perpetual novelty of original creation and radical recommencement. At this level, *Über-lieferung* is a matter of "being delivered over" into the domain where human experience "catches on," begins. To be sure, repetition or rethinking of the tradition plays a preparatory role here, but it always stands under the measure of the event anticipated in the forethought, which by leaping to the unique limit of its possibilities at once outlines or de-fines their scope. The questioning which does violence in translating the sense of the traditional texts finds its guide through "listening for the promise of that which is to come in the question" (US 175). "To ask: How does it stand with Being? is nothing less than to *re-peat* the incipience of our historical-spiritual *Dasein* in order to transmute it into another incipience. This is possible. It is even, in its giving of measures, the decisive form of history, because it takes its onset from the ground event" (EM 29).

At times, Heidegger even restricts the term "history" to these epochal breakthroughs to immediacy, no doubt because it is here that the very source of history is laid bare. At this level, the *Über of Überlieferung* is not mediated but sprung. But such a radical discourse with the tradition occurs only once in a great while (*je-weils*), and one may be permitted to wonder what happens in the long interims. At other times, he appears to accept other more customary ways of regarding history. Thus he distinguishes between the historical *conversations* which wend their way on the level of what is said, and his own kind of *discourse* which plunges into the unexpressed source of the tradition (WD 110). Most interpretations of texts, not only philosophical, are conversations which, in general, are sufficient for their exposition. Whereas the conversation with the tradition according to Hegel had the character of the sublimation of what was already said, Heidegger's discourse with the tradition involves a backtracking into its unspoken

Wesen or source (Id 43-45). In this sense, the break with the forward continuity of the tradition is precisely the way to remain in the tradition more profoundly. But even the conversation has a hidden relation to the unsaid, and is accordingly a disguised modification of the rare discourse. And the occasional emergence of the immediate in epochal abruptness for which the discourse disposes itself requires a long preparation. "Yet this unmediated character of the incipience, the special character of the leap out of the unmediatizable, does not exclude but rather includes the longest and entirely unobtrusive preparation of the incipience" (HW 63). Not the explicit preparation of repetition here, but something "entirely unobtrusive." Could it be that this long preparation occurs in the more normal conversations with the tradition, through the mediation of language, "entirely unobtrusively," as Gadamer's account tries to show? Heidegger's attempt to overcome Hegel does not mean that he absolutely denies the possibility of a "mediation within identity" (ID 15),[13] or "the possibility of a natural change in language" (US 276) as described by Wilhelm von Humboldt. He only insists that there is a final leap *through* the normal conversation with the tradition to the creative event, which does not abide by previously established laws, but creates its own norms that bestow a unique bearing on the original thinker and changes the normal course of history fundamentally. The great thinker is of course influenced by his tradition, but only because he lets himself be influenced according to that unique insight which is to be thought by him (WD 39).[14] His translation of a text from its idiom to his own is based on a displacement into the ineffable source of all idioms. The trans-lation from one language to another here becomes the "carrying over" of language itself to its source (WD 140-41, HW 312).

And it is here, in the mysterious relation between language and Being, that the secret of the hermeneutic happening resides (US 96). For both thinkers, this occurrence takes place in the discourse which takes its course according to the subject matter. But in these parallel descriptions, one notes a nuance of difference which now becomes all important. Whereas Gadamer always speaks of "the coming-to-language of the subject matter" (360, 439, 446, 450), Heidegger orients himself toward the "unspoken bidding" of its "place of sojourn" (WD 110), in which "the course of such a discourse must have its own character, according to which it would be more silent than spoken" (US 152). In both instances it is a matter of the inaugural event of the upsurge of the unsaid into the said. Yet Heidegger's dwelling on the unsaid could strike us as perverse if we were not already aware of the deliberate reversal which he sees as essential for that rare discourse which is intended to be radical.

Their difference in emphasis becomes more striking in their explicit remarks on the relation between language and Being. Gadamer describes it as a speculative unity of mirroring, where Being displays itself in language, so that language *is* Being in its self-display; and Being, far from being a "speechless pre-given," comes to language for just this display.

> What comes to language is indeed something other than the spoken word itself. But the word is only a word through that which comes to language in it. It is there in its own sensuous Being only in order to sublimate itself into what is said. But in turn, that which comes to language is not a speechless pre-given, but rather receives its determination in the word. (450)

But Heidegger asserts in almost identical terms that "the sayable word receives its determination from the unsayable" (N II 484). And it is the ineffable itself which somehow finds its way into words, an ineffable not in the objective sense of *an sich*, but as the most comprehensively immediate of human experiences which, because of this, is unmediatizable *in itself* and the medium which permeates all other experiences, "the hold of all holds, the relation of all relations" (US 267: *Ver-hältnis*). And the ineffable "speaks" (US 266): Not a language in any recognizable sense, except as a pure and simple showing which always withdraws in favor of that which shows itself. To describe its manifestation as a melodic modulation has the advantage of the less tangible, nonsubstantial character of the auditory over the visual metaphor of the mirror used by Gadamer. (Is this because Gadamer is more concerned with the written word?) Nevertheless Heidegger's account trails off into the cryptic here, and many have parted ways with him at this point,[15] just as Husserl lost his following when he pushed toward the groundlessness of the transcendental ego. But can we really deny the validity of the resolute endeavor to get to the bottom of things, even if that bottom falls out and opens onto an abyss? Must not such an endeavor at least be attempted to see where it might lead? Perhaps the most useless of endeavors, this "descent into the poverty of thought," but perhaps because of this the most philosophical, or as Heidegger would prefer to put it, the most "thoughtful."

Instead of the regress into the birthplace of language, Gadamer prefers to situate the "horizon of a hermeneutical ontology" (415) in language itself, the familiar language of the world and not the silent "language" of Being. Rather than trying to catch a glimpse of the mysterious other side of the horizon, he finds all that is necessary in the linguistic world horizon itself. For the acquisition of a particular language, through which we become familiar with the world, far from binding us to a particular world view, endows us with the possibility of fusing with any other language and its world horizons. And does this not indicate the infinite power of language which knows no bounds in its capacity to say all? Hence a language in which metaphysics happened to be expressed is not thereby doomed to speak only in the objectifying terms of the subject-predicate relations of classical grammar. Hegel's doctrine of the speculative sentence already suggests other directions. But to acknowledge the universality of language does not mean to accept his conception of the absolute transparency of spirit. Heidegger's crucial discovery of a *Wesen* which involves not only presence (*Anwesen*) but also absence (*Abwesen*) applies particularly to the essence of language, in which what is said always involves at once the unsaid of a totality of meaning. This linguistic relation to the whole thus always preserves the possibility of thinking that which cannot be thought ahead of its time. The new is there with the old, for with the first words of a language all is already said, even though all is still to be said. Hence no leap, reversal, special event or abrupt mission is needed to account for the emergence of the new from the old.[16]

To describe this process, Gadamer finds his clues not only in Heidegger but in the tradition from Hegel back to Plato, in the notion of speculative dialectic, but now no longer a subjective dialectic of the spirit or an objective dialectic of becoming, but rather a dialectic in the variegated display of language. One could then describe the movement of the conversation of tradition in the way in which Gadamer characterizes the essence of the Hegelian dialectic, that it is "an immanent development in which the concepts move themselves more and more toward ever greater differentiation and concretization,"[17] but without distinguishing so sharply between the concept and its expression and representation in the word. The dialectic for Gadamer is finite insofar as it never ends in complete knowledge and perfect identity of consciousness and object, but continually opens onto ever new experiences through its unceasing questioning. Yet this very openness is described as a relation to the infinite, to the inexhaustibility of an "inner dimension of multiplication" (434) of the word, to a totality of meaning. Nothing essential is ever lost or left behind, old meanings are at least latently integrated into new and broader possibilities of meaning as the situation changes and the receivers of the tradition are new and different (423–24, 437–38). The *Über-setzung* of tradition is thus more a matter of mediation of past and present rather than a displacement toward a radically new future. The discontinuity that demands an amalgam of the horizons of past and present is ultimately only presumptive (289). The temporal distance is not really a yawning abyss, but is filled with the continuity of that which is mediated by the tradition (281).

But at this point, one begins to feel restive in the face of the lack of emphasis of a sense of the erratic, of the possibility of failure and of all the other contingencies that enter into human existence. Even if it may be true that on the level of language, the healing power of time filters out the sources of error that accrue from being too close to an issue, it would seem that other levels of experience need to be invoked to complete a hermeneutic ontology, to indicate, for example, the necessity for the "demystifying" movement of hermeneutic.

But one could perhaps say the same for Heidegger's radical hermeneutic, and therefore "one-sided" in its leap over all forms of intermediate hermeneutics. And perhaps Heidegger is not far from Gadamer after all. Gadamer and other commentators have long pointed to the submerged Hegelian elements in Heidegger's thought. True, his basis for history is not absolute knowledge, but the erratic mysterious. Yet the attempt to grasp history comprehensively is there. And the continual interplay between the determinate and the indeterminate, truth and untruth, said and unsaid, are all reminiscent of Hegel's framework of Being and nothing mediating themselves into the truth of concrete becoming.[18] Are we not once again on the threshold between finite and infinite? In his latest efforts, Heidegger no longer appears to insist on an inexorable finitude. How can he, in the face of an indeterminable event which he identifies as the One and All, hidden totality, inexhaustible fullness?[19]

But when this whole is aboriginal Being instead of the historical life world, does this not radically alter the character of the unsaid into its impossible asymptote, the unsayable? Or is it that, when Gadamer refers to language as a process of making oneself at home in the world and Heidegger points to its relation to the aboriginal mystery, they are dealing with obverse sides of the same phenomenon or "horizon," the relation between *Heimat* and *Geheimnis*? When Gadamer sees an "inner infinity" in language because it knows no limits to its possibilities of expression, and Heidegger looks for "not a new language, but a changed relationship to the source of the old one,"[29], are they not in accord in the conviction in the inexhaustible wealth of language? Just as Hegel's speculative sentence realized possibilities beyond the metaphysical subject-object relation, so Heidegger's circular sentences (The source of truth is the truth of the source; The source of speech: the speech of the source) and monological sentences (The thing things, the world worlds, the event e-vents) explore possibilities toward a new epoch for the old language, not only directed toward uncovering what cannot be said ahead of time, but oriented toward the ineffable as such. By what warrant can we assert in advance that such an endeavor is impossible, if the attempt is not made?

But does not the task first need a long preparation? And is this to be achieved only by a comprehensive hermeneutic, or do we not also need the complementary experiences of lesser hermeneutics, which aim at exposing the unsaid in one or another region of human endeavor? Perhaps some of these too are "forest trails" which will bring us to the "simplicity of the manifold dimensions of Being."

NOTES

1. An initial version of this paper was presented to the Heidegger Circle on April 26, 1968, at the University of Pittsburgh. I wish to thank the members of the Circle for their helpful comments and candid criticisms. One of the participants, Richard Palmer, generously gave me access to manuscript portions of his recently published book, *Hermeneutics* (Evanston; Ill.: Northwestern University Press, 1969).

2. Hans-Georg Gadamer, *Wahrheit und Methode: Gründzuge einer philosophischen Hermeneutik*, 2nd ed., expanded through a supplement (Tübingen: J. C. B. Mohr, 1965). The first edition was published in 1960. The foreword to the second edition, in which Gadamer replies to his critics, is especially clarifying. Reference to this work, our central source, is hereafter simply to the pages only.

Further significant clarifications of *Wahrheit und Methode* are to be found in Gadamer's recently published *Kleine Schriften* I: *Philosophie: Hermeneutik;* II: *Interpretationen* (Tübingen: J. C. B. Mohr, 1967), to which a third volume, including a complete bibliography of Gadamer's work, is soon to be added. Since these texts were received after the main body of this paper was drafted, I have incorporated some of the most striking of these clarifications in the notes. Hereafter referred to as KS.

3. By thus following Heidegger, Gadamer's hermeneutic is fundamentally ontological rather than epistemological, inasmuch as the issue centers on the "Being of history" rather than on the "possibility of science" (KS I, 4). Gadamer, who was a student of Heidegger's in those "white hot" days of philosophical intensity immediately preceding *Being and Time*, sees the real question even in *Being and Time* as not centered on the understanding of Being but on the Being of understanding, i.e., "in what way understanding is Being (KS I, 74). For if understanding is at once thrown, it is not considered simply as an activity of the conscious self, but as a happening of Being. And since already in *Being and Time* understanding is also at once discursive, this movement of Being is a happening of language, which is precisely where Gadamer's hermeneutic finally plumbs for its most original soundings.

4. Hans-Georg Gadamer, *Le Problème de la conscience historique*, Claire Cardinal Mercier no. 2, 1957 (Publications universitaires de Louvain, 1963). Four lectures given at Louvain in 1958, presenting some of the material later published in *Wahrheit und Methode*, but with varying nuances. Hereafter cited as PCH.

5. Certain variants to this account of the circle and the following account of temporal distance can be detected by comparing the above references with Gadamer's article in the Heidegger *Festschrift:* "Vom Zirkel des Verstehens," *Martin Heidegger zum siebzigsten Geburtstag* (Tübingen: Neske, 1959), pp. 23–34.

6. The interpreter's encounter with a text, the so-called "hermeneutic situation," begins to take on the character of an existential *Grenzsituation!* Those acquainted with Heidegger will recognize here the essentials of his discussion of *Ent-schlossenheit* as the total openness of a radical questioning that lets be. The most originative thinking begins in astonishment or *Angst*, responds by questioning, and ends by listening for the unspoken message promised in the question. But even though the listening takes precedence over the questioning as the most "authentic gesture of thinking" (US, 175), even more fundamental than the interpretive exposure of the message is the event of the advent of the message itself, happening as it does beyond human guidance and methodical manipulation. Accordingly, "the hermeneutical does not first signify the exposition, for even before this there is the bringing of the message and tidings" (US, 122).

For Gadamer, the "hermeneutic *Ur*-phenomenon" (KS I, 107) is located in the dialectical relation between answer and question. Accordingly, an assertion is truly understood only when it is seen as the spoken answer to an unspoken question (KS I, 99, 142). But every question is in its turn a motivated background of presuppositions whose hardened crust must at times be broken up in order to stir up new questions (KS I, 54). Such is the function of the genuine researcher, who has the ability to uncover the truly productive questions (KS I, 108). His is the ability to discover *in* the articulated tradition of his field what is yet to be said. Hence all research work really involves hermeneutics, for whenever it is a matter of listening for the unsaid in the said, there is hermeneutic.

It seems that this would apply in some sense to the tradition of natural science as well, where the "language" is mathematical and the "text" is "Nature," though the hermeneutic issue probably lies primarily on the level of guiding presuppositions expressed (whenever they are expressed) in much more mundane language, as indicated in the works of N. R. Hanson, T. S. Kuhn, S. Toulmin, et al.

7. Heidegger speaks of "the silent course of a conversation that moves us." *Discourse on Thinking*, trans. J. M. Anderson and E. H. Freund (New York: Harper & Row, 1966), p. 70. And Heidegger's conversation with a Japanese friend "about" language turns out to be a discourse "from," and in this sense "by," language (US, 149–50).

8. But the Heideggerian conception of repetition is very relevant here. The issue is central: how to comprehend the fact that the same subject matter is understood differently at different times? For repetition not only appropriates what is transmitted, but also transmutes or "destroys" it.

9. In this regard, Gadamer has, ever since his student days, been fascinated with the Heideggerian theme of the forgetfulness which necessarily precedes and underlies recollection, for his part emphasizing its concealment (*Verbergung*) positively as a preservation (*Bergung*) in the shelter of language, the "house of Being," which thus provides continuity to history (KS I, 86–90, 160). Rather than unhiddenness, which Gadamer considers to be more Greek than Heideggerian, Heidegger's most significant thought concerns the forgetting involved in familiar experiences like instrumentality which hermeneutic phenomenology is called upon to draw out of implicitness. In its lived execution, i.e., *actus exercitus*, language in use is overlooked and passed over in silence, like a tool in its unobtrusive service. But as a medium without which man cannot function as a man, language is much more encompassing than a tool that can be put down and taken up as its function is required (KS I, 95–98). Not being under our control like a tool, language in effect overwhelms man and takes on its own *actus exercitus* or historicity, which Gadamer now describes as the continual synthesis between past and present

horizons (KS I, 57). Nevertheless this "house" is our secret familiarity with the world (*zu Hause*), our home (*Heimat*) in all of its mystery (*Geheimnis*).

10. Hegel's doctrine of the "speculative sentence" (Preface to *The Phenomenology of Mind*, Baillie translation, pp. 118–24) is the touchpoint for this terminology. Without accepting the absolute self transparency of *Wissen*, Gadamer nevertheless sees in Hegel's *Geist* an initial attempt to transcend the subject-object dichotomy of metaphysics, corresponding to the role of language in his own philosophy. For Gadamer, the phenomenon of language provides a finite relation to the infinite much more appropriate to human experience, thus still "infinite like *Geist* and yet finite like any happening" (KS I, 148). The infinity of meaning here is described in other contexts as the "totality of meaning" (441). One is reminded of the formula *totum sed non totaliter* which the medievals used to comprehend the Aristotelian statement that "the soul is in a way all." And it is after all this issue of the "infinite correspondence between soul and Being" (KS I, 64) which is now being approached by way of language (434 ff.).

11. Wittgenstein's phrase is no accident here. Though Gadamer's conception of the play of language is much broader, encompassing as it does the whole of language rather than localized idioms, he finds a kindred spirit in Wittgenstein on this issue, inasmuch as he emphasizes the pure functionality of the word as the proper character of language (KS I, 146). Cf. Gadamer's "Die phänomenologische Bewegung," *Philosophische Rundschau* II, 1963, pp. 1–45, esp. pp. 41–45. For an account of the historicity of language which in certain respects dovetails with Gadamer's, see Michael Polanyi, *Personal Knowledge* (New York: Harper Torchbook, 1964), pp. 104–17.

12. Cf. also Heidegger's *Vorbemerkung* to *Wegmarken* (Frankfurt am Main: Vittorio Klostermann, 1967). Gadamer often makes the same point, in opposition to Schleiermacher's psychologistic hermeneutic (e.g., 280).

13. At another point, he even gives a nuance of encouragement to interpret the character of the conversation with past philosophers as a dialectic, at least at some level: "Whether the dialogue is necessarily a dialectic *and when* [it is so], this we leave open." *Was ist das—die Philosophie?* (Pfullingen: Neske, 1960), p. 31 (my emphasis). And in his discussion of speculative dialectic in the Gadamer *Festschrift*, Heidegger points out that revelation for man is not through man but "through the logos" (p. 55), i.e., *dia-logos* (p. 45). But his *logos* is a more primordial (and elusive) conception of language than Gadamer's. "Hegel und die Griechen," *Die Gegenwart der Griechen in neueren Denken* (Tübingen: J. C. B. Mohr, 1960), pp. 43–57. Since published in *Wegmarken*, op. cit., pp. 255–72). A few hints of Heidegger's version of an acceptable dialectic are given in HW, 169 and WD, 101.

14. And furthermore, "the thinker can never say what is most his own. It must remain unsaid, because the sayable word receives its determination

from the unsayable" (N II, 484). And nevertheless, conversely, "Every incipient and authentic naming utters the unspoken, and indeed in such a way that it remains unspoken" (WD, 119). The unsayable is somehow said!

We might recall here Bergson's essay on philosophical intuition, in which he calls for reading the history of philosophy not simply in terms of a chain of influences, whereby the individual philosopher is reduced to a synthesizer of the currents of his day, but more importantly in terms of the unique intuition which the philosopher spends his life trying to express without ever succeeding. Moving beyond the levels of reading the history of philosophy in terms of influence-relations and individual intuition to the level of the "loving strife" of the conversation between thinkers, in which "the philosophers of the past are constantly changing their meanings" through "renovating interpretations," Paul Ricoeur goes one step further and locates the unity of this history in "the *Being* preliminary to the questioning" which prompts and permeates all the questions in the long conversation and yet always itself eludes being said. What the conversation is about and what initiated the conversation in the first place itself exceeds the conversation. "And yet we have no other access to the *One* than the debate of one philosophy with another." *History and Truth*, trans. C. A. Kelbley (Evanston, Ill.: Northwestern University Press, 1965), pp. 52–53.

15. For example, Laszlo Versenyi, *Heidegger, Being, and Truth* (New Haven, Conn.: Yale University Press, 1965), pp. 159–76.

In order to avoid "the harassing backward flight of thought in search of the first truth" and "to escape the difficulties of a radical beginning of philosophy," Ricoeur locates his hermeneutic in existing language, "in which everything has already been said in some fashion." "From the midst of speech, to remember." But Ricoeur restricts his hermeneutic field to something less than the entirety of language in focusing on the multivocal symbols of myth, dream, and poetry. *The Symbolism of Evil*, trans. E. Buchanan (New York: Harper & Row, 1967), pp. 348–49.

Ricoeur's hermeneutic aphorism, "the symbol gives rise to thought," bears illuminating resemblances as well as differences to certain remarks by Heidegger, e.g., "withdrawal is that which truly gives rise to thought" (WD, 55). For Ricoeur, it is not the indeterminate but the overdetermined content of a surplus of sense in the symbol that provides food for thought. Likewise, for Heidegger, "withdrawal" cannot be considered as a purely negative term referring to the indeterminate "there is" without keeping in mind its inexhaustible power to "give."

16. "Anmerkungen zu dem Thema 'Hegel und Heidegger,'" *Natur und Geschichte: Karl Löwith zum 70 Geburtstag* (Stuttgart: Kohlhammer, 1967), pp. 123–31. See pp. 129–31. This is Gadamer's most extensive critique of Heidegger in relation to his own thought. On the universality of language, KS I: 31–32, 57–58, 99–100, 111, 175.

17. "Hegel und die antike Dialektik," *Hegel-Studien* 1, 1961, pp. 173–99. See p. 197.

18. *Natur und Geschichte*, op. cit., pp. 124–25.

19. William J. Richardson, S.J., *Heidegger: Through Phenomenology to Thought* (The Hague: M. Nijhoff, 1963), p. 640.

20. Preface to Richardson, op. cit., p. xxiii.

CODE TO ABBREVIATIONS OF REFERENCES TO HEIDEGGER'S TEXTS

EM	*Einführung in die Metaphysik* (Tübingen: Niemeyer, 1958)
HD	*Erläuterungen zu Holderlins Dichtung* (Frankfurt a. M.: Klostermann, 1951)
HW	*Holzwege* (Frankfurt a. M.: Klostermann, 1957)
ID	*Identität und Differenz* (Pfullingen: Neske, 1957)
N II	*Nietzsche*, zweiter Band (Pfullingen: Neske, 1961)
SG	*Der Satz vom Grund* (Pfullingen: Neske, 1958)
SZ	*Sein und Zeit* (Tübingen: Niemeyer, 1957)
US	*Unterwegs zur Sprache* (Pfullingen: Neske, 1960)
VA	*Vorträge und Aufsätze* (Pfullingen: Neske, 1959)
WD	*Was heisst Denken?* (Tübingen: Niemeyer, 1954)

2. HERMENEUTICS AND TRUTH

David Ingram

Recently, some philosophers in the Anglo-American and Continental traditions, having rid themselves of the antiquated presuppositions and taxonomies of classical epistemology and metaphysics, have turned their attention toward various holistic doctrines to account for the nature of truth and being. Classical epistemology held that truth was a property which denoted the adequation, or correspondence, of knowledge and reality, conceived as absolutely self-subsisting, univocal being. Attempts to explain this correspondence invariably invoked such metaphors as mirroring, picturing, reflecting, etc.[1]

The major difficulties with the correspondence theory of truth became perspicuous, the holists maintain, with the advent of post-Cartesian philosophy. It is Descartes to whom we owe the idea that the *cogito* and the peculiar conviction which accompanies it are to be regarded as the *sine qua non* of knowledge as such. The path leading from immediate subjectivity to external reality is now to be guaranteed by way of indubitable evidence. Henceforth, epistemology becomes the chief concern of philosophy, which is delegated the task of showing how our knowledge claims (or mental representations) can be justified as objectively valid.

According to the holists, neither transcendental nor empirical epistemologies have satisfactorily carried out this task. As Quine and others pointed out, the 'theory-ladenness' of observation statements — the fact that meaning and reference are a function, not of atomic acts of ostensive definition, but of syncategorematic inclusion within a specific semantic totality — necessarily frustrates any attempt to define the meaning of so-called referring expressions in terms of a neutral operationalist description of expected sensory presentations.[2]

To be sure, the transcendental approach to the problem inaugurated by Kant was intended to obviate the aforementioned difficulties encountered by empiricism through the postulation and deduction of *a priori* categories. Hegel notwithstanding, however, the assumption that all particular conceptual worldviews are commensurable and converge upon an absolute set of Archimedian points has been dealt a serious blow by philosophers of science such as Kuhn and Feyerabend.

This takes us to the topic of my paper. The significance of hermeneutics for the problem of truth, I shall argue, is two-fold. On the one hand, contemporary philosophical hermeneutics is the pre-eminent defender of epistemological holism. The major proponents of this posture argue that truth-claims which purport to say something about reality are relative to irreducible interpretative schemas. The lack of a universal language in terms of which every epistemic frame of reference might be univocally translated in turn seems to entail relativism — an implication which Rorty and Derrida wholeheartedly embrace and defend. On the other hand, the philosophical hermeneutics developed by Gadamer is introduced as an alternative to the holistic relativism advanced by Rorty (though Rorty conveniently elides this fact in his commentary of the former's work). Gadamer, I contend, not only seeks to refute the classical theory of truth and its correlative methodological presuppositions but he also undertakes the justification of a different concept of truth which still retains a link to the idea of universal agreement.

The question addressed by this essay is whether Gadamer's concept of truth fully succeeds in overcoming holistic relativism. My investigation of this problem will proceed as follows. In section one I will examine Heidegger's defense of hermeneutic holism and his theory of historicity with the aim of demonstrating its implications for a theory of truth. Section two will join the issue of truth as it is taken up by Gadamer in *Wahrheit und Methode*. I shall endeavor to show that Gadamer elaborates a dialogical model of hermeneutic experience which draws its basic impetus from Heidegger's theory of historicity and Hegel's concept of experience. Finally, section three will conclude with a critical examination of the problem of deriving normative conditions from hermeneutic experience.

I

In *Sein und Zeit* Heidegger addresses the separate issues of truth and being as aspects of the same problem. By improperly formulating the question of being as one of substance ontology replete with its taxonomic division of beings into hierarchies of genera and species, Western metaphysics, Heidegger observes, concealed from itself the primary question of being as the *ground* and *possibility* of beings.[3] The classical notion of being conceived as an independently subsisting substratum of intrinsically determinate properties—what Aristotle called *hypokeimenon*—abstracts from the contextual background against which discrete 'things' appear as possible beings. Hence, the difficulty arises concerning the relation of correspondence which obtains between two separate existents, *res* and *intellectus*.[4]

According to Heidegger, beings are not originally encountered as isolable objects with substantive properties such as color, weight, extension, etc., but are rather disclosed as implements of use, what he calls *ready-to-hands (Zuhanden)*. The disclosure of pragamata, which includes such items as tools, equipment, construction materials etc., is essentially teleological and practical, viz., their *meaning* and *identity* are defined with reference to a *totality* of assignments and functions, all of which are referred back to the intentional vector of our aims.[5]

Heidegger elaborates the holistic nature of experience by designating *understanding (Verstehen)* as the primary structure of our insertion in the world. Understanding so conceived is neither a subjective faculty of sympathetic concern nor a specific epistemic method for deciphering symbolic objectifications, but rather denotes the way in which human beings inhabit a world. For Heidegger, understanding is assigned the status of an ontological 'clearing' whereby a world-horizon, or contextual background, is originally projected. The anticipatory, protensive orientation of projection (*Entwerfen*) is analogous to that foresight which guides our reading of a text. In the case of textual comprehension, the meaning of each sentence is syncategorematically determined by situating it within a not-yet-completed sequence of interrelated actions and events which are tied together in a coherent totality by way of an anticipatory completion of the narrative. Similarly, from an ontological perspective, specific involvements with persons and entities are thrown into relief against the anticipatory projection of a world-horizon. In both instances there exists a semantic interdependence of part and whole.[6]

The significance of Heidegger's hermeneutic holism for the problem of truth can be grasped once we understand the derivative nature of the proposition as that which refers to an object. In the pre-propositional circumspective concern (*Umsicht*) which typifies our 'sighting' of tools, there is no contemplative detachment separating 'subject' from 'object'; the implement is inconspicuous and merges with the manipulator. Though it is impossible to piece together the tool from an isolated subject and object, one can trace the emergence of the 'thing', or *present-at-hand*, in breakdowns and disruptions within the equipmental network. Once the tool loses its functionality, the unity of the referential *Gestalt* dissolves and we are left with a lifeless 'object' which manifests itself as a potential subject of predicates.

The origin of the thing, then, roughly coincides with the possibility of the proposition as that which explicitly predicates properties of an object.[7] Once the proposition is further removed from immediately indicating something within our experiential horizon and is reified into a piece of information for purposes of transmission, it becomes possible to view it as a thing to be compared with an objective state-of-affairs. Hence, just as 'thinghood' is revealed as a limited manner of projecting a scientific, theoretical world which is parasitic on an *a priori* matrix of practical involvements, so too, Heidegger argues that the correspondence theory of truth is likewise possible only against the background of a more universal experience of truth conceived as 'disclosedness' (*aletheia*).[8] Heidegger's analysis of truth as disclosedness is essentially congruent with our commonsensical understanding of the notion. Heidegger asserts that the truth of a proposition manifests itself when it is demonstrated to be true. Such demonstration has nothing to do with comparing proposition with object, but involves providing evidence in support of the proposition, e.g., by pointing something out or by proffering reasoned justification. The fact that the truth of a proposition is a function of its being *warranted* rather than of its being related in some mysterious way to brute sense-data shows that a prior *context of discourse* determining the semantic domain of reference is already presupposed. The presentation of evidence in support of a proposition, for example, merely singles out those salient aspects of the data that have already been previously located by an agreed upon set of conventional signifiers. In other words, ostensive reference presupposes that the referent already be semantically highlighted, named, and thereby ontologically determined *vis-à-vis* the entire linguistic totality of which the atomic signifiers are but a part.[9]

Now it is Heidegger's contention that understanding is itself ontologically embedded in a prior, culturally determined matrix of presuppositions which delimit the range of possible meaningfulness. This dimension of Heidegger's theory of understanding, which will occupy the remainder of our treatment of his hermeneutic theory, leads directly to a confrontation with the issue of relativism.

According to Heidegger, presuppositions operate below the threshold of conscious intent as a *vis a tergo* which comprises the familiar referential background guiding our search for possible meaning. This dependence upon a pre-reflective sedimentation of orientations, what Heidegger calls the *facticity* of human existence, signifies the state of being delivered over to a situation, a mood, a cultural identity, etc.[10] Now Heidegger believes that this dependency has ontological import for the way in which human being and world are codeterminative. Projected possibilities which do not facilitate understanding, or in some other way fail to mesh with the horizon of expectations, exert a counterthrust that alters this horizon, and therewith, our self-identity.[11] The reciprocal reinterpretation of world and self (*Auslegung*), which transpires as a result of this critical interplay is further elaborated by Heidegger in his discussion of historicity (*Geschichtlichkeit*).

The linguistic forms and traditions that are inculcated in us map out a sort of destiny (*Geschick*) or pre-determined manner of viewing reality in terms of which we understand ourselves and our world. Not only is the being of individuals and their world relative to tradition, but this ontological circle is itself modulated through cultural transmission. A cultural heritage is not a static accumulation of anachronisms, but is a dynamic process whereby what is handed down and preserved is necessarily reinterpreted in light of the interests and concerns of the present.[12]

We can summarize the preceding discussion by saying that Heidegger's holistic account of truth conceived as a contextual clearing for possible denotation is essentially tied to the way in which historical languages and traditions open-up horizons of meaning. From a synchronic perspective, particular entities appear in a determinate light only insofar as they are hermeneutically located within a referential *Gestalt* that ultimately refers back to our purposes and aims. Seen diachronically, however, these referential totalities are themselves determined by historical possibilities that have been handed down.

The aforementioned account of truth clearly has relativistic implications. If disclosure is structurally defined by an ontological circle in which every interpretation continually discloses new possibilities and thereby transcends itself, then understanding and truth will necessarily be *partial* and *incomplete*. There can in principle be no final, absolute interpretation of reality which escapes revision in view of the open horizon of future projects. Indeed, because world-horizons are projections of sedimented presuppositions, they essentially remain relative to concrete historical circumstances.

II

Heidegger's hermeneutic holism undermines the foundations of classical epistemology in both its empirical and transcendental forms. The semantic interdependence which obtains between isolated propositions and the linguistic totality entails that objective reference and correlatively, ontological commitment, can hardly be conceived as a function of ostensive grounding in reality any more than can verification be regarded as a function of adducing interpretation-free sense-data statements in support of objective facts.[13]

The correspondence criterion of truth is operational only as long as the categories determining ontological commitments are shared alike by one and all. For this reason, Rorty correctly observes that traditional epistemology is possible only within the parameters of a shared discourse.[14] As the framework progressively succeeds in expanding its explanatory purview to include ever new horizons of discourse, it can be said to approach asymptotically an ideal of universal agreement. Charles Peirce, for one, believed that the hypothetico-deductive methodology of the natural sciences established the possibility for achieving such an ideal consensus, though as Kuhn and Feyerabend have pointed out, there is no rational consensus regarding the acceptance of this paradigm.[15] Nevertheless, there is no gainsaying the fact that hermeneutic holism condones coherence, or consensus, as a criterion of truth. The progressive translation of alien discourses into the unitary idiom of a given paradigm in a manner which enhances the overall explanatory power and consistency of the system also facilitates pragmatic utility.[16]

Transcendental idealism, however, rests its case on the existence of a *consensus gentium* concerning such pragmatic values. Recently, Jürgen Habermas and K.-O. Apel have attempted to revive the transcendentalist program by grounding the methodologies of the natural sciences, the humanities, and the social sciences in distinct *a priori* cognitive interests (*kenntnisleitende Interesse*).[17] Though such interests straddle the line separating biological instincts and cultural dispositions, these philosophers concede that their precise meaning and value is contingent upon historically variable interpretations. Assuming that Heidegger is correct, the historicity of human understanding would indeed preclude the possibility of attaining a complete consensus uniting all historical interpretations. Because living languages undergo constant mutation in the open horizon of possible interpretation, the Hegelian project of sublating all historical worldviews to a unified system appears to be a fantastic chimera.

The incompleteness and relativity of cultural horizons brings into question the very possibility of discovering a viable model of truth. Nietzsche, we know, took the perspectivalism of our condition as proof of the infeasibility of such a notion. "Truth is the kind of error without which a certain species of living being could not live."[18] Derrida, following Nietzsche, has drawn the most radical conclusions from the hermeneutic interdependence which subsists between the signifier and the signified. According to Derrida, every signifier is a metaphor for the signified. Referent, symbol, and concept (meaning) are co-determinative and the total signifier only acquires a meaning metonymically by way of further reference to the entire system of signs.

> There is thus no phenomenality reducing the sign or the representer so that the thing signified may be allowed to glow finally in the luminosity of its presence. The so-called "thing itself" is always already a *representamen* shielded from the simplicity of intuitive evidence. The *representamen* functions only by giving rise to an *interpretant* that itself becomes a sign and so on to infinity.[19]

In opposition to structuralism, Derrida maintains that the system of signs — the field of possible reference — is indefinite and infinite. The semiological enterprise of connecting *nominatum* and sense as dual functions of the sign must give way to a grammatological study of the geneology of infinitely extending sign chains which never refer beyond themselves to a pristine signified. For Derrida, the primacy of spoken communication (conceived as immediate comprehension of a plenitude of meaning complete in itself) over writing must be reversed. Language is essentially haunted by the "trace" of "arche-writing" (*ar-*

chiécriture), namely, a fundamental alterity (*différance*) or spacing which designates both the inclusion of every sign within the semantic horizon of every other sign and the internal dialectical structure of the sign itself.[20] As a unity of difference and identity, the sign opens-up an exteriority (the world of extant signifieds) which in its very "otherness" and opacity reflects the alterity within the semantic interiority of the sign. Is this radical alterity which resides at the heart of the sign not already present in Heidegger's notion of historicity?

If human understanding, as an event of linguistic disclosure, is a continually self-transcending movement which loses itself in the indefinite horizon of possible interpretation, then the hermetic relativity of self-enclosed sign structures is indeed shattered, but only at the expense of dissolving into a play of de-centered acts of signification. Lacking a transcendental referent, it appears that no possible notion of truth can be salvaged out of this arbitrary play of signifiers.

There remains, however, an alternative to this radical relativism. Gadamer observes that the process of interpretation "which we are" is itself teleologically oriented toward a state of openness (*Offenheit*) and mutual recognition. Even Rorty, who bases his understanding of hermeneutics principally on Gadamer's work, acknowledges that hermeneutic holism entails a commitment of sorts to refrain from epistemological reductionism.

> . . . hermeneutics is an expression of hope that the cultural space left by the demise of epistemology will not be filled — that our culture should become one in which the demand for constraint and confrontation is no longer felt. The notion that there is a permanent neutral framework whose "structure" philosophy can display is the notion that the objects to be confronted by the mind, or the rules which constrain inquiry, are common to all discourse, or at least to every discourse on a given topic. Thus epistemology proceeds on the assumption that all contributions to a given discourse are commensurable. Hermeneutics is largely a struggle against this assumption.[21]

Despite this admission, Rorty denies that hermeneutics is in the business of showing that discourse and interpretation in general presuppose a consensus regarding the very rules of hermeneutic interplay. Hermeneutics, he informs us, has relinquished the search for absolutes and is content to "settle back into the 'relativism' which assumes that our only useful notions of 'true' and 'real' and 'good' are extrapolations . . . from practices and beliefs."[22]

No doubt, if truth is conceived as correspondence to an *antecedently* existing ground of agreement, one which is itself removed from the historical process of interpretation, then Rorty and Gadamer would concur that the search for such a truth must be in vain. Nevertheless, though there may not be any discourse which is capable of uniting speakers standing in incommensurable world-horizons, there still remains the *meta-hermeneutical* pre-condition which binds them together in a common effort to achieve agreement, namely, mutual recognition and openness. This pre-condition, Gadamer argues, is not adventitiously related to the process of generating consensus, notwithstanding the fact that it has only become a conscious demand since the "practices and beliefs" of the Enlightenment. That Gadamer himself espouses a faith in reason reminiscent of his predecessors in the German Idealist tradition is certainly ignored by most of his commentators, who prefer to concentrate their attention upon his more notable objection to the Enlightenment's "prejudice against prejudices"—a fact which may explain why they have strangely ignored the teleological dimension of his hermeneutics. Consequently, a propaedeutic examination of his hermeneutic theory must begin with a discussion of this objection in order to place it in proper perspective.

Romantic hermeneutics, Gadamer maintains, succumbs to historicism precisely because it never entirely succeeded in extricating itself from the enlightenment credo of scientific objectivity. The hermeneutic tradition extending from Schleiermacher to Dilthey viewed cultural artifacts as spiritual objectivities whose very being was alien to the interpreter in much the same way that extended substance was regarded as alien to the subjectivity of the scientist by post-Cartesian empiricism.[23] Dilthey, whose *Lebensphilosophie* laid the epistemological foundations of the tradition, uncritically appropriated the classical idea of truth in his transcendental deduction of the *Geisteswissenschaften*, insisting that the proper aim of textual interpretation be methodologically secured by way of an empathetic re-living (*Nacherleben*) of the original *Weltanschauungen* of alien spiritualities.[24] Buttressing this methodology was the assumption that human understanding is capable of transcending its own horizon of cultural prejudices, a presupposition which stands discredited from the standpoint articulated in *Sein und Zeit*.[25] Retrieving the Kerygmatic orientation of biblical hermeneutics, Gadamer argues that human understanding is not to be conceived as an act of psychological transposition, but is rather like a conversation in which a shared understanding (agreement) is reached that resists reduction to either of the interlocutors' privileged intentions.[26]

It will be recalled that Heidegger's analysis of historicity overcomes the hermetic relativism of historicism by showing that the semantic elisions separating the past from the present, the interpreter from tradition, subject and object, etc., are at least partially bridged in a continuous movement of reinterpretation. Nevertheless, the lack of closure endemic to our ever changing protensive reflection upon our past introduces a new element of relativity. Gadamer's *Wahrheit und Methode*, I believe, can be seen as an attempt to justify a theory of truth which takes into consideration this new relativity without, however, abandoning the idea of a teleological advance.

For Gadamer, true understanding is dialectical rather than reductive, viz., it is neither a blind repetition of an alien spirituality—a self-defeating act which, if possible, would only succeed in retaining meaningless anachronisms—nor an uncritical assimilation to the parochial present, which would equally obscure the novel meaning of the past. True understanding occupies a middle ground which preserves tradition as of vital consequence for the present only by critically excising both parochial prejudices and anachronisms.

Gadamer observes that the temporal distance separating the interpreter from tradition establishes the setting for hermeneutical reflection in two senses. First, the opacity of something which is partially anachronistic and resists immediate assimilation to one's familiar horizon of discourse challenges one's prejudices and stimulates critical reflection. Second, whatever universal value the text may have beyond what was understood by its original audience only emerges *ex post facto*, from the vantage point of a retrospective comprehension of the totality of past interpretations.[27] Finally, the true meaning of the text, Gadamer reminds us, is not identifiable with any one canonical interpretation, but is essentially relative to a changing horizon of discourse.

> . . . the discovery of the true meaning of (tradition) is never finished; it is, in fact, an infinite process. Not only are fresh sources of error constantly excluded, so that the true meaning has filtered out all kinds of things that obscure it but there emerge continually new sources of understanding which reveal unsuspected elements

of meaning . . . the filtering process is not a closed dimension, but is itself undergoing constant movement and extension.[28]

The continuity which ties together diverse historical interpretations in the unitary phenomenon of a cultural truth may be illustrated in a number of ways, so long as the eternal 'contemporaneity' of the phenomenon is not construed as an immutable Platonic essence.[29]

Gadamer's wedding of temporality and truth strikes one *prima facie* as nothing more than a re-affirmation of relativism. However, what Rorty and others lose sight of is that Gadamer also conceives the temporal dimension as teleological in nature.

In *Sein und Zeit* Heidegger already realized that the possibility of true (or authentic) understanding presupposed making "a reciprocative rejoinder to the possibility of that existence which has already been there."[30] Gadamer further adumbrates the contours of such a hermeneutic reciprocity in terms of the concept of *Bildung*, which informs Hegel's treatment of experience in the *Phenomenology of Spirit*.[31]

Bildung denotes a process of cultivation, or education whereby egoistic individuality is elevated to the moral plane of free, universal self-consciousness. Hegel observes that civic acculturation is a necessary condition for individual freedom because the private moral conscience which follows its own dictates must inevitably encounter the resistance of other such agents. This objective resistance is only overcome at the level of political life where individuals conduct themselves in accordance with legally promulgated norms and customary codes which they collectively acknowledge as representing their mutual interest.[32] If one continues one's *Bildung* further by familiarizing oneself with the languages, customs, and literary accomplishments of other historical peoples, one may even achieve a modicum of freedom from the narrow outlook of one's own cultural horizon and, by so doing, gradually learn to open oneself up to even broader horizons of fresh experience. Contrary to Dilthey, freedom from parochial prejudices is not achieved by methodologically eclipsing one's entire cultural background and restoring it to the state of a *tabula rasa*. Rather, growth into cultural horizons and the freedom which is thereby acquired is possible only by translating the unfamiliar into the familiar. Stated differently, freedom is not an event which transpires *sub specie aeternitatis* but is only actuated in the play of historical possibilities.[33]

Gadamer elucidates the structure of *Bildung* with respect to two concepts which recall Hegel's concept of experience: synthesis (*Aufhebung*) and dialogue. Gadamer compares *Bildung* to a progressive *fusion of horizons* in which interpreter and tradition are elevated to participation in a higher universality. This fusion is at once the cancellation of both the parochial prejudices of the interpreter which impede access to the unique message of the tradition and the dead anachronisms implicit in the latter as well as the *preservation* and *extension* of what is common to both of them.[34] The moment of cancellation results in a dual negation whereby both the being of the interpreter and the being of the tradition are altered.[35] However, in contradistinction to Hegel's dialectic of experience, hermeneutic experience does not culminate in a complete identity of subject and object (absolute knowledge) but only issues in progressively higher states of reflexive openness, what Gadamer calls *effective-historical consciousness (Wirkungsgeschichtliches Bewusstsein)*.[36]

The reflexivity of hermeneutic experience has the structure of a dialogue. Figuratively speaking, the interpreter and the text can be regarded as advancing potentially conflicting truth claims. The ebb and flow of questions and answers which arises from this encounter is like a game (*Spiel*) in which the play, more than the conscious intentions of the players, determines what happens. As in any conversation, what is said is "put at risk"; one's answer may not elicit the expected response from the other, but the dialogical process continues with the aim of achieving as much agreement as possible.[37]

Significantly, Gadamer argues that openness and mutual recognition are necessary conditions of true dialogue and he underscores the importance of this concept for hermeneutic theory by defining it in the normative phraseology of political rights.

> The experience of the 'thou' throws light on the idea of effective historical experience. The experience of the 'thou' also manifests the paradoxical element that something standing over against me asserts its own rights and requires absolute recognition and in that very process is understood. . . . It is the same with tradition.[38]

Again, hermeneutic reciprocity enjoins against any reductionistic attempt on the part of the interpreter to assimilate the meaning of the other by 'prejudging' it in advance.

In human relations the important thing is . . . to experience the 'thou' as 'thou', i.e., not overlook his claim and listen to what he has to say to us. To this end openness is necessary. Without this kind of openness to one another there is no human relationship.[39]

III

In retrospect, Gadamer's theory of truth reaffirms relativism, albeit, not without qualification. To be sure, the "hermetic" relativism typical of historicist doctrines of truth loses much of its appeal once the historicity of cultural transmission is acknowledged. Nevertheless, the relativity of truth-claims with respect to culture-bound discourses which cannot in principle command universal assent is not thereby discounted. Even if there were to exist a clear etymological descent linking historically disparate traditions so that a "shared meaning" were to emerge, it is apparent that each concrete interpretation of this meaning would yield an irreducibly unique and, therefore, different content. The meaning which is preserved and extended in cultural transmission is not an immutable essence, but undergoes cultural alteration in application to new historical circumstances. The higher universality of meaning which arises from the concourse of traditions is no more reducible to its constitutive cultural "moments" than is a vital organism reducible to its molecular, inorganic components. Gadamer cites Aristotle's example of natural law to illustrate the relativity of universal truth-claims, which are neither entirely conventional in the way that traffic regulations are nor absolutely unchangeable and independent of human convention in the way that physical laws are.[40] Moreover the achievement of a universal consensus uniting all present discourses would hardly mitigate the problem of relativism, for such a consensus would itself require reinterpretation in light of future events. Subsequently, it cannot be denied that Gadamer's theory of truth is inimical to traditional epistemic absolutism.

Despite the above conclusion, Gadamer's elucidation of the *process* of human understanding does contain something of a qualification of relativism. To recapitulate, according to Gadamer every successful clarification of the "thou" which truly captures its provocative meaning without distortion or diminution involves hermeneutical reflection. The latter, in turn, contributes to a process of *Bildung* whereby our parochial horizons are liberated from restrictive prejudices and broadened. The maturation of free, self-conscious, universal spirituality is itself impelled by a dialogical interplay of prejudices which progressively evolves higher levels of openness and reciprocity. Thus, the very *modus operandi* of human understanding is teleologically oriented toward a recognition of the "thou" as one whose individuality merits an equal right to be respected and understood. Though such an attitude no doubt informs any search for new meaning, it is especially definitive of communicative understanding. Indeed, Gadamer regards reciprocity as in some sense a transcendental condition for the very possibility of human communication as such.

Might not Gadamer's analysis of reciprocity procure for humanity a *normative* direction which is not subject to the relativistic vicissitudes of time and place? Unfortunately, Gadamer does not give us an unequivocal response to this question. On the one hand, he endorses the view that dialogical reciprocity is a necessary and universal condition founding all possible communication. On the other hand, he just as emphatically repudiates the possibility of any transcendentally justified ethic.[41] Wherein, then, does the normative status of reciprocity reside?

In his social and political writings, Gadamer occasionally likens the fundamental consensus which unites and harmonizes the different social strata of a community (*Gemeinschaft*) to the equilibrium (*Gleichgewicht*) of forces which secures the well-being of a biological organism.[42] Language is here regarded as the ultimate medium of consensual solidarity and organic metaphors are introduced to underscore the egalitarian interaction which constitutes its syncretic unity. Language is a "game of interpretation" in which "everyone is at the center."[43] The egalitarianism of this dialogue is primarily a reflection of the primacy of social process over individual and corporate will. Inasmuch as social life consists of a vast web of intersecting contracts, norms and other forms of mutual agreement linking a plurality of autonomous wills, it essentially extends beyond the unitary control of particular agencies. Even totalitarian governments, it would seem, must respect established customs and practices which foster harmonious interaction if their authority is to be freely recognized as legitimate. The tendency of this line of thought is to treat relations of authority and inequality, to the extent that they typify stable communities, as epiphenomenal manifestations of a prior consent freely given by those occupying subordinate positions in the social hierarchy. Consequently, we find Gadamer arguing, for example, that the rhetorical hegemony which corporate powers apparently exercise with respect to formation of public opinion is illusory because it is dialogically checked and countered by individual consumers whose scales of preference function as the decisive factor regulating production in the free market.

On the above reading, the normative scope of dialogical reciprocity is universal and necessary for all "true" (i.e., harmonious) communities, regardless of the specific forms of institutionalized authority and inequality they possess. Because the meaning of reciprocity has now been extended to cover a seemingly *indefinite* range of social arrangements, it is doubtful whether any *concrete, prescriptive* content can be generated from it. Gadamer reminds us that this is in perfect keeping with the general tenor of his philosophical hermeneutics, which extrudes methodological and prescriptive considerations in favor of *ontological description*.[44] Habermas here correctly observes that Gadamer's ontological hermeneutics harbours a neo-Kantian prejudice which perpetuates a suspect dichotomy separating facts and values.[45] The corollary to such a view is a relativism which condones all *de facto* social consensus, no matter how *ideologically* constrained it might be due to covert disparities in economic and political power, as dialogically well-founded so long as it is sustained by tacit consent.[46]

Notwithstanding this rather negative assessment of Gadamer's theory of truth, it is perfectly obvious that Gadamer does attach some prescriptive import to dialogical reciprocity. This is particularly evident in his debate with Habermas, where he argues that there is an *a priori* limit to social engineering, including the kind of psychotherapeutic sociology advocated by Habermas, which ostensibly authorizes the "critic of ideology" to question others as pathologically affected, as lacking the qualifications for rational accountability, and, therefore, as unreliable in matters of speech. Apropos of the above remark, Gadamer has pointed out that Habermas's critical sociology has the paradoxical consequence of subverting the very fabric of societal reciprocity which it seeks to restore under the aegis of therapy.[47] Yet, one can detect in his more recent pronouncements concerning the deleterious impact of mass-media manipulation something of a rapprochement with the "critical" position espoused by his opponent.[48] Gadamer now submits that even in modern Western democracies which formally institutionalize procedural rules guaranteeing freedom of speech and association, the balance of dialogical give and take is so tilted in favor of corporate powers that the *lingua franca* by means of which society as a whole reaches consensus is inevitably distorted. This is a surprising admission, for Gadamer here seems to be saying that true dialogical reciprocity is *not* compatible with a state of affairs in which socio-economic disparities and political privileges constrain the "natural equilibrium" of dialogical checks and balances — *be they acknowledged legitimate or otherwise.*

> The real political activity of the citizen has become . . . restricted to the participation in elections . . . In the old days it was the personal participation of the citizens in the administrative work which controlled and neutralized the impact of special interest groups . . . on the common welfare. Today it is much more difficult to control and neutralize the organization of powerful economic interests. Even the opinions which form the patterns of social life and constitute the conditions for solidarity are today dominated to a great extent by the technical and economic organizations within our civilization.[49]

Eschewing a social psycho-therapeutic solution to the problem of post-modern dystopia, Gadamer prefers to advocate mutual restraint on the part of would-be social engineers and media technocrats. Rhetorical manipulation, Gadamer concludes, though indispensable as a means of generating societal consensus, needs to be counterbalanced by greater dialogical self-determination.

> Both rhetoric and the transmission of scientific knowledge are monological in form; both need the counterbalance of hermeneutical appropriation, which works in the form of dialogue. And precisely and especially practical and political reason can only be realized and transmitted dialogically. I think, then, that the chief task of philosophy is to justify this way of reason and to defend practical and political reason against the domination of technology based upon science . . . it vindicates again the noblest task of the citizen . . . decision-making according to one's own responsibility . . .[50]

Is the above citation not a moral *recommendation* to promote the cause of a more democratic society? If so, how can it be squared with Gadamer's earlier contention that philosophical hermeneutics essentially prescinds from value commitments?

There are two possible ways to interpret Gadamer on this score which will render his hermeneutics consistent. On the one hand, it is possible to construe his recommendation as a particular, culture-bound interpretation of an *a priori* pre-condition which lends it vital, imperative significance for the historical present. However, the peculiar egalitarian and libertarian contours of this interpretation could not on this view of the matter be themselves transcendentally justified. Whatever authority these values command for the present age must be seen as accruing to them in virtue of their historical relation to past tradition, especially the secular rationalism of our Enlightenment heritage. This is just to say that an ideal of uncoercive dialogue would be legitimated to the degree that this legacy is accepted as a convincing source of value which has "proven" its worth for contemporary society.

The above interpretation of Gadamer's position is unsatisfactory chiefly because it would have him defend a *philosophically sanctioned* ethics on the basis of a particular historical tradition whose "worth" is clearly questionable to him and whose acknowledged authority is limited to a rather small segment of humanity. The other alternative is to interpret Gadamer's ontological hermeneutics as axiological in the strong sense of the word, i.e., as implying a *definite* normative commitment. This is the option pursued by Habermas, who takes as his point of departure Heidegger's analysis of the "fore-completion" of interpretative understanding. In his review of *Wahrheit und Methode*, Habermas insisted that the protensive orientation of understanding necessarily ties every historical and sociological interpretation of human action to the anticipated future. The historian is not a mere chronicler of events, but ties them together into a coherent narrative. Some intimation about the significance of entire cultures, their relation to one another in the broader expanse of human history *as a whole*, and what the latter, *qua* process striving for completion, means to the individual historian gives his own practical situation (e.g., the arena in which human emancipation is achieved, the setting for the eschatological redemption of the world, etc.) implicitly if not explicitly informs the narrative colligation of data into a meaningful whole. Thus, historical narrative, like literary criticism, involves evaluation as well as description. Inasmuch as philosophical hermeneutics too seeks to understand the meaning of human being it cannot renounce the projection of a universal history from a practical standpoint. For Habermas, the practical standpoint which imposes itself on us with compelling force is none other than a visionary interest in an emancipated speech community in which dialogical reciprocity is substantively guaranteed.[51]

In his rejoinder to Habermas, Gadamer did not contest the view that "the goal, the end-thought of freedom" possesses a "compelling evidentness" which "one can as little get beyond" as "one can get beyond consciousness itself."[52] In a more recent reply he agrees that the "living idea of reason" cannot renounce the ideal of a general agreement grounded in "a shared life under conditions of uncoercive communication."[53] However, he qualifies these remarks by denying that a *fixed* end-point of the historical process can be determined once and for all. The projection of a universal history is always provisional, for it is subject to revision in light of new circumstances. Despite this important qualification, there is no getting around the fact that Gadamer does subscribe to a teleology which specifies, if not the *terminus ad quem*, at least the *terminus a quo*, i.e., the ideal presupposition and direction, of all human understanding. Surely, this is tantamount to a transcendental justification of a norm having considerable prescriptive, critical impact.[54]

In effect, the aforementioned reconciliation of ontology and axiology which one increasingly detects in Gadamer's recent philosophy provides something of an "absolute" reference point for human practice, albeit, one which cannot entirely escape the historical relativity of finite understanding. Every general ethical principle, regardless of its status, must be reinterpreted to accommodate the unique circumstances of our historical condition. The parameters of ethical conduct, however, are nonetheless definite, even if they do permit an indeterminate number of possible responses. Indeed, it is only in and through the living application of tradition that continuity and value are preserved. But following Hegel, is this not to concede that history is at once the realization and the Golgotha of the absolute, that the advent of truth is only played out in the eternal recurrence of concrete interpretation? If I am not mistaken, our reflection on hermeneutics inexorably leads to this conclusion. Consequently, it is appropriate to end this essay by recalling the dialectic of truth which resonates in the denouement of *Wahrheit und Methode:*

> In understanding we are drawn into an event of truth and arrive, as it were, too late if we want to know what we ought to believe.[55]

NOTES

1. Cf. Augustine, *Confessions*, I. 8. and L. Wittgenstein, *Tractatus Logico-Philosophicus* (London, 1922).

2. Quine argues that the analytic/synthetic distinction and the verificationist theory of truth are untenable because they presuppose a bogus distinction between semantics, language, and logic on the one hand, and practice, experience, and psychology on the other. (W. V. O. Quine, "The Two Dogmas of Empiricism" in *From a Logical Point of View* [New York, 1953].) In connection with this critique of epistemological atomism also see Wittgenstein's refutation of the ostensive theory of meaning. (L. Wittgenstein, *Philosophical Investigations* [New York: Macmillan, 1953].)

3. M. Heidegger, *Being and Time*, trans. E. Robinson and J. Macquarrie (New York, 1962), pp. 21–24, 30–32.

4. Ibid., p. 258.

5. Ibid., pp. 96–102.

6. Ibid., pp. 182–88.

7. Ibid., pp. 102–7, 189–203. Clearly, everyday practical understanding and "know-how" does not get articulated in the mind in the form of explicit propositions—a point which Gilbert Ryle eloquently makes in *The Concept of Mind* (New York, 1949, pp. 25–61).

8. Ibid., pp. 114–24, 262–93. There has been much controversy generated by Heidegger's etymological derivation of *aletheia* understood as disclosedness. Cf. "Friedlander vs. Heidegger: *Aletheia* controversy," by C. S. Nwodo in the *Journal of the British Society for Phenomenology* 2 (1979).

9. *BT*, pp. 261, 269–73. Cf. G. Schufrieder, "Art and the Problem of Truth," *Man and World* 13 (1980), for a discussion of the different levels of truth in the Heideggerian corpus.

10. *BT*, pp. 174, 435–36.

11. Ibid., p. 192.

12. Ibid., pp. 434–36.

13. Cf. J. Fell, *Heidegger and Sartre: An Essay on Being and Place* (New York, 1979), pp. 395–98.

14. R. Rorty, *Philosophy and the Mirror of Nature* (Princeton, 1979), p. 317.

15. For Peirce, the superiority of the scientific method of investigation resides in its capacity to generate an uncompelled and permanent consensus about reality. (C. Peirce, "The Logic of 1873," VII, p. 319 in *Collected Papers* [Cambridge, 1931–35].) Kuhn and Feyerabend, however, deny that the methods, values, and standards which inform modern scientific research have any privileged claim over other methods of discovering the truth in this respect. Cf. T. Kuhn, *The Structure of Scientific Revolutions* (Chicago, 1961), pp.

108–9, and Feyerabend "Against Method, Outline of an Anarchistic Theory of Knowledge," *Minnesota Studies in the Philosophy of Science* IV (1970).

16. Cf. L. Versenyi, *Heidegger, Being, and Truth* (New Haven, 1965), pp. 49–51.

17. J. Habermas, *Knowledge and Human Interests*, trans. J. Shapiro (Boston, 1971), p. 196. K.-O Apel, "The A Priori of Communication and the Foundations of the Humanities," *Man and World* 3 (1975).

18. F. Nietzsche, *Will to Power*, trans. W. Kaufmann (New York, 1968), p. 272.

19. J. Derrida, *Of Grammatology*, trans. G. Chakravorty Spivak (Baltimore, 1976), p. 49.

20. Ibid., p. 70.

21. Rorty, loc. cit., pp. 315–16.

22. Ibid., p. 377.

23. H.-G. Gadamer, *Truth and Method* (*TM*), trans. G. Garret and J. Cumming (New York, 1975), p. 210.

24. W. Dilthey, *Pattern and Meaning in History*, ed. and trans. H. P. Rickman (New York: 1962), pp. 72–74.

25. Ibid., pp. 167–68. Also see *TM*, p. 200.

26. *TM*, pp. 158–59.

27. Ibid., p. 365. Though Gadamer states that true understanding is possible only when *all* relations to the past have faded away, this would, as he notes elsewhere, render understanding impossible. For the importance of sharing a common tradition and the possibility of cross-cultural understanding, see *TM*, p. 425.

28. Ibid., pp. 265–66.

29. Claus von Bormann notes that there remains a residual element of Platonism in *TM*. ("Die Zweideutigkeit der hermeneutischen Erfahrung" in *Hermeneutik und Ideologiekritik* (*HI*, [Frankfurt, 1971], p. 93–94.)

30. *BT*, p. 438.

31. *TM*, pp. 306–8 (*TM*, p. 15).

32. Cf. *Vernunft im Zeitalter der Wissensschaft* (Frankfurt, 1976), p. 64.

33. *TM*, p. 273. (*TM*, p. 272.)

34. *TM*, p. 318. (*TM*, p. 319.)

35. *TM*, p. 320.

36. Ibid., p. 245.

37. Ibid., pp. 259, 320.

38. Ibid., p. 324.

39. Ibid., pp. 233–34.

40. *TM*, p. 285.

41. Cf. H.-G. Gadamer, "Über die Möglichkeit einer philosophischen Ethik" in *Kleine Schriften* I (Tübingen, 1967), pp. 184–88.

42. H.-G. Gadamer, "Uber die Planung der Zukunft," in *Kleine Schriften* I, pp. 172–74.

43. H.-G. Gadamer, "On the Scope and Function of Hermeneutical Reflection," in *Philosophical Hermeneutics*, ed., D. Linge (Berkeley, 1976), p. 32.

44. *TM*, p. xvi.

45. Cf. J. Habermas, *Zur Logik der Sozialwissenschaften* (Frankfurt, 1967), p. 291. It was the unresolved tension between axiology and ontology in Hegel's own philosophy that led to the controversy among his followers posing "conservative" right Hegelians against "critical" left Hegelians — a controversy which bears striking resemblance to the Gadamer/Habermas debate. Echoing the conservatives, Gadamer asserts that philosophical hermeneutics retraces the path marked out by Hegel's *Phenomenology of Spirit*, which describes the *substance* of social life from the vantage point of a retrospective synopsis (*TM*, p. 269). The problem for historical practice arises because understanding can only grasp the true meaning of history in its dead past, not in its living present or future. According to Habermas (and Marx), the contemplative objectivity of philosophy is contested by the fact that it, too, is an activity situated in practical life and therefore, anticipates the ideal fulfullment of that life. Hence, in contrast to the conservative's emphasis upon the justification of the present in terms of the past the radical is inclined to criticize the present in terms of its unfulfilled promises. Rudiger Bubner ("Theory and Practice in Light of the Hermeneutic-Criticist Controversy" in *Cultural Hermeneutics* 2 [1975], 240–42) and Paul Ricoeur (*The Conflict of Interpretations* [Evanston, Ill., 1974], pp. 13–14 and "Ethics and Culture," *Philosophy Today* 17 [1973], 153–75) attempt to bridge the hiatus separating the conservative and critical aspects of hermeneutical reflection.

46. *TM*, p. 289.

47. H.-G. Gadamer, "On the Scope and Function of Hermeneutical Reflection" in *Philosophical Hermeneutics*, trans. D. Linge, 1976, pp. 40–41.

48. The major shortcomings of Gadamer's ontological conception of dialogue, Habermas avers, is that it ignores the socio-economic constraints which covertly impinge upon the equilibrium of democratic checks and balances from outside the context of dialogue (*KHI*, pp. 314–15). Habermas's more recent attempts to combine philosophical hermeneutics and the speech act theories of Austin and Searle have led him to develop a consensus theory of truth which shows how our interest in an emancipated speech community constitutes an essential condition of human knowledge. The *Ideal speech situation* articulates the pragmatic conditions of rational discourse, which specify a symmetrical distribution of chances to select and employ speech acts without hindrance from external coercion (e.g., threats of violence, economic and political pressure, etc.) and internal ideological constraint. (J.

Habermas, "Wahrheitstheorien," in *Wirklichkeit und Reflexion: Festschrift für Walter Schulz* [Pfullinger, 1973], pp. 245–58),

49. H.-G. Gadamer, *Vernunft im Zeitalter der Wissenschaft* (Frankfurt, 1976), p. 64.

50. H.-G. Gadamer, "Hermeneutics and Social Science," *Cultural Hermeneutics* 2 (1975), p. 314.

51. *Knowledge and Human Interest*, p. 284 (cf. ft. 50). Also see Arthur Danto, *Analytical Philosophy of History* (Cambridge, 1965), p. 115.

52. H.-G. Gadamer, "On the Scope and Function of Hermeneutical Reflection" in *Philosophical Hermeneutics*, trans. D. Linge, p. 37.

53. See my dissertation, "Truth, Method, and Understanding in the Human Sciences: The Gadamer/Habermas Controversy," University of California, 1980.

55. *TM*, p. 446.

3. PHILOSOPHY IN THE CONVERSATION OF MANKIND

Richard J. Bernstein

I

Richard Rorty has written one of the most important and challenging books to be published by an American philosopher in the past few decades.[1] Some will find it a deeply disturbing book while others will find it liberating and exhilarating—both, as we shall see, may be right and wrong. Not since James and Dewey have we had such a devastating critique of professional philosophy. But unlike James and Dewey (two of Rorty's heroes), who thought that once the sterility and artificiality of professional—and indeed much of modern philosophy since Descartes—had been exposed, there was an important job for philosophers to do; Rorty leaves us in a much more ambiguous and unsettled state. I will examine Rorty's book from a variety of perspectives, beginning with a general overview and then moving to more finely meshed descriptions. My aim is not only to illuminate the power and subtlety of Rorty's analysis and to show its inner unity, but to locate basic issues that are left unresolved.

In a book that is filled with all sorts of "jolts" and apparently outrageous claims, one of the first is Rorty's declaration that the three most important philosophers of the twentieth century are Wittgenstein, Heidegger, and Dewey. Grouping these three together may appear to be something of a "category mistake" because according to the common wisdom, it would be hard to imagine three thinkers who are as far apart in philosophical temperament, style, and concern. What they share in common, according to Rorty, is that "each tried, in his early years, to find a new way of making philosophy 'foundational'— a new way of formulating an ultimate context for thought." But eventually,

> Each of the three came to see his earlier effort self-deceptive, as an attempt to retain a certain conception of philosophy after the

notions needed to flesh out that conception (the seventeenth-century notions of knowledge and mind) had been discarded. Each of the three, in his later work, broke free of the Kantian conception of philosophy as foundational, and spent his time warning us against those very temptations to which he himself had once succumbed. Thus their later work is therapeutic rather than constructive, edifying rather than systematic, designed to make the reader question his own motives for philosophizing rather than to supply him with a new philosophical program. (p. 5)

This passage indicates Rorty's intellectual affinities and what he wants to stress in these "three most important philosophers of our century." But he is not primarily concerned with the thought of Wittgenstein, Heidegger, and Dewey, except in the sense that he sees himself as doing, in a far more modest and concentrated way, the type of "philosophical therapy," "deconstruction," and "overcoming of tradition" that typifies the essential thrust of their later work. Rorty's primary focus is contemporary analytic philosophy—especially the philosophy of mind and epistemology—its historical origins, the ways in which it emerged out of the womb of seventeenth-century notions of mind and knowledge, the ways in which analytic philosophy has become increasingly sterile and remote from the "conversation of mankind," and its (possible) demise. He seeks to show that the self-image or self-conception that many analytic philosophers share—that we have finally discovered the right methods and the correct way of stating philosophical problems so that they can be solved—is a self-deception, a grand illusion. On the contrary, sophisticated analytic philosophers are themselves caught in metaphors such as "our glassy essence" and "mirroring" nature or reality that have gone stale. The very issues that seem so vital in analytic philosophy—problems of mind-body identity, whether knowledge can or cannot be characterized as justified true belief, the theory of reference and meaning—are themselves bound up with historical assumptions that can be exposed and questioned. These are "problems" not to be solved but to be dissolved or deconstructed. The way to perform this type of therapy is to dig deep into the language games in which they are embedded and to see how these language games are themselves the result of a series of historical accidents, options, and confusions. Roughly speaking, Rorty uses a two-stage strategy in carrying out his critique. The first stage is a "softening up" technique where he addresses the problems and positions that are currently being debated and shows that as we sharpen the issues and points of difference, the various controversies fall apart (and do not lead to significant new foundational philosophical truths). These are the sections that will probably capture the imagination of analytic philosophers. They will recognize types of arguments with which they are familiar and will pounce upon — as they rightfully should — what is sound and unsound, convincing and unconvincing in Rorty's arguments. But although the book is filled with arguments, many of which are brilliant and ingenious, Rorty at several points warns against the love of argument that has characterized *one* strand in philosophy ever since Plato. What is unsettling and disturbing about Rorty's argumentative style is that he refuses to play the game that can be recognized as "normal" philosophy, i.e., he doesn't seem to be primarily concerned with carefully stating issues in such a manner so that one can proceed to develop the strongest arguments in support of a correct "position." Rather he wants to show that there is something wrong with the whole approach to philosophy as a discipline that deals with basic problems and advances by clarifying and solving these problems. As one follows the nuances of his arguments, it begins to dawn on the reader that just when he thinks he is getting down to the hard core of these disputes, he discovers that there is no core.

But assuming for the moment that Rorty is successful in this deconstructive technique, the question naturally arises, how did philosophers ever get themselves into a situation of thinking that something extremely important is at issue in advancing a theory of reference or meaning, or stating the necessary and sufficient conditions for what is to count as knowledge, or solving the mind-body problem. This highlights the second stage or aspect of Rorty's strategy. He exposes the *historical* origins of what we now take to be standard philosophical problems and he searches for the historical roots of those philosophical "intuitions" that play such a primary role in philosophical debate. If Rorty is right, then most analytic philosophers are not only wrong, they are self-deceived about what they are doing — at least insofar as they think of "their discipline as one which discusses perennial, eternal problems — problems which arise as soon as one reflects" (p.3). Indeed, it should be clear that if Rorty is right then most systematic philosophers — past and present — have misunderstood what they have been doing. We can already see that although Rorty focuses on recent analytic philosophy, there are much broader ramifications to his critique — a critique that finally turns into a mediation on the philosophical enterprise itself.

In order to carry out this critique, Rorty develops a historical reconstruction of modern philosophy which is the context from which analytic philosophy emerges. Rorty is sufficiently impressed by Heidegger to be aware of how we might trace the source of the trouble back to Plato, but for his purposes he begins his "history" with the founders of modern philosophy, Descartes, Locke, and Kant. The "ideal type" of what philosophy as a discipline is supposed to be that Rorty wants to undermine and debunk may be stated as follows:

> Philosophy can be foundational in respect to the rest of culture because culture is the assemblage of claims to knowledge, and philosophy adjudicates such claims. It can do so because it understands the foundations of knowledge and it finds these foundations in the study of man-as-knower, of the "mental processes" or the "activity of representation" which make knowledge possible. To know is to represent accurately what is outside the mind; so to understand the possibility and nature of knowledge is to understand the way in which the mind is able to construct such representations. Philosophy's central concern is to be a general theory of representation, a theory which will divide culture up into areas which represent reality well, those which represent it less well, and those which do not represent it at all (despite their pretense to do so). (p. 3)

This conception of philosophy which may appear to be intuitive and obvious is one that has a long, complicated, and devious history.

> We owe the notion of a "theory of knowledge" based on an understanding of "mental processes" to the seventeenth century, and especially to Locke. We owe the notion of "the mind" as a separate entity in which "processes" occur to the same period, and especially to Descartes. We owe the notion of philosophy as the tribunal of pure reason, upholding or denying the claims of the rest of culture to the eighteenth century, and especially to Kant, but this Kantian notion presupposed general assent to Lockean notions of mental processes and Cartesian notions of mental substance. (pp. 3–4)

These notions which we have inherited from the seventeenth and eighteenth centuries do *not* represent great breakthroughs or discoveries which set philosophy on a secure path. Rather they were "inventions" — the invention of distinctions and problems that were blended with potent metaphors which captured the imagination of philosophers and set the direction for "normal" philosophizing.

One of the many spinoffs of Rorty's reflections is a distinctive understanding of how the history of philosophy has developed. He rejects the view that there are perennial problems of philosophy which arise as soon as we begin to reflect. He is equally relentless in his criticism of a variant of this which takes the more "charitable" view that our philosophic ancestors were dealing with basic problems, but the trouble is that they did so in an obscure and confused manner. Rorty displaces this self-congratulatory understanding of the history of philosophy (as the dialectical unfolding of problems) which he claims has had a distortive influence on the writing of the history of philosophy and a mystifying effect on our understanding of philosophy as a discipline.

His alternative, which can be seen as a novel blending of themes suggested by Heidegger, Derrida, Foucault, Kuhn, and Feyerabend, may be stated as follows: There are moments in history when, because of all sorts of historical accidents — like what is going on in some part of culture such as science or religion — a new set of metaphors, distinctions, and problems is invented and captures the imagination of followers. For a time, when a particular philosophical language game gets entrenched, it sets the direction for "normal" philosophizing. After a while, because of some other historical accidents — like the appearance of a new genius or just plain boredom and sterility — another cluster of metaphors, distinctions, and problems usurp the place of what is now seen as a dying tradition. At first the abnormal talk of some new genius may be dismissed as kookiness or as not being "genuine" or "serious" philosophy. But sometimes this abnormal talk will set philosophy off in new directions. It is an illusion to believe that we are always dealing with the same basic problems of philosophy. We must resist the Whiggish temptation to rewrite the history of philosophy in our own image — where we see our predecessors as "really" treating what we now take to be fundamental problems. The crucial point is to realize that a philosophical paradigm does *not* displace a former one because it can better formulate the problems of a prior paradigm.

Rather, because of a set of historical contingencies, it "nudges" the former paradigm aside. This is what happened in the seventeenth century when within a relatively short period of time the entire tradition of scholasticism collapsed and no longer seemed to have much point. After such a revolution or upheaval occurs, philosophers have a difficult time figuring out what was the point of the elaborate language game that had evolved. If they don't dismiss it out of hand, they are ineluctably tempted to reinterpret it as an anticipation of their present concerns. While Rorty refuses to make any predictions about what will happen next in philosophy, he certainly suggests that this is likely to happen again with the problematic of modern philosophy and its offspring, analytic philosophy. To understand a historical movement such as analytic philosophy or even the whole tradition of modern philosophy, one must uncover the set of metaphors, distinctions, confusions, and problems that are characteristic of the language games or the forms of life that established the patterns for normal philosophizing. Briefly stated, the history of modern philosophy is the history of the rise and fall of the "mind" and the prized philosophical discipline — "epistemology."

II

Rorty's book is divided into three parts and consists of eight chapters: part 1, *Our Glassy Essence*, comprises two chapters, "The Invention of the Mind," and "Persons Without Minds"; part 2, *Mirroring*, which is the central part of the book, contains four chapters, "The Idea of a 'Theory of Knowledge,' " "Privileged Representations," "Epistemology and Empirical Psychology," and "Epistemology and Philosophy of Language"; and part 3, *Philosophy*, concludes with two chapters, "From Epistemology to Hermeneutics," and "Philosophy Without Mirrors." In the next three sections I will treat some of the highlights of each of these parts and show how Rorty seeks to get back to (and behind) those "intuitions" and pre-analytic distinctions that seem to arise as soon as we begin to reflect. Thus, for example, the mind-body problem is taken to be a basic problem for philosophy because it appears to be intuitively evident that there is some important distinction between what is "mental" and what is "physical," even though we may be perplexed about how to characterize this distinc-

tion and what to make of it. But, Rorty tells us, "In my Wittgenstein-
ian view, an intuition is never anything more or less than familiarity
with a language-game, so to discover the source of our intuitions is
to relive the history of the language-game we find ourselves playing"
(p. 34). Now every philosopher who wants to get clear about the mind-
body problem is obliged to ask what are the criteria for distinguishing
the "mental" and the "physical." In what I called the "softening up"
stage of Rorty's strategy he quickly runs through several of the major
criteria that philosophers have invoked to characterize the "mental":
intentionality, nonspatiality, immateriality, temporality, the presumed
"phenomenal quality" of pains and other "raw feels." He concludes
his survey with the claim that

> the only way to associate the intentional with the immaterial is
> to identify it with the phenomenal, and that the only way to iden-
> tify the phenomenal with the immaterial is to hypostatize univer-
> sals and think of them as particulars rather than abstractions from
> particulars—thus giving them a non-spatial-temporal habitation.
> (p. 31)

Consequently if we refuse to make this hypostatization, and see through
the trap of invoking a specious metaphysical distinction, then we would
have an easy dissolution of the mind-body problem. As Rorty himself
points out, it is a bit too quick and easy. Furthermore, carrying out
his therapeutic analogy, he tells us "What the patient needs is not a
list of his mistakes and confusions but rather an understanding of how
he came to make these mistakes and become involved in these confusions" (p. 33). If we are ever finally to get rid of the mind-body problem we need to be able to give a satisfactory answer to such a question as:

> How did these rather dusty little questions about the possible
> identity of pains and neurons ever get mixed up with the ques-
> tion of whether man "differed in kind" from the brutes—whether
> he had dignity rather than merely value? (p. 33)

Posing a question like this should already make us realize that "the
mind-body" problem is a misnomer. At best it is a label for a cluster
of quite distinct and different problems that have become fused and
confused together. We can see this by considering the partial list that
Rorty gives "of the features which philosophers have, at one time or
another, taken as marks of the mental":

1. ability to know itself incorrigibly ("privileged access")
2. ability to exist separately from the body
3. nonspatiality (having a nonspatial part or "element")
4. ability to grasp universals
5. ability to sustain relations to the inexistent ("intentionality")
6. ability to use language
7. ability to act freely
8. ability to form part of our social group, to be "one of us"
9. inability to be identified with any object "in the world" (p. 35).

Confusion is compounded, because all too frequently when it is argued that a given feature simply will not serve to mark off the "mental" — the response has been that the feature in question is not the *really* important or essential feature. For heuristic purposes, Rorty distinguishes three clusters of issues: the problem of consciousness, the problem of reason, and the problem of personhood. Clarifying the differences and the interrelations among these problems is one of Rorty's primary aims. In part 1, *Our Glassy Essence*, Rorty concentrates on the problem of consciousness, focusing on 1, 2, and 3 in his list. One reason for this is that many contemporary analytic philosophers have written as if the problem of consciousness *is* the heart of the mind-body problem. One need only think of Smart's opening statement in his article that set off so much of the contemporary debate:

> There does seem to be, as far as science is concerned, nothing in the world but increasingly complex arrangements of physical constituents. All except for one place; in consciousness. That is, for a full description of what is going on in man you would have to mention not only physical processes in his tissues, glands, nervous system, and so forth, but also his states of consciousness; his visual, auditory and tactual sensations, his aches and pains. . . . So sensations, states of consciousness, do seem to be the one sort of thing left outside the physicalist picture, and for various reasons I just cannot believe that this can be so. That everything should be explicable in terms of physics . . . except the occurrence of sensations seems to me to be frankly unbelievable.[2]

In unraveling the problem of consciousness, Rorty's task is to show how this problem arose and how we became preoccupied with "rather dusty little questions about the possible identity of pains and neurons." The story he unfolds goes back to Plato and Aristotle. But the point of his historical excursion into classical and scholastic philosophy is to make us keenly aware of how different the so-called mind-body problem was before and after Descartes — to show us that what we now (after Descartes) take to be obvious and intuitive distinctions did not exist prior to Descartes's "invention" of the mind. Descartes invented the mind in the sense that it is only after Descartes that the problem of *consciousness* became a central problem for philosophy. What then for Descartes was the essential feature or criterion of the "mental"? According to Rorty's reconstruction, Descartes's effective criterion is an appeal to "indubitability." Despite Descartes's own conviction that he had hit upon a rock bottom metaphysical distinction between the mind and the body, Descartes, by appealing to indubitability, sowed the seeds for transforming (or creating) the mind-body problem into an epistemological issue about the nature and consequences of indubitability — which is itself the origin of the contemporary obsession with incorrigibility and privileged access.

Now one can imagine a critic of Rorty objecting at this point (at the end of his first chapter) as follows: Despite the historical learning and imagination that is evidenced in Rorty's history of the origin of the problem of consciousness, and despite the rhetoric about "dusty little questions," the tables can easily be turned on Rorty. For this exercise in historical reconstruction doesn't dissolve anything. On the contrary, Rorty's narrative can be read as showing just why the problem of consciousness is the nub of the mind-body problem — why it is so important to clarify the relation between pains and neurons. Nothing Rorty has said thus far indicates that the problem is either unimportant or has yet been satisfactorily resolved.

I think that Rorty is perfectly aware that this is the "natural" objection to make at this point. The aim of his second chapter, "Persons Without Minds," is to meet the objection squarely — to show that when we work through all the major twists and turns in contemporary analytic debates about the status of consciousness the entire problematic dissolves. He does this in a most ingenious fashion. He invents a science fiction tale where the general characters are Antipodeans who live on the other side of the galaxy and seem to be just like us in all respects with one great difference. For them neurology and biochemistry had been the first disciplines in which technological breakthoughs were achieved. Unlike us they do not make any first person or third person reports about pains, "raw feels," and minds. Where we use "mentalese" they speak about the stimulation of neurons and C-fibers. In the twenty-first century some of our tough-minded analytic philosophers visit the Antipodeans and confront the problem of trying to figure out whether the Antipodeans have minds, and whether they experience consciousness in the way in which we do. The device is imaginative and playful but the point is deadly serious. For Rorty uses it to work through virtually all the major moves that have been made by philosophers — both substantive and metaphilosophical — in the debate that has gone on from Feigl to Kripke. In what is one of the densest chapters of the book, we have nothing less than a re-enactment of the attempts by analytic philosophers to state and solve the problem of consciousness. Rorty argues that all attempts to invent imaginative thought-experiments or resolve the issues by an appeal to the analysis of meanings fail. As the discussion gets more heated and sharper, Rorty focuses on the notion of a "phenomenal property" and smokes out what he takes to be the key principle involved:

> P) Whenever we make an incorrigible report on a state of ourselves, there must be a property we are presented with which induces us to make the report (p. 84).

As he phrases it, this principle "enshrines the Cartesian notion that 'nothing is closer to the mind' than itself, and involves an entire epistemology and metaphysics, a specifically dualistic one" (p. 84). So the problem becomes what to make of and what to do with this principle (P). Indeed most of the positions that have been taken on the mind-body problem (as the problem of consciousness) can be characterized in relation to the stand that they take to (P) — including behaviorism, various forms of materialism, and linguistic dualisms. So Rorty runs through the various "positions" in order to show that while they can be interpreted as containing important insights, none of them bring us any closer to a resolution of the outstanding issues.

Despite Rorty's disclaimers, it begins to look as if he himself is doing what he keeps telling us we should not do — that he is in effect advocating a "substantive" position on the mind-body problem — a position that looks like a sophisticated form of materialism. In a way he is and in a way he isn't.

What the principle (P) shows is how the contemporary problem of consciousness depends on the status of incorrigibility and privileged access. But at this point, Rorty makes what might seem to be a surprising move. He claims that the proper response is *not* to argue for or against principle (P), but to drop it altogether "and thus be neither dualists, skeptics, behaviorists, nor 'identity theorists' " (p. 97). The denouement comes when Rorty declares:

> The real difficulty we encounter is, once again, that we are try-ing to set aside the image of man as possessor of a Glassy Essence, suitable for mirroring nature with one hand while holding on to it with the other. If we could ever drop the whole cluster of images which Antipodeans do not share with us, we would not be able to infer that matter had triumphed over spirit, science over privacy, or anything over anything else. These warring op-posites are notions which do not make sense outside a cluster of images inherited from the Terran seventeenth century. No one except philosophers, who are professionally obligated to take these images seriously, will be scandalized if people start saying "The machine told me it didn't really hurt — it only, very horribly seemed to." Philosophers are too involved with notions like "on-tological status" to take such developments lightly, but no other part of culture is. . . . Only the notion that philosophy should provide a permanent matrix of categories into which every possi-ble empirical discovery and cultural development should be fit-ted without strain impels us to ask unanswerable questions like "Would this mean that there were no minds?" "Were the An-tipodeans right in saying 'There never were any of these things you call "raw feels" '?" (p. 123)

The above passage sums up the substance of what Rorty has to say about the problem of consciousness. But one might still want to ob-ject that this only shows that Rorty is really a materialist (and the passage appears in a section entitled "Materialism without Mind-Body Iden-tity"). Such a claim would not be wrong, but it would certainly miss the point. For the triumphal verdict that Rorty is a materialist *man-qué* only gains its rhetorical force because we are infected by a set of images and categories that Rorty is urging us to set aside. If we insist on clinging to talk about materialism (and Rorty might ask, why bother?) then the point is to realize how innocuous and how unphilosophical "materialism" really is. It amounts to the unphilosophical claim that someday our great-grandchildren may talk and act like Antipodeans and relegate the problem of consciousness to the dustbin of historical curiosities.

III

Part 2, *Mirroring*, deals with the rise, nature, and demise (and some recent attempts to salvage) epistemology. The moral of this part is a variation on part 1 and deepens Rorty's argument. Just as the modern notion of "mind" has its origins in the seventeenth century, so does epistemology which is so frequently taken to be either identical with philosophy or the heart of philosophy. Just as we can already envision the passing of the obsession with the "mind," so Rorty argues that we already have the grounds for envisioning the collapse of epistemology.

Rorty begins his examination of epistemology by probing its origins and the way in which it has thrived upon a central confusion that has plagued the theory of knowledge ever since — the confusion between the *causal* conditions of the genesis of knowledge and the *justification* of knowledge claims. He also argues that by the end of the nineteenth century, epistemology became so well fixed that it became virtually identical with philosophy as a discipline. For the past hundred years, it has seemed that the first task of philosophers is to resolve epistemological issues before any progress can be made with other problems and areas of philosophy. The historical probing of the origins of epistemology is followed by what Rorty himself considers to be the central chapter of the book, "Privileged Representations" which deals with the work of Sellars and Quine. Once we fully appreciate the force and consequences of Sellars's critique of the "Myth of the Given" and Quine's skeptical arguments about the language-fact distinction, then we have grounds for not only abandoning the major distinctions that have set the context for modern philosophy but also questioning analytical philosophy. But Rorty isn't finished. The final two chapters of this part examine what he considers two misguided attempts to "save" epistemology by finding successor disciplines — empirical psychology and the philosophy of language — which might replace traditional epistemology and presumably answer the "real" problems that our epistemological predecessors were trying to answer.

Since Rorty considers his discussion of Sellars and Quine as the centerpiece of his book, I want to concentrate on the novel interpretation that he offers of their work. According to Rorty's historical reconstruction of epistemology, it is basically the "Kantian picture of concepts and intuitions getting together to produce knowledge" (p. 168) that makes sense of the idea of a "theory of knowledge" as a specifically philosophical discipline distinct from psychology.

> This is equivalent to saying that if we do not have the distinction between what is "given" and what is "added by the mind" or that between the contingent (because influenced by what is given) and the "necessary" (because entirely "within" the mind and under its control), then we will not know what would count as a "rational reconstruction" of our knowledge. (p. 169)

Although these two related distinctions were attacked throughout the history of the analytic movement, it is only with the arguments of Sellars and Quine that they have been fully discredited. Sellars and Quine invoke the same argument in their critiques, "one which bears equally against the given-versus-nongiven and the necessary-versus-contingent distinctions. The crucial premise of this argument is that we understand knowledge when we understand the social justification of belief, and thus have no need to view it as accuracy of representation" (p. 170). Unlike many critics of Sellars and Quine who think they have gone too far with their holistic tendencies, Rorty claims that they have not gone far enough. The consequence of their arguments is *not* to advocate a better way of doing epistemology, or even to see that epistemology can now be replaced by a "legitimate" scientific inquiry, but simply to put an end to epistemology *tout court*.

> It is as if Quine, having renounced the conceptual-empirical, analytic-synthetic, and language-fact distinctions, were still not quite able to renounce that between the given and the postulated. Conversely Sellars having triumphed over the later distinction, cannot quite renounce the former cluster. Despite courteous acknowledgement of Quine's triumph over analyticity, Sellars's writing is still permeated with the notion of "giving the analysis" of various terms or sentences, and with a tacit use of the distinction between the necessary and the contingent, the structural and the empirical, the philosophical and the scientific. Each of these two men tends to make continual, unofficial, tacit, heuristic use of the distinction which the other has transcended. It is as if analytic philosophy could not be written without at least *one* of the two great Kantian distinctions, and as if neither Quine nor Sellars were willing to cut the last links which bind them to Russell, Carnap, and "logic as the essence of philosophy." (pp. 171–72)

I cannot go into the details of Rorty's interpretation, defense, and critique of Sellars and Quine. Rorty develops an extremely perceptive analysis of their work, a strong defense of their claims against many of the objections that have been raised by others, and at the same time a penetrating critique. For example, many critics have argued that Quine's later work, especially his reflections on the indeterminacy of translation, reveals a blatant contradiction — or at least a deep tension — with his own pragmatic and holistic arguments. Rorty locates and specifies this tension better than anyone else (see p. 202). I am primarily interested in how Rorty "uses" Sellars and Quine — the role that they play in the dramatic narrative he is unfolding. Sellars and Quine complete the critique of the Kantian legacy of epistemology and lead us to a "holistic" view of knowledge, to what Rorty labels "epistemological behaviorism." (The choice of these terms "holism" and "epistemological behaviorism" are unfortunate because they suggest that we are dealing with a new and better epistemological position. Every time we are tempted to make this move, i.e., to replace one position by what now seems to be a better philosophical position, Rorty pulls the rug from under our feet.) How then are we to understand what Rorty means by "epistemological behaviorism" and "holism"?

> Explaining rationality and epistemic authority by reference to what society lets us say, rather than the latter by the former, is the essence of what I shall call "epistemological behaviorism," an attitude common to Dewey and Wittgenstein. This sort of behaviorism can best be seen as a species of holism — but one which requires no idealist metaphysical underpinnings. It claims that if we understand the rules of a language-game, we understand all that there is to understand about why the moves in that language-game are made. . . . If we are behaviorist in this sense, then it will not occur to us to invoke either of the traditional Kantian distinctions. (p. 174)

In short, to advocate "epistemological behaviorism" is not to advocate a new subtle epistemological position; rather it is to see through and to abandon epistemology, to see that the whole project only makes sense if we accept some form of the Kantian distinctions which have now been rejected. As for "holism," Rorty warns us that "A holistic approach to knowledge is not a matter of antifoundationalist polemic, but a distrust of the whole epistemological enterprise" (p. 181). Consequently "to be a behaviorist in epistemology . . . is to look at the normal scientific discourse of our day bifocally, both as patterns adopted for various historical reasons, and as the achievement of objective truth, where "objective truth" is no more and no less than the best idea we currently have about how to explain what is going on" (p. 385).

Anticipating the charge that epistemological behaviorism and holism require abandoning objectivity, truth, and the growth of knowledge, Rorty insists:

> For the Quine-Sellars approach to epistemology, to say that truth and knowledge can only be judged by the standards of the inquirers of our own day is not to say that human knowledge is less noble or important, or more "cut off from the world" than we had thought. It is merely to say that nothing counts as justification unless by reference to what we already accept, and that there is no way to get outside our beliefs and our language so as to find some test other than coherence.
>
> To say that the True and the Right are matters of social practice may seem to condemn us to a relativism which all by itself, is a *reductio* of a behaviorist approach to either knowledge or morals. . . . Here I shall simply remark that only the image of a discipline — philosophy — which will pick out a given set of scientific or moral views as more "rational" than the alternatives by appeal to something which forms a permanent neutral matrix for all inquiry and all history, makes it possible to think that such relativism must automatically rule out coherence theories of intellectual and practical justification. One reason why professional philosophers recoil from the claim that knowledge may not have foundations, or rights and duties an ontological ground, is that the kind of behaviorism which dispenses with foundations is in a fair way toward dispensing with philosophy. (pp. 178–79)

There are many analytic philosophers who share Rorty's skepticism about traditional epistemology. But for them the basic trouble is that genuine philosophic issues have been obscured by epistemological formulations. We need to reformulate the relevant issues in a "purified" philosophy of language or a scientific empirical psychology. But Rorty is relentless in his critique of those who think epistemology can be salvaged in this way. In the last two chapters of *Mirroring*, he exposes two attempts to found successor disciplines to epistemology. Neither "empirical psychology" nor the "new philosophy of language" help to solve epistemological problems. Once again there are striking inversions. (Rorty's use of this technique, where he shows how things turn out to be the very opposite of what they purport to be, is a variant of Hegel's own use of this dialectical strategy.) From Rorty's perspective, the new concern with the issue of "realism" and the belief that the way to deal with the foundations of philosophy is through "formal semantics" do *not* represent advances in philosophy. On the contrary, Putnam insofar as he temporarily misled us into thinking that the issue of metaphysical realism is an important one for philosophy, and Dummett insofar as he thinks that Frege has shown us the way to get at the foundations of philosophy turn out to be arch reactionaries. It would be hard to imagine a more antithetical understanding of modern philosophy and analytic philosophy than that presented by Dummett and Rorty. Dummett, acknowledging that philosophers have mistakenly claimed that they have discovered the "real" foundations of philosophy, is nevertheless convinced that there are real foundations and that we have now discovered how to go about finding them.[3] From Rorty's point of view this is a despairing attempt to save analytic philosophy — one that can't quite give up holding on to the "problem of representation" and the belief that there is something to be preserved from the metaphor of mirroring reality.

IV

There will be some readers who when they reach this point in Rorty's book (after 311 densely argued pages) will breathe a sigh of relief. They may not be acquainted with the latest subtleties in the analytic controversies about the mind-body problem, or the pros and cons of a causal theory of reference, or why so many professionals are excited by the work of Davidson, Putnam, Kripke, Dummett, and their colleagues. But they may have felt that somehow philosophy took a wrong turn with the analytic movement. They may feel some satisfaction that Rorty has written the type of critique that could only be written by an "insider," and that he has shown that the emperor has no clothes — or at least is scantily clad. If only Anglo-American philosophers had taken a different turn; if only, for example, they had followed the lead of Husserl who opened up the field of phenomenology, then we might have avoided the tangled mess which has consumed so much technical competence. But if this is the way they have read Rorty, they have *misread* him and they have missed the real sting of his critique. Rorty is not denigrating the contribution of analytic philosophers, despite the severity of his critique. The first two parts of the book employ (with novel twists) the insights and arguments of analytic philosophers to show how they lead to surprising and unexpected conclusions. But even more important, Rorty has dropped enough hints along the way to show how his critique can be generalized. "Professional philosophy" is not to be identified with any school in philosophy but cuts across schools. Many of Rorty's most incisive criticisms are just as relevant to those continental philosophers who think of themselves as having taken the "transcendental turn." From Rorty's perspective, the differences between Russell and Husserl are insignificant when compared with what they share in common. Each in his distinctive way played a crucial role in reinforcing the image of philosophy as a foundational discipline. Furthermore, it should now be clear that Rorty's primary object of attack is any form of systematic philosophy which shares the conviction that there are real foundations that philosophy must discover and that philosophy as a discipline can transcend history and adumbrate a permanent neutral matrix for assessing all forms of inquiry and all types of knowledge.

Nevertheless, for those who think in terms of Anglo-American philosophy and Continental philosophy, it will be noticeable that in the final part, *Philosophy*, a new set of characters, and a new set of problems enter the stage. Heidegger, Gadamer, Sartre, Habermas, Apel, Foucault, and Derrida are discussed along with Kuhn and Feyerabend. Rorty now takes up such familiar "continental" distinctions as that beween Spirit and Nature, *Geisteswissenschaften* and *Naturwissenschaften*. But there is no change of theme. In this carefully orchestrated work all this material is integrated into a reflection on philosophy itself — a reflection that emerges from the first two parts of the book. What is provocative and refreshing about Rorty is that he cuts across the stale polemic and the irritable defensiveness that characterize much of the nondialogue between Anglo-American and Continental philosophy. He is equally devastating and equally illuminating about both sides of this great divide.

In order to get this last part into clear focus, it may be helpful to raise a number of doubts and suspicions that will surely have occurred to many readers. Is Rorty simply engaging in a destructive critique or does he have anything constructive to say? It certainly looks as if he is leading us to historicism, skepticism, relativism, and nihilism. At times, Rorty even uses these labels to characterize his project. Presumably we all know that these are philosophic dead ends and can be refuted by carefully constructed self-referential arguments. How then does Rorty get out of this bind? How does he meet the objection that any critique must take a stand someplace on what is True and Right — and this stance itself demands some sort of philosophic justification? One of the main purposes of the final part of his book is to answer these doubts and to adumbrate an alternative understanding of philosophy as a voice in the conversation of mankind. But before turning to Rorty's own self-understanding of the philosophical enterprise, I want to clarify the sense in which the above "labels" do and do not apply to Rorty.

If by historicism we mean that history itself is a foundational discipline, that the explanations that philosophers seek can only be found in the study of history, or even if we understand by historicism the curious variant that Popper attacked where a historicist is supposed to be someone who believes that there are laws of history which enable us to predict the future, then Rorty is certainly *not* a historicist. On the contrary, he has presented some of the strongest arguments against such a position. For he has been arguing and trying to show us that there is *no* foundational discipline — neither history, nor philosophy, nor science, nor poetry. There is no part of culture that is more privileged than any other part — and the illusion that there *must* be such a discipline is one that needs to be exorcised. Further, given Rorty's insistence on historical accidents, contingencies, and options, it doesn't make any sense to think that history could ever aspire to be a predictive discipline. But if by historicism we mean that a healthy historical sense of how philosophic language games arise, get entrenched, and pass away may cure us of the belief that there are perennial philosophical problems, then Rorty is certainly a historicist and tells us that this is the moral of his book.

If by skepticism we mean the type of epistemological doctrine that insists that we can never really know what is beyond the "veil of ideas" and that our claims to knowledge can never "really" be justified, then it is difficult to imagine a more forceful attack on such skepticism. Such an epistemological skepticism gains its force from accepting the very metaphors that Rorty urges us to abandon. If Rorty's therapy were successful, if we could rid ourselves of the desire for constraint and compulsion and the fear that unless we discover the (nonexistent) foundations of knowledge we are faced with intellectual and moral chaos, then epistemological skepticism would no longer be a position to be "refuted" — it would simply wither away. If by skepticism we mean that we have grounds for being suspicious of all attempts to escape history, to discover the foundations of knowledge, language, or philosophy, and to delineate a permanent neutral framework for evaluating all claims to knowledge, then this is what Rorty has been advocating.

If by relativism we mean that there is no truth, objectivity, and standards for judging better and worse arguments or moral positions, then Rorty is certainly *not* a relativist, and suggests that such a relativism has become something of a straw man for philosophers to attack. Rorty's aim is not to deny or denigrate "truth" and "objectivity" but to demystify these "honorific" labels. If by relativism we mean epistemological behaviorism, that there is no other way to justify knowledge claims or claims to truth than by appealing to those social practices which have been hammered out in the course of human history and are the forms of inquiry *within* which we distinguish what is true and false, what is objective and idiosyncratic, then Rorty advocates such a relativism. But this does not mean that "anything goes."

If by nihilism we mean that whether we are dealing with knowledge or morals, anything is just as good or as true as anything else, then again Rorty is *not* a nihilist. On the contrary, such a position is frequently adopted by those who think this is the only alternative to the claim that knowledge and morals have foundations. But if nihilism means being liberated from the illusion that there is something to which we can appeal which will or ought to command universal assent, that there is no way of escaping from human freedom and responsibility in making moral decisions, and no ultimate support to which we can appeal in making such decisions, then Rorty happily thinks of himself as a nihilist.

The point I am emphasizing can be stated in a slightly different way. "Historicism," "Skepticism," "Relativism," and "Nihilism," are typically thought to be so objectionable because they are taken to be positions to which we are driven when we give up the claim that there are "real" foundations for truth, objectivity, knowledge, and morals. They are all shaped in the image of what might be called the "Cartesian Anxiety" — the grand Either/Or — either there is some basic foundational constraint or we are confronted with intellectual and moral chaos. Rorty is *not* advocating that we take sides on this fundamental dichotomy that has shaped the Cartesian-Lockean-Kantian tradition. Rorty's main therapeutic point is to liberate us from this Either/Or, to help us to see through it, and to set it aside.

But still we want to know what function, if any, philosophers can perform and what type of self-understanding of philosophy emerges if we give up these various "self-deceptions" that Rorty exposes. In the final part of the book where Rorty seeks to answer this question, he "works through" what initially seems to be a bewildering array of distinctions: Spirit and Nature, *Geisteswissenschaften* and *Naturwissenschaften*, commensurability and incommensurability, normal and abnormal discourse, familiarity and unfamiliarity, epistemology and hermeneutics, systematic and edifying philosophy, and philosophy as inquiry and philosophy as conversation. Rorty's "asides" are frequently as illuminating and incisive as his main points. But I want to touch on the significance of some of these distinctions only insofar as they enable us to grasp Rorty's own understanding of philosophy.

By "commensurable" Rorty means "able to be brought under a set of rules which will tell us how rational agreement can be reached on what would settle the issue on every point where statements seem to conflict. These rules tell us how to construct an ideal situation, in which all residual disagreements will be seen to be 'noncognitive' or merely verbal, or else merely temporary—capable of being resolved by doing something further" (p. 316). Modern philosophy shaped by the Cartesian-Lockean-Kantian tradition in *both* its analytic and continental forms has been obsessed with the search for commensuration. This is the quest that is characteristic of epistemology. Hermeneutics, as Rorty understands it, is not the name of a new method or discipline, an alternative way to achieve commensuration, but rather largely a struggle against the assumption that all contributions to culture are commensurable. Hermeneutics "is an expression of hope that the cultural space left by the demise of epistemology will not be filled—that our culture should become one in which the demand for constraint is no longer felt" (p. 315). The distinction between the "commensurable" and the "incommensurable," which Rorty takes over from recent debates in the philosophy of science, is one that he generalizes. It is applicable to all domains of discourse, whether they be science, philosophy, poetry, or literary criticism.

Earlier, when characterizing Rorty's understanding of the history of philosophy, I indicated that he sees it as consisting of periods of "normal discourse" where there is agreement about problems, procedures, and the "correct" way of finding solutions followed by periods of abnormal discourse when strange and new ways of speaking and writing appear. He radicalizes Kuhn's distinction of "normal" and "abnormal" discourse because Rorty sees this as a feature of all discourse and culture (as Kuhn himself sometimes suggests.) It is during periods of "normal" discourse that epistemology thrives, because these are the times when there is agreement, when it does appear as if *all* discourse might be commensurable and philosophy might be able to clarify the rules of commensuration. But there is always a danger of confusing what is historically stable with the permanent and eternal, or in thinking that the domain in which such stability has been achieved is the measure for all other domains. (Rorty even envisions the possibility that other parts of culture such as morals or poetry might be taken as our paradigms of normality rather than science, just as there was a time in the West when theological discourse played this role.) By introducing such bland distinctions as the "normal" and the "abnormal" or the "familiar" and the "unfamiliar," Rorty deliberately wants to make us aware of how "relative" these distinctions are to the changing scene of culture.

Throughout his book Rorty has been attacking the "Cartesian-Lockean-Kantian" tradition of modern philosophy, but implicitly and explicitly he has been contrasting this tradition with another attitude toward philosophy. He speaks of

> figures who, without forming a "tradition," resemble each other in their distrust of the notion that man's essence is to be a knower of essences. Goethe, Kierkegaard, Santayana, William James, Dewey, the later Wittgenstein, the later Heidegger are figures of this sort . . . These writers have kept alive the suggestion that, even when we have justified true belief about everything we want to know, we may have no more than conformity to the norms of the day. They have kept alive the historicist sense that this century's "superstition" was last century's triumph of reason, as well as the relativist sense that the latest vocabulary, borrowed from the latest scientific achievement, may not express privileged representations of essences, but be just another of the potential infinity of vocabularies in which the world can be described. (p. 367)

The mainstream of philosophers Rorty calls "systematic philosophers," and the peripheral ones—following Kierkegaard—he calls "edifying philosophers." What is common to edifying philosophers is that they use every means they can to voice their skepticism about the "whole project of commensuration."

> In our time, Dewey, Wittgenstein, and Heidegger are the great edifying, peripheral thinkers. All three make it as difficult as possible to take their thought as expressing views on traditional philosophical problems, or as making constructive proposals for philosophy as a cooperative and progressive discipline. They make fun of the classic picture of man, the picture which contains systematic philosophy, the search for universal commensuration in a final vocabulary. They hammer away at the holistic point that words take their meaning from other words rather than by virtue of their representative character, and the corollary that vocabularies acquire their privileges from the men who use them rather than from their transparency to the real. . . .
>
> Edifying philosophers want to keep space open for the sense of wonder which poets sometimes cause—wonder that there is something new under the sun, something which is *not* an accurate representation of what was already there, something which (at least for the moment) cannot be explained and can barely be described. (pp. 368–70)

Now it might seem as if Rorty is casting his lot with edifying philosophy (although he realizes that there is something paradoxical about the very notion of an edifying philosopher). Edifying philosophy is always reactive and parasitic upon the pretentions of systematic philosophy. Edifying philosophers are frequently Rorty's heroes, and he himself admires and emulates their use of satire, ridicule, and paradox. But this is not quite where Rorty leaves us. He suggests a new metaphor for understanding philosophy and the role that it can play in culture— philosophy as *conversation* rather than philosophy as *inquiry*. Rorty is alluding to Oakeshott's conception of conversation in "The Voice of Poetry in the Conversation of Mankind." Philosophy like poetry is best understood as one of the many voices in the conversation of mankind. A conversation can be civilized, illuminating, intelligent, revealing, exciting. Truth may be relevant to a conversation, but so can many other things, and a conversation is not to be thought of as a disguised inquiry into truth or the discovery of foundations. To view philosophy as a form of conversation which is itself part of the larger conversation of mankind is to begin "to get the visual, and in particular the mirroring, metaphors out of speech altogether" (p. 371). It also means recognizing that as culture changes one or another voice may play a more significant role in the conversation. From this perspective we can view edifying philosophers as conversational partners rather than "seeing them as holding views on subjects of common concern" (p. 372). "One way of thinking of wisdom as something of which the love is not the same as that of argument, and of which the achievement does not consist in finding the correct vocabulary for representing essence, is to think of it as the practical wisdom necessary to participate in a conversation" (p. 372). Rorty concludes his book with an eloquent plea for dropping the notion of "philosophers as knowing something about knowing which nobody else knows so well" and dropping the notion that their voice "always has an overriding claim on the attention of the other participants in the conversation" (p. 392). Instead we should be frank about the "useful kibitzing" that philosophers sometimes provide. Rorty's entire book can be read as an ironic variation on the Peircian theme of not blocking the road to inquiry. For it is not open inquiry that needs defense today, but open civilized conversation. Rorty thinks it is idle to speculate about what will happen next in philosophy, but in his final sentence he tells us "The only point on which I would insist is that philosophers' moral concern should be with continuing the conversation of the West, rather than with insisting upon a place for the traditional problems of modern philosophy within that conversation" (p. 394).

V

Rorty never becomes shrill or strident in his critique of "professional philosophy," "modern philosophy," and "analytic philosophy." With the possible exception of Quine, there hasn't been an American philosopher since William James who has written with as much wit, humor, playfulness, and seductive eloquence. All this is combined with a moral seriousness and passion that seeks to unmask pretensions, illusions, and self-deceptions, that seeks to make us aware of our historical limitations—or to use a classical turn of phrase—to make us aware of our human finitude. Although I am sympathetic with his powerful and challenging critique, there is something fundamentally wrong with where Rorty leaves us. In this final section I want to argue that the moral of the tale he tells is not quite the one that he suggests. In a manner similar to the way in which Rorty uses Sellars and Quine (against themselves) I want to show that Rorty himself does not quite see where his best insights and arguments are leading him. Much of this book is about the obsessions of philosophers and the pictures that hold them captive. But there is a sense in which Rorty himself is obsessed. It is almost as if he can't quite "let go" and accept the force of his own critique. It is as if Rorty himself has been more deeply touched by what he is attacking than he realizes. Rorty keeps pointing to and hinting at an alternative to the foundationalism that has preoccupied modern philosophy without ever fully exploring this alternative. Earlier I suggested that one way of reading Rorty is to interpret him as trying to help us to set aside the Cartesian anxiety—the Cartesian Either/Or—that underlies so much of modern philosophy. But there is a variation of this Either/Or that haunts this book—Either we are *ineluctably* tempted by foundational metaphors and the desperate attempt to escape from history *or* we must frankly recognize that philosophy itself is at best a form of "kibitzing." Suppose, however, that Rorty's therapy were really successful; suppose we were no longer held captive by metaphors of "our glassy essence" and "mirroring," suppose we accepted that knowledge claims can never be justified in any other way than by an appeal to social practices, suppose we were purged of the desire for constraint and compulsion, then what? The scene of culture and the voice of philosophy in the conversation of mankind look very different from the one that Rorty proposes. To flesh out what I mean, I will begin with what might seem to be external and peripheral matters and then move closer to the heart of Rorty's vision.

I can isolate Rorty's obsession by comparing him with one of his heroes, John Dewey. Rorty thinks that Dewey is one of the three most important philosophers of our century because while in his early work he tried to provide a new foundation for philosophy, he—like Heidegger and Wittgenstein—came to see this earlier effort as self-deceptive. Dewey in his later work "spent his time warning us against these very temptations to which he had succumbed." From what Rorty says here and in other places, the story is a bit more complicated, for according to Rorty, Dewey himself was briefly tempted — or bullied — into thinking he had to supply a new metaphysical foundation for his own naturalistic vision.[4] But as might be suspected, this is the "bad" Dewey, and his lasting contribution is "therapeutic rather than constructive, edifying rather than systematic, designed to make the reader question his own motives for philosophizing rather than supply him with a philosophical program." But this interpretation of Dewey is a gross distortion, one that is more revealing about Rorty than it is about Dewey. It is true as far as it goes, but Dewey was not nearly as obsessed with attacking epistemology and the "spectator theory of knowledge" as is Rorty. What Rorty leaves out — or fails to give its just due — is that Dewey was primarily concerned with the role that philosophy might play *after* one had been liberated from the obsessions and tyrannies of the "problems of philosophy." Dewey would certainly agree with Rorty that all justification involves reference to existing social practices and that philosophy is not a discipline that has any special knowledge of knowing or access to more fundamental foundations. But for Dewey this is where the real problems begin. What are the social practices to which we should appeal? How do we discriminate the better from the worse? Which ones need to be discarded, criticized and reconstructed? Dewey sought to deal with these problems without any appeal to "our glassy essence," "mirroring," or foundational metaphors. According to Rorty's own analysis, these are genuine problems, but Rorty never quite gets around to asking these and related questions. He tells us, of course, that there is no special philosophical method for dealing with such issues and no ahistorical matrix to which we can appeal. But accepting this claim does not make these issues disappear. Whatever our final judgment of Dewey's success or failure in dealing with what he called the "problems of men," Dewey constantly struggled with questions which Rorty never quite faces — although his whole reading of modern philosophy is one that points to the need for reflective intellectuals to examine them. Sometimes Rorty writes as if any philosophic attempt to sort out the better from the worse, the rational from the irrational (even assuming that this is historically relative) must lead us back to foundationalism and the search for an ahistorical perspective. But Rorty has also shown us that there is nothing inevitable about such a move. Following Rorty, we do not have to see this enterprise as finding a successor foundational discipline to epistemology, but rather as changing the direction of philosophy, of giving the conversation a different turn. Ironically, for all his critique of the desire of philosophers to escape from history and to see the world *sub species aeternitatis*, there is a curious way in which Rorty himself slides into this stance. He keeps telling us that the history of philosophy, like the history of all culture, is a series of contingencies, accidents, of the rise and demise of various language games and forms of life. But suppose we place ourselves *back* into our historical situation. Then a primary task is one of trying to deal with present conflicts and confusions, of trying to sort out the better from the worse, of focusing on which social practices ought to endure and which demand reconstruction, of what types of justification are acceptable and which are not. Rorty might reply that there is no reason to think that the professional philosopher is more suited for such a task than representatives of other aspects of culture. But even this need not be disputed. We can nevertheless recognize the importance and the legitimacy of the task of "understanding how things in the broadest possible sense of the term hang together in the broadest possible sense of the term."[5]

In saying this, I do not think that I am saying anything that Rorty himself doesn't suggest, but he does not grapple with these issues. In part, I think this is due to his own unwarranted anxiety that philosophers can't quite help getting caught in the snares of the type of foundationalism which he has so devastatingly criticized. This is why Rorty himself is still not liberated from the types of obsessions which he claims have plagued most modern philosophers. The point can be approached from a slightly different perspective by examining a central example that Rorty gives to support his type of historicism.

In his discussion of Kuhn's work in sorting out what he takes to be right and wrong in the controversies between Kuhn and his critics, Rorty takes up what might be considered the hard case — the controversy between Galileo and Bellarmine.

> But can we then find a way of saying that the considerations advanced against the Copernican theory by Cardinal Bellarmine — the scriptural descriptions of the fabric of the heavens — were "illogical or unscientific"? This, perhaps, is the point at which the battle lines between Kuhn and his critics can be drawn most sharply. Much of the seventeenth century's notion of what it was to be "rational" turns on Galileo's being absolutely right and the church absolutely wrong. To suggest that there is room for rational

disagreement here — not simply for a black-and-white struggle with reason and superstition — is to endanger the very notion of "philosophy." (p. 328)

Rorty points out that Kuhn does not give an explicit answer to the question. However, Kuhn's writings provide an "arsenal of argument for a negative answer." "In any case, a negative answer is implied by the argument of the present book" (p. 328). It is important to clarify just what Rorty is and is not claiming. He is certainly not suggesting that the issues raised in the dispute between Galileo and Bellarmine are unimportant. On the contrary, the fate of European culture was affected by the resolution of issues raised in this debate. But Rorty argues that there are no permanent standards, criteria, or decision procedures to which one could univocally appeal which would declare Galileo on the side of truth, objectivity, and rationality, and sharply distinguish Galileo's arguments from Bellarmine's "irrationality."

> The conclusion I wish to draw is that the "grid" [to use Foucault's term] which emerged in the later seventeenth century and eighteenth century was not there to be appealed to in the early seventeenth century, at the time that Galileo was on trial. No conceivable epistemology, no study of the nature of human knowledge, could have "discovered" it before it was hammered out. The notion of what it was to be "scientific" was in the process of being formed. If one endorses the values — or perhaps the ranking of competing values — common to Galileo and Kant, then indeed Bellarmine was being "unscientific." We are heirs of three hundred years of rhetoric about the importance of distinguishing sharply between science and religion, science and politics, science and art, science and philosophy, and so on. This rhetoric has formed the culture of Europe. It made us what we are today. We are fortunate that no little perplexity within epistemology, or within the historiography of science, is enough to defeat it. But to proclaim our loyalty to these distinctions is not to say that there are "objective" and "rational" standards for adopting them. (pp. 330–31)

Rorty insists that it is an illusion to think that philosophers stand as neutral third parties to this significant debate, and that they are able to score points for one side or the other by appealing to ahistorical standards of rationality and objectivity. But it is instructive to see what

Rorty passes over all too rapidly. Suppose we try the thought experiment of imagining ourselves back into the context of this debate, and suppose too that we are liberated from thinking that the issues can be resolved by an appeal to permanent epistemological standards. What then? Certainly the issues don't disappear. Our task is precisely to "hammer out" the relevant issues involved, to clarify them and to try to sort out what are the better and worse arguments. This is not a matter of arbitrarily endorsing one set of values over competing values, but rather trying to give the strongest "historical reasons" to support one side or the other. The issues *cannot* be resolved simply by appealing to existing social practices, for the heart of the controversy is the genuine and serious conflict of competing social practices. How are we to understand what are the relevant "historical reasons" — or even what we mean by "historical reasons"? What is revealing about the above passage is the way in which Rorty's language itself reflects what he is presumably opposing. When he places "objective" and "rational" in scare quotes and contrasts this with "three hundred years of rhetoric" he is implicitly aping those who think that either there are rock bottom permanent standards of objectivity and rationality or there is only "mere" rhetoric. But Rorty himself has deconstructed this sense of objectivity and rationality. He distinguishes two senses of "objective" and "subjective."

> "Objectivity" in the first sense was a property of theories, which, having been thoroughly discussed, are chosen by a consensus of rational discussants. By contrast, a "subjective" consideration is one which has been, or would be, or should be, set aside by rational discussants — one which is seen to be, or should be seen to be, irrelevant to the subject matter of the theory. . . . For a consideration to be subjective, in this sense, is simply for it to be unfamiliar. So judging subjectivity is as hazardous as judging relevance.
>
> In a more traditional sense of "subjective," on the other hand, "subjective" contrasts with "corresponding to what is out there" and thus means something like "a product only of what is in here" (in the heart, or in the "confused" portion of the mind which does not contain privileged representations and thus does not accurately reflect what is out there). In this sense "subjective" is associated with "emotional" or "fantastical," for our hearts and our imaginations are idiosyncratic, while our intellects are,

at their best, identical mirrors of the self-same external objects. (pp. 338–39)

Throughout the history of philosophy these two different senses of "objective" and "subjective" have been confused and tangled together. "In this way, the tradition since Plato has run together the 'algorithm versus no algorithm' distinction with the 'reason versus passion' distinction" (p. 339). While there is an innocuous sense in which we employ the second distinction, Rorty has argued that we are on the very brink of misunderstanding when philosophers try to blow this up into something like the issue of realism versus idealism. It is the first distinction that is the effective distinction for sorting out what is "objective" and "subjective." This is a variable and changeable distinction both with respect to different historical epochs and with respect to different fields of inquiry. But the key reference here is to a consensus chosen by *rational discussants*. How are we to decide who are the rational discussants and in what sense they are "rational"? This is not "merely" a rhetorical question, but frequently the most vital question to be confronted. What we learn from Rorty is that philosophers do not have any special knowledge or any special access to permanent standards to answer this question. Sorting out rational discussants from those who are judged to be irrational is precisely the type of issue that needs to be "hammered out." But nothing that Roty says lessens the importance of the question. Indeed everything he says and shows indicates that this is the sort of question that philosophers or, if one prefers, "reflective intellectuals" ought to be addressing.

There is something askew in Rorty's emphasis. Throughout he argues as if we are confronted with two alternatives: *Either* all justification, whether in matters of knowledge or morals, appeals to social practices *or* to illusory foundations. He has been primarily concerned with criticizing the second alternative because he rightly thinks that this is the one to which most modern philosophers have been drawn — disputing only what are the foundations and how they are to be known. But suppose we reject this second alternative and concentrate on the one that Rorty advocates. As Rorty well knows any defense of a consensus view is open to the criticism of how are we to distinguish a rational from an irrational consensus. His constant references to the "best" social practices and to what "rational" discussants would accept indicates his awareness of this problem. But he has very little to say about it. For to deny that there is some absolute or definitive way of making this distinction is not to deny that there is a vital distinction to be made. Sometimes it seems as if Rorty himself is guilty of a version of the "Myth of the Given"—as if social practices are the sort of thing that are *given*, and that all we need to do is to look and see what they are. But surely this is an illusion. To tell us, as Rorty does over and over again, that "to say the True and Right are matters of social practice" (p. 179) or that "justification is a matter of social practice" (p. 186) or that "objectivity should be seen as conformity to norms of justification we find about us" (p. 361), will not do. We want to know how we are to understand "social practices," how they are generated, sustained, and pass away. But even more important we want to know how they are to be *criticized*. For in any historical period we are confronted not only with a tangle of social practices, but with practices that make competing and conflicting demands upon us. There is danger here of reifying the very idea of a social practice and failing to appreciate that our very criticisms and arguments about what is rational and irrational are constitutive of traditions and social practices.

Rorty seems to be deeply ambivalent about the prospects for philosophy. The moral of his work is to suggest and to advocate a need for a turn in the role that philosophy plays in the conversation of mankind. Even his "historicism" points to a way in which philosophy can play a much more vital and central role when we accept our historical limitations but nevertheless try to make sense of the conflicts and confusions that confront us and to gain a critical perspective. At the same time he draws back from taking this seriously, from entering the very area of problems that he has opened up for us.

There is the same lack of balance in the moral decisionism that runs through the book. For all his criticism of Kant, Rorty praises Kant for helping us to see that the

> attempt to answer questions of justification by discovering new objective truths, to answer the moral agent's request for justifications by descriptions of a privileged domain, is the philosopher's form of bad faith—his special way of substituting pseudo-cognition for moral choice. Kant's greatness was to have seen through the "metaphysical" form of this attempt, and to have destroyed the traditional conception of reason to make room for moral faith. Kant gave us a way of seeing scientific truth as something which can never supply an answer to our demand for a point, a justification, a way of claiming our moral decision about

what to do is based on *knowledge* of the nature of the world. (p. 383)

Unfortunately, according to Rorty, Kant misled us into thinking that there is nevertheless a decision procedure for moral choice. But here too Rorty seems to be presupposing what he has so effectively criticized, viz., that "justifying" moral (and social and political) choices is *either* a matter of deceiving ourselves into thinking there is some ultimate ground to which we can appeal *or* a matter of personal (arbitrary?) decision. One would have thought that this is just the type of misleading either/or that he wants to expose. For sometimes we can and do try to justify or warrant our moral decisions by giving the best reasons we can give to support them even when we recognize that there can be disagreements about what constitutes good reasons. And sometimes we are forced to reflect on what does and ought to count as good reasons even when we recognize that there is no algorithm or eternal standards to which we can appeal to settle the relevant issues. If we accept Rorty's claim that all justification, whether of knowledge or moral choices, cannot hope to escape from history and only makes sense with reference to social practices, we are still faced with the critical task of determining which social practices are relevant, which ones ought to prevail, be modified, or abandoned. "Hammering this out" is not a matter of "mere" rhetoric or "arbitrary" decision, but requires argumentation.

One perspective for understanding the moral of Rorty's book is to see his work as an attempt to recover the notion of *phronesis* — the type of practical reasoning that Aristotle sketched for us which doesn't make any appeal to ultimate foundations, eternal standards, or algorithms. But Aristotle also sowed the seeds for the distrust that philosophers have of *phronesis* by contrasting it in the strongest possible way with the contemplative understanding of *noesis*. Rorty not only questions this contrast, but more significantly, he shows us that the more we understand what goes on in theoretical and scientific reasoning, the more we realize how closely it resembles the forms of reasoning and decision making exemplified by the person who exhibits *phronesis*. This is a major reversal or an inversion. For typically philosophers have taken *theoria* — or more accurately their images of what *theoria* is supposed to be like — to be the standard by which practical wisdom is to be judged. Once we make the turn Rorty advocates, once we realize that we are dealing with forms of discourse which differ from each other in degree and not in kind, once we realize that effective rationality is always a form of *rational* persuasion which can never attain a definitive ahistorical closure, then the reflective task would seem to be to clarify the different forms of *phronesis* and *rational* persuasion.

One might imagine Rorty replying that it is not his intention to deny that there are genuine conflicts, problems created by competing social practices, and uncertainties that demand reflective understanding. These are all involved in the image of philosophy as conversation that he wants to substitute for philosophy as the inquiry into foundations. Rather his main point is to challenge the presumption that philosophers have some special knowledge or method which enables them to do this better than anyone else. He also claims that a healthy historical sense reveals that there have been times when theologians, poets, scientists, and literary critics have performed this function better than professional philosophers. But I do not want to dispute these claims nor even Rorty's skepticism about the way in which professional philosophy has become a marginal voice in the conversation of mankind. I do want to urge that we can give a very different twist to Rorty's critique of philosophy. We can see it as a type of therapy that can liberate us from stale metaphors and fundamental misconceptions about what philosophy can achieve. Despite many rearguard actions and misguided attempts to salvage traditional problems or to reformulate them in new and sophisticated ways, we can see that there are many signs of playing out the legacy of notions inherited from the seventeenth century. Underneath the polemic between various advocates of "objectivism" and "relativism," one can detect that philosophers themselves are increasingly coming to realize that there is something wrong with the entire framework and the categorial distinctions that keep these debates alive.

The choice that confronts us is not one of opting for philosophy as "kibitzing" or playing out a few more variations on the same old tired themes. Rorty worries about and warns against the temptation of philosophers to think that they must come up with "constructive programs" which turn out to be new self-deceptive apologies for foundational disciplines. He himself is obsessed with the obsessions of philosophers. But he has shown us that we can set aside these obsessions and need not be tempted to answer unanswerable questions. But there are plenty of questions concerning justification, objectivity, the scope of disciplines, the proper way of distinguishing rational from irrational discussants, and *praxis* that are answerable and demand our attention—even when we concede that any answers are themselves subject to historical limitations. Rorty's book can be read as helping to bring about a turning in philosophy and in seeing how ideas which were once liberating have become intellectual straitjackets. But once we make this turning, once we are liberated from the metaphors and pictures that have held us captive, once we set aside the anxieties about constraint and compulsion that have been so powerful in philosophy, then the scene of culture and the potential contribution of the voice of philosophy in the conversation of mankind becomes far more alive and dramatic.

NOTES

1. Richard Rorty, *Philosophy and the Mirror of Nature* (Princeton, N.J.: Princeton University Press, 1979). References to this work are cited in the text by page number only.

2. "Sensations and Brain Processes," reprinted in *The Philosophy of Mind*, ed. V.C. Chappell (Englewood Cliffs, N.J.: 1962), p. 161.

3. In his essay, "Can Analytical Philosophy Be Systematic, and Ought It to Be?" Dummett says, "Only with Frege was the proper object of philosophy finally established; namely, first that *thought*, secondly that the study of *thought* is to be sharply distinguished from the study of the psychological process of *thinking*; and finally, that the only proper method for analyzing thought consists in the analysis of *language* . . . it has taken nearly a half century since his death for us to apprehend clearly what the real task of philosophy, as conceived by him involves." *Truth and Other Enigmas* (London: Duckworth, 1978), p. 458.

4. See Richard Rorty, "Dewey's Metaphysics," in *New Studies in the Philosophy of John Dewey*, ed. Steven M. Cahn (Hanover, N.H.: University of New England Press, 1977).

5. Wilfrid Sellars, "Philosophy and the Scientific Image of Man," *Science, Perception, and Reality* (New York: Humanities Press, 1963), p. 1.

PART II

Traditions, Knowledge, and Truth

4. EPISTEMOLOGICAL BEHAVIORISM AND THE DE-TRANSCENDENTALIZATION OF ANALYTIC PHILOSOPHY

Richard Rorty

1. INTRODUCTION

Analytic philosophy is traditionally associated with empiricism and scienticism, and thus is often opposed to transcendental philosophy. This seems to me seriously misleading. It is more helpful, I think, to see the career of analytic philosophy from Russell to Sellars and Davidson as describing the same trajectory as that of pragmatism from Peirce to Dewey, of Wittgenstein's thought from the *Tractatus* to the *Investigations*, and of Heidegger's from the project of *Fundamentalontologie* to that of *Andenken*. In each case the trajectory is marked by what I shall call "de-transcendentalization." A project of thought which starts off by announcing that it will construct a permanent neutral framework for the criticism of culture, consisting of apodictic truths (usually identified as "logical" or "structural") differing in kind from those found outside of philosophy, "de-transcendentalizes" itself by gradually blurring the distinctions between logic and fact, structure and content, atemporal essence and historical accident, theory and practise, philosophy and non-philosophy. The impulse to make "logic the essence of philosophy" which motivated the early Russell is the same impulse which led Peirce to derive the pragmatic maxim as a corollary from the logically-demonstrable "reality of Thirdness." It is a special form of the impulse to "put philosophy upon the secure path of science" which motivated Kant, which in turn is the impulse to solve all the problems of philosophy at once (as Wittgenstein announced the *Tractatus* had done). Conversely, the impulse which led James and Dewey to disregard Peirce's formalism, the older Wittgenstein to mock the notion that "logic is something sublime," Heidegger to take his *Kehre*, Quine to denounce the idea of "first philosophy," and Davidson to deplore the "adventitious philosophical puritanism" which sullies semantics, is an impulse away from these pretensions.[1] It is an impulse towards seeing the continuity between philosophy and the rest of culture, away from the Kantian image of the philosopher presiding over a tribunal of pure reason before which the other areas of culture must appear.

As I shall be using the term, "transcendental philosophy" is marked by

(a) the attempt to group philosophy together with mathematics and logic as "apodictic" and "non-empirical";
(b) the notion that there is something called "the nature of human knowledge" which is capable of being known by some specifically philosophical, and thus non-empirical, means;
(c) the claim that philosophical truths about the nature of human knowledge can be used to divide culture into areas according to the legitimacy of the knowledge-claims made therein.

Obviously not all philosophies usually called (by themselves or others) "transcendental" bear all of these marks. Hegel and Habermas, e.g., would protest at being saddled with (a), and I would argue that Hegel's principal contribution was the *Phenomenology's* de-transcendentalization of Kant. But I am not sure that there are more than family resemblances between all the various philosophical projects which have been labeled "transcendental." At any rate, I despair of finding a set of necessary and sufficient conditions which would encompass Hegel and Russell, Fichte and Husserl, Carnap and Apel. So I shall rest content with the point that (a) all three of these marks are borne by Kant, by Peirce, by the early Wittgenstein, and by Russell and Carnap, and that (b) the repudiation of all three is characteristic of Dewey, the later Wittgenstein, and the presently dominant figures within analytic philosophy. These points suffice, I hope, to make defensible my use of the term "de-transcendentalization" to describe the career of analytic philosophy.

Three developments within analytic philosophy have been of almost equal importance in this de-transcendentalization. They are

(1) the abandonment of the notion of epistemology as first philosophy, as a result of criticism of the notion that certain representations (sense-data on the one hand, meanings on the other) are privileged and foundational;

(2) the reaction against formalism among the "Oxford philosophers," and their realization that the diagnosis of the causes of philosophical perplexity could ride free of concern with the question of how to use the first-order predicate calculus as a matrix for the sentences of English;

(3) the separation, within recent American philosophy of language, of problems about how to interpret the sentences of English as fitting into such a matrix from epistemologically-centered issues, such as the need to give "empiricist analyses" of various terms.

The result of these developments, I believe, has been to disjoin analytic philosophy almost entirely from its empiricist and positivist beginnings. All that remains of "hard core" analytic philosophy is the philosophy of language. That area of study has become a self-contained and autonomous discipline which feels no allegiance either to the metaphilosophical slogan that "philosophical questions are questions of language" or to the nominalist and extensionalist intuitions of, e.g., Carnap and Russell. Philosophy of language, in short, no longer has much to do with "linguistic philosophy." The other inquiries making up analytic philosophy in America at present (e.g., the "theory of action," Rawlsian moral philosophy, Gettierology) are not united by any common metaphilosophical standpoint, nor any empiricist or scientistic bias, nor any special strategies of argumentation that are peculiarly "analytic," much less "linguistic" or "logical". "Analytic philosophy" has become, in fact, a sociological description which conveys no knowledge of the interests or motives or predilections of those who practise it. It merely denotes membership in a certain tradition — acquaintance with certain writings and lack of acquaintance with others. When a movement is de-transcendentalized to the extent that analytic philosophy has been, it ceases to have any clear self-image, and becomes merely the "philosophy of the schools" — the analogue of what Kuhn calls "normal science." Once the process of detranscendentalization has gone on as long as it has in this case, a certain lack of coherence becomes inevitable.

In this paper, I shall be focusing almost exclusively on the first of the three developments I have listed. The full story of what has happened to analytic philosophy in America would need to take into account all three developments, and would pay particular attention to the role of Wittgenstein, Austin, and Strawson in connection with the second, and of Davidson and Putnam in connection with the third.

I shall have space only to discuss the overthrow of foundational epistemologies (and thus, I would claim of epistemology itself) which I
regard as chiefly due to the efforts of Quine and Sellars. I shall not —
again for reasons of space — present and defend particular Sellarsian
or Quinean doctrines. Rather, I shall ask the reader to assume the cogency of Quine's attack on the distinctions between language and
theory, meaning and fact, analytic and synthetic, and of Sellars' attack
on the Myth of the Given. Instead of defending either philosopher
against his critics (or purifying their doctrines in order to make this
defense more successful), I want simply to offer an interpretation of
their achievements which supports my claim about their role in the
de-transcendentalizing process.

In the next section, I shall take a step backwards and say something
about the notion of "logic" as the study of certain privileged representations. This notion was essential in the initial phases of analytic
philosophy. Then I shall try to make clear why Sellars' attack on "sensory givenness" and Quine's on "meaning" were attacks on the two
sorts of privileged representations needed to give content to the notion of "philosophy as logical analysis." In the following section, I shall
dub the common denominator of Sellars' and Quine's positions "epistemological behaviorism" and try to show how this "behavioristic" or
"pragmatist" standpoint contrasts with the "transcendental" one common to their predecessors. Finally, in section 4, I shall try to show how
epistemological behaviorism makes it impossible to think of "language"
as a field of transcendental inquiry, or of the philosophy of language
or "linguistic analysis" as a new sort of transcendental philosophy. In
the concluding section, I shall add a few brief remarks to connect what
I have been saying with certain other discussions of transcendental
argumentation, and of the possibility of transcendental philosophy,
which I shall not have space to discuss in detail.

2. APODICTIC TRUTH, PRIVILEGED REPRESENTATIONS, AND ANALYTIC PHILOSOPHY

At the end of the nineteenth century, philosophers were justifiably
worried about the future of their discipline. On the one hand, the
tradition of British empiricism had lent philosophical significance to
the rise of empirical psychology and to the question "what do we need

to know about knowledge which psychology cannot tell us?" Ever since Descartes's attempt to make the world safe for clear and distinct ideas and Kant's to make it safe for synthetic a priori truths, ontology had been dominated by epistemology. So the "naturalization" of epistemology by psychology suggested that a simple and relaxed physicalism was the only sort of ontological view needed. On the other hand, the tradition of Hegelian idealism had become — in England and America — what has been well described as "a continuation of Protestantism by other means." The idealists saved the "spiritual values" which physicalism seemed to neglect by invoking Berkelean arguments to get rid of material substance and Hegelian arguments to get rid of the individual ego, while resolutely ignoring Hegel's historicism. The earnest reductionism of Bain and Mill and the equally earnest romanticism of Royce drove aesthetical ironists like James and Bradley, as well as social reformers like the young Dewey, to proclaim the irreality of traditional epistemological problems and solutions. They were provoked to radical criticism of "truth as correspondence" and "knowledge as accuracy of representations," thus threatening the entire Kantian notion of philosophy as meta-criticism of the special disciplines. Simultaneously, Europeans like Nietzsche, Bergson, and Dilthey were undermining some of the same Kantian presuppositions. For a time, it seemed as if philosophy might turn away once and for all from epistemology, and from the quest for certainty, structure and rigor.

The spirit of playfulness which seemed about to enter the subject around 1900 was nipped in the bud. It was mathematics which inspired Plato to invent philosophy, and it was to mathematical logic that serious-minded philosophers turned for rescue from the exuberant satire of their critics. The paradigmatic figures in this attempt to recapture the mathematical spirit were Husserl and Russell. The young Husserl saw philosophy as trapped between "naturalism" and "historicism," neither of which offered the sort of "apodictic truths" which Kant had assured philosophers were their birthright.[2] Russell joined Husserl in denouncing the psychologism which had infected the philosophy of mathematics and announced that logic was the essence of philosophy.[3] Driven by the need to find something to be apodictic about, Russell discovered "logical form" and Husserl discovered the "purely formal" aspects of the world which remained when the nonformal had been "bracketed." The discovery of these privileged representations began once again a quest for seriousness, purity, and rigor.[4]

This quest made it possible to defer a reconsideration of the Image of Philosophy for another two generations. But in the end, heretical followers of Husserl (Sartre and Heidegger) and heretical followers of Russell (Sellars and Quine) raised the same sorts of questions about the possibility of apodictic truth which Hegel had raised about Kant. Phenomenology gradually became transformed into what Husserl despairingly called "mere anthropology,"[5] and analytic philosophy of science (under the influence of Hanson, Kuhn, Feyerabend, and Harré) has become increasingly historicist and decreasingly "logical." So, seventy years after Husserl's *Philosophy as Strict Science* and Russell's "Logic as the Essence of Philosophy," we are back with the same putative dangers which faced the authors of these manifestoes: if philosophy becomes too naturalistic, hard-nosed positive disciplines will nudge it aside; if it becomes too historicist, then intellectual history, literary criticism, and similar soft spots in "the humanities" will swallow it up.[6]

Although both Husserl and Russell wished to differentiate themselves sharply from Kant and from traditional epistemology, nevertheless their projects contained all three of the marks of "transcendentality" which I have listed above. The central element in the complex of notions which both men inherited from Kant is that of a distinction between scheme and content—the distinction which Davidson has recently called the "third, and perhaps the last, dogma of empiricism"[7] and which is, I have argued elsewhere,[8] constitutive of the notion of a specifically philosophical discipline called "the theory of knowledge." This distinction is presented by Kant as that between two sorts of representations—the intuitive and the conceptual—and recurs as a distinction between thought and its object, language and the world, "posits" and the stimuli with which they cope, and the like. If one does not have the distinction between what is "given" and what is "added by the mind," nor that between the "contingent" (because influenced by what is given) and the "necessary" (because entirely "within" the mind and under its control), then one will not know what would count as a "rational reconstruction" of our knowledge. These two distinctions were attacked at intervals throughout the history of the analytic movement. But the former had been subject to much more suspicion than the latter. Neurath had questioned Carnap's appeal to the given, and doubts had often been expressed about Russell's notion of "knowledge by aquaintance" and Lewis' "expressive language." These doubts came to a head in the early 50s, with the appearance of Wittgenstein's

Philosophical Investigations, Austin's mockery of "the ontology of the sensible manifold," and Sellars' "Empiricism and the Philosophy of Mind." The distinction between the necessary and the contingent—revitalized by Russell and the Vienna Circle as the distinction between "true by virtue of meaning" and "true by virtue of experience"—went substantially unchallenged, however, and formed the least common denominator of "ideal language" and "ordinary language" analysis. However, in the early 50s Quine's "Two Dogmas of Empiricism" challenged *this* distinction, and with it the standard notion (common to Kant, Husserl, and Russell) that philosophy stood to empirical science as the study of structure to the study of content. Given Quine's doubts (buttressed by similar doubts in Wittgenstein's *Investigations*) about how to tell when we are responding to the compulsion of "language" rather than that of "experience," it became difficult to explain in what sense philosophy might have the desired apodictic character. In what follows, I shall drop Husserl and phenomenology, and confine myself to discussing two radical ways of criticizing the Kantian foundations of analytic philosophy—Sellars' behavioristic critique of "the whole framework of givenness" and Quine's behavioristic approach to the necessary-contingent distinction. It is a familiar fact that holism and contextualism have been the chief weapons of critics of logical empiricism, just as they were Hegel's chief weapons against Kant and T.H. Green's chief weapons against Mill and his followers. As long as knowledge is conceived of as accurate representing—as the Mirror of Nature—holistic doctrines (such as Quine's "*any* statement is subject to revision" and Sellars' "there may turn out to be no colored objects") sound pointlessly paradoxical. So the response to Sellars on givenness and Quine on analyticity is that they have "gone too far"—that they have allowed holism to sweep them off their feet and away from common sense. I shall be trying to show that there is a single argument which bears equally against the given-interpretation and the necessary-contingent distinctions, and that the premises of this argument amount to a repudiation of the notion of knowledge as accuracy of representation. I hope thereby to show that Sellars' and Quine's points cannot be effectively defended within the Image of the Mirror of Nature, but that once that Image is broken, the notion of philosophy as the discipline which looks for *privileged* representations among those constituting the Mirror becomes unintelligible. A thorough-going holism has no place for the notion of philosophy as "conceptual," as "apodictic," as picking out the "foundations" of the rest of knowledge, as explaining which representations are "purely given" or "purely conceptual," as presenting a "canonical notation" rather than an empirical discovery, as isolating "trans-framework heuristic categories," — nor, *a fortiori*, as "transcendental." If one sees knowledge as a matter of social practice rather than of holding a mirror up to nature, one will not be likely to envisage a meta-practice which will be the critique of all possible forms of social practice. So holism suggests, as Quine has argued in detail and Sellars has said in passing, a conception of philosophy which has nothing to do with the quest for certainty.

Neither Quine nor Sellars, however, has developed a new conception of philosophy in any detail. Quine, after arguing that there is no line between science and philosophy, tends to assume that he has thereby shown that science can replace philosophy. But it is not clear what task he is asking science to perform. Nor is it clear why natural science, rather than the arts, or politics, or religion, should take over the area left vacant. Further, Quine's conception of science is still curiously instrumentalist. It is based on a distinction between "stimuli" and "posits" which seems to lend aid and comfort to the old intuition-concept disinction, and yet Quine transcends both distinctions by granting that stimulations of sense-organs are as much "posits" as anything else. It is as if Quine, having renounced the conceptual-empirical, analytic-synthetic, and language-fact distinctions, is still not quite able to renounce that between the given and the postulated. Conversely, Sellars, having triumphed over the latter distinction, could not quite renounce the former cluster. Despite courteous acknowledgement of Quine's triumph over analyticity, Sellars' writing is still permeated with the notion of "giving the analysis" of various terms or sentences, and with a tacit use of the distinction between the necessary and the contingent, the structural and the empirical, the philosophical and the scientific. Each of the two men tends to make continual, unofficial, tacit, heuristic use of the distinction which the other has transcended. It is as if analytic philosophy could not be written without at least *one* of the two great Kantian distinctions, and as if neither Quine nor Sellars were willing to cut the last links which bind them to Russell, Carnap, and "logic as the essence of philosophy."

Analytic philosophy *cannot*, I suspect, be written without one or the other of these distinctions. If there are no intuitions into which to resolve concepts (in the manner of the *Aufbau*) nor any internal relations among concepts to make possible "grammatical discoveries" (in the manner of "Oxford philosophy"), then indeed it is hard to imagine what an "analysis" might be. Wisely, few analytic philosophers any longer try to explain what it is to offer an analysis. Although there was a great deal of metaphilosophical literature in the 30s and 40s under the aegis of Russell and Carnap, and another spate of such literature in the 50s which took the *Philosophical Investigations* and *The Concept of Mind* as paradigms,[9] there is now little attempt to bring "analytic philosophy" to self-consciousness by explaining how to tell a successful from an unsuccessful analysis.

The present lack of metaphilosophical reflection within the analytic movement is, I think, symptomatic of the sociological fact that analytic philosophy is now, in several countries, the entrenched school of thought. Thus in these countries *anything* done by philosophers who employ a certain style, or mention certain topics, counts (*ex officiis suis*, so to speak) as continuing the work begun by Russell and Carnap. Once a radical movement takes over the establishment against which it revolted, there is less need for methodological self-consciousness, self-criticism, or a sense of location in dialectical space or historical time.

As I have already said, I do not think that there any longer exists anything identifiable as "analytic philosophy" except in some such stylistic or sociological way. But this is not a disparaging remark, as if some legitimate expectation had been disappointed. The analytic movement in philosophy (like any movement in any discipline) worked out the dialectical consequences of a set of assumptions, and now has little more to do. The sort of optimistic faith which Russell and Husserl shared with Kant—that philosophy, its essence discovered at last, had finally been placed upon the secure path of a science—is not something to be mocked or deplored. Such optimism is only possible for men of high imagination and daring, the heroes of their times.

3. BEHAVIORISM, JUSTIFICATION, AND HOLISM

The simplest way to describe the common features of Quine's and Sellars' attack on logical empiricism is to say that both raise behaviorist questions about the epistemic privilege which logical empiricism claims for certain assertions, *qua* reports of privileged representations. Quine asks how an anthropologist is to divide the sentences to which natives whole-heartedly and eternally assent into contingent empirical plat-itudes on the one hand and necessary conceptual truths on the other. Sellars asks how the authority of first-person reports of, e.g., how things appear to one, the pains from which one suffers, and the thoughts that drift before one's mind differ from the authority of expert reports on, e.g., metal stress, the mating behavior of birds, or the colors of physical objects. If one lumps all those together and asks "How do one's peers know which of one's assertions to take one's word for and which to look for confirmation of?" then one is asking the same sort of question as Quine's. It would seem enough for the natives to know which sentences are unquestionably true, without knowing which are true "by virtue of language." It would seem enough for our peers to believe there to be no better way of finding out our inner states than our reports, without their knowing what "lies behind" our making them. It would also seem enough for *us* to know that our peers have this acquiescent attitude — this alone seems sufficient to give us that inner certainty about our inner states which the tradition has explained by "immediate presence to consciousness," "sense of evidence," and other forms of the view that reflections in the Mirror of Nature are intrinsically better known than Nature itself. For Sellars, the certainty of "I have a pain" is a reflection of the fact that nobody cares to ques-tion it, not conversely. Just so, for Quine, the certainty of "All men are animals" and of "There have been some black dogs." Quine thinks that "meanings" drop out as wheels that are not part of the mechan-ism,[10] and Sellars thinks the same of "self-authenticating non-verbal episodes."[11] More broadly, if assertions are justified by society rather than by the character of the inner representations they express, then there is no point in attempting to isolate *privileged* representations.

Explaining rationality and epistemic authority by reference to what society lets you say, rather than the latter by the former, is the essence of behaviorism when applied to human knowledge. It is a species of holism which requires no idealist or panpsychist metaphysical under-pinnings (as did Green's and Dewey's). Behaviorism claims that if you understand the rules of a language-game, you understand all that there is to understand about why moves in that language-game are made. (All, that is, save for the extra understanding you get when you engage in various research programs which nobody would call epistemological — into, for example, the history of the language, the structure of the brain, the evolution of the species, and the political or cultural am-biance of the players.) If one is behaviorist in this sense, then it would not occur to one to invoke either of the traditional Kantian distinctions. But can one just go ahead and be behaviorist? Or, as Quine's and Sellars' critics suggest, doesn't behaviorism simply beg the question?[12] Is there any reason to think that fundamental epistemic notions *should* be explicated in behavioral terms?

This last question comes down to: can we treat epistemology as the study of certain ways in which human beings interact, or must we find an ontological foundation (involving some specifically philosophical way of describing human beings) for epistemology? Shall we take "S knows that p" (or "S knows non-inferentially that p," or "S believes incorrigibly that p" or "S's knowledge that p is certain") as a remark about the status of S's reports among his peers, or shall we take it as a remark about the relation between subject and object, between Nature and its Mirror? The first alternative leads to a coherence theory of a truth and a therapeutic approach to ontology (in which philosophy can straighten out pointless quarrels between common sense and science, but not contribute any arguments of its own for the existence or inexistence of something). For Quine, to say that something is a necessary truth is to say that nobody has given us any interesting alternatives which would lead us to raise questions about it. For Sellars, to say that a report of a passing thought is incorrigible is to say that nobody has yet suggested any way of predicting and controlling human behavior which does not involve taking first-person contemporary sincere reports of thoughts at face-value. The second alternative leads to "ontological" explanations of the relations between minds and meanings, minds and immediate data of awareness, universals and particulars, thought and language, consciousness and brains, and so on. For philosophers like Chisholm and Bergmann, such explanations *must* be attempted if the realism of common sense is to be preserved. The aim of all such explanations is to make truth something more than what Dewey called "warranted assertability": more than what one's peers will, *ceteris paribus*, let one get away with saying. Such explanations, when ontological, usually take the form of a redescription of the object of knowledge so as to "bridge the gap" between it and the knowing subject. To choose between these approaches is to choose between truth as "what it is good for us to believe" and truth as "contact with reality."

So, it seems that the question of whether one can be behaviorist in one's attitude toward knowledge is not a matter of the "adequacy" of behaviorist "analyses" of knowledge-claims or of mental states. Rather, it is a matter of whether philosophy has more to offer than common sense (supplemented by biology, history, etc.) about Truth. The question is not whether necessary and sufficient behavioral conditions for "S knows that p" can be offered; no one any longer dreams they can. Nor is the question whether such conditions can be offered for "S sees that p," or "It looks to S as if p" or "S is having the thought that p." To be behaviorist in the large sense in which Sellars and Quine are behaviorist is not to offer reductionist analyses, but to refuse to attempt a certain sort of explanation: the sort of explanation which not only interposes a notion such as "acquaintance with meanings" or "acquaintance with sensory appearances" between the impact of the environment on human beings and their reports about it, but uses such notions to explain the reliability of such reports.

But, once again, how is one to decide whether such notions are needed? It is tempting to answer: on the basis of an antecedent decision about the nature of human beings—a decision on whether we need such notions as "mind," "stream of consciousness," and the like to describe them. But this would be the wrong answer. To be behaviorist in epistemology is not the same as being reductionist in the philosophy of mind. One can take the Sellars-Quine attitude towards knowledge while cheerfully "countenancing" raw feels, a priori concepts, innate ideas, sense-data, propositions, and anything else which an explanation of human behavior might find it helpful to postulate.[13] What one *cannot* do is to take knowledge of these "inner" or "abstract" entities as *premises* from which our knowledge of other entities is normally inferred, and without which the latter knowledge would be "ungrounded." The difference is between saying that to know a language is to be acquainted with the meanings of its terms, or that to see a table is to have a rectangular sense-impression, and explaining the *authority* of tokens of "All men are animals" or "That looks like a table" by virtue of the prior (internal, private, non-social) authority of a knowledge of meanings or of sense-impressions. Behaviorism in epistemology is not a matter of metaphysical parsimony, but of whether one thinks that authority can attach to assertions by virtue of relations of "acquaintance" between persons and, e.g., thoughts, impressions, universals, and propositions, or whether such authority is always a matter of social practice.

The difference between the Quine-Sellars and the Chisholm-Bergmann outlook on these matters is not the difference between lush and spare landscapes, but more like the difference between moral philosophers who think that rights and responsibilities are a matter of what society bestows and those who think that there is something inside a man which society "recognizes" when it makes its bestowal. The two schools of moral philosophy do not differ on the point that human beings have rights worth dying for. What they differ about is whether, once one has understood when and why these rights have been granted or denied, in the way in which social and intellectual historians understand this, there is more to understand. They differ, in short, about whether there are "ontological foundations for human rights," just as the Sellars-Quine approach differs from the empiricist and rationalist traditions about whether, once one understands when and why various beliefs were adopted or discarded (as historians and sociologists of knowledge do), there is something called "the relation of knowledge to reality" left over to be understood.

This analogy with moral philosophy lets one focus the issue about behaviorism in epistemology yet again: the issue is not adequacy of explanation of fact, but rather whether any practice of justification can be given a "grounding" in fact. The question is not whether human knowledge in fact has "foundations," but whether it makes sense to suggest that it does – whether the idea of epistemic or moral authority having a "ground" in nature is a coherent one. For the pragmatist in morals the claim that the customs of a given society are "grounded in human nature" is not one which he knows how to argue about. He is a pragmatist because he cannot see what it would be like for a custom to be so grounded. For the Quine-Sellars approach to epistemology, to say that truth and knowledge can only be judged by the standards of the inquirers of our own day is not to say that human knowledge is less noble or important, or more "cut off from the world," than we had thought. It is merely to say that nothing counts as justification unless by reference to what we already accept, and that there is no way to get outside our beliefs and our language so as to find some test other than coherence for our assertions.

To say that the True and the Right are matters of social practice may seem to condemn one to a *relativism* which, all by itself is a *reductio* of a behaviorist approach to either knowledge or morals. But only the impulse toward transcendental philosophy, the hope for a discipline which will pick out a given set of scientific or moral views as more "rational" than the alternatives by appeal to something which forms a permanent neutral matrix for all inquiry and all history, makes it possible to think of coherence theories of intellectual and practical justification as "relativist." One reason why professional philosophers recoil more violently than most men from the claim that knowledge may not have foundations, nor rights and duties an ontological ground, is that the kind of behaviorism which dispenses with foundations is in a fair way towards dispensing with philosophy. For the view that there is no permanent neutral matrix within which the dramas of inquiry and history are enacted has as a corollary that criticism of one's culture can only be piecemeal and partial—never "by reference to eternal standards." The urge to say that assertions and actions must not just cohere with other assertions and actions, but also "correspond" to something apart from what people are saying and doing, has some claim to be called *the* philosophical urge. It is the urge which drove Plato to say that Socrates' words and deeds, failing as they did to cohere with current theory and practice, nonetheless corresponded to something which the Athenians could barely glimpse. The residual Platonism which Quine and Sellars are opposing is not the hypostatization of non-physical entities, but the notion of "correspondence" with such entities as the touchstone by which to measure the worth of present practice.[14]

I am claiming, in short, that the Quine-Sellars attack on the Kantian notion of two sorts of representations—intuitions "given" to one faculty, and concepts (or meanings) "given" to another—is not the attempt to substitute one sort of account of human knowledge for another, but an attempt to get away from the notion of "an account of human knowledge." It amounts to a protest against an archetypal philosophical problem: the problem of how to reduce norms, rules, and justifications to facts, generalizations, and explanations.[15] There is no way in which one might find some neutral metaphilosophical ground on which to argue the issues Quine and Sellars raise. For they are not offering an "account" to be tested for "adequacy" but pointing to the futility of offering an "account." The point may be brought out by noting that to refuse to justify assertions by appeal to behavioristically unverifiable episodes (in which the mind recognizes its own direct acquaintance with an instantiation of blueness or with the meaning of "blue") is just to say that justification must be holistic. If we are not to have a doctrine of "knowledge by acquaintance" which will give us a foundation, and if we are not simply to deny that there is such a thing as justification, then one will claim with Sellars that "science is rational not because it has a foundation, but because it is a self-correcting enterprise which can put *any* claim in jeopardy, though not all at once."[16] One will say with Quine that knowledge is not like an architectonic structure but like a field of force,[17] and that there are no assertions which are immune from revision. One will be nihilistic not because one has a taste for wholes, any more than one is behaviorist because of a distaste for "ghostly entities," but simply because justification has always *been* behavioristic and holistic. Only the professional philosopher has dreamed that it might be something else, for only he is frightened by the epistemological sceptic. An holistic approach to knowledge is not a matter of anti-foundationalist polemic, but a distrust of the whole epistemological enterprise. A behavioristic approach to episodes of "direct awareness" is not a matter of anti-mentalistic polemic, but a distrust of the Platonic quest for that special sort of certainty associated with visual perception. The Image of the Mirror of Nature, a mirror more easily and certainly seen than that which it mirrors, stereoscopically reinforces, and is reinforced by, the search for a transcendental standpoint.

4. THE LINGUISTIC TURN, PRACTICE, AND THEORY

What Gustav Bergmann called "the linguistic turn" in philosophy was taken by many to have freed the philosopher once and for all from dependence upon empirical science, enabling him to retain his traditional Platonic role as spectator of time and eternity. For if knowledge of apodictic truth is the result of inspection of the meanings of words, and if empirical knowledge can be "rationally reconstructed" by formulating conditions for asserting sentences in terms of the occurrence of certain privileged representations (e.g., sense-data), then one can understand all about the nature of knowledge without leaving one's armchair. By examining "the limits of language," one can draw Kantian conclusions without fearing Hegelian relativization of those conclusions. Quine's and Sellars' behaviorist attacks upon privileged representations, however, have let us see that once we have the notion of the world (not the thing-in-itself, but the collection of objects currently countenanced by common sense, science, and culture) on the one hand, and of linguistic behavior on the other, we do not need privileged representations to account for knowledge claims. Thus we do not need the notion of "intuition" nor of "concept," nor that of "epistemology." But neither do we need the notion of "language," where this is a special, permanent, neutral, philosophical, formal field of study, yielding "conceptual truths."

But this is not to say that the linguistic turn was fruitless. On the contrary, the substitution of "language" for "thought" or "mind" or "reason" has permitted philosophers to take the relativity of knowledge and culture to conceptual frameworks, paradigms, and pictures more seriously than such relativity has ever been taken before. In good Hegelian fashion, the logical empiricist version of Kantian philosophy not only contained the seeds of its own destruction, but permitted the development of a vastly improved version of Hegel's replies to Kant. The quest for universality and objectivity which Plato took as definitory of philosophy has led us (by way of logical empiricism —a detour made in a final attempt to make philosophy a source of apodictic truth) to a still better understanding of why Plato's dream will not come true. For as long as there seemed to be a human nature, conceived of as an eye to which things (ideas, natures, meanings, sensations) are present, the Platonic project made some sense. The greatest single contribution which linguistic philosophy has made to culture was an involuntary one. It helped us to see through the Platonic notions of "objectivity," and "necessity" and "reason" and "human nature," and to substitute notions of man as a self-changing being, *capable of remaking himself by remaking his speech*. It has helped us break down the distinction between theory and practice in a way which was impossible for the nineteenth century.

To see this, it is helpful to return once again to Kant and Hegel, and to the contrast between the *ésprit de finesse* which preceded the rise of analytic philosophy and the *ésprit de géometrie* which marked its most flourishing period. Kant, by insisting on knowledge as a product of activity rather than of passive contemplation, was the first to seriously endanger the complex of Platonic epistemological notions which stemmed from taking mathematics as the model for all inquiry.[18] But Kant thought that inquiry was pretty much over, and could be *known* to be over by detecting the forms which our subjectivity had necessarily imposed. Newtonian physics and the ethics of the Enlightenment could be viewed as objective, not in the sense of corresponding to reality, but as something which we cannot help ourselves from constructing. Hegel's insistence that physics and ethics, like everything

else imaginable, could have alternatives, was the first attempt to trans-
form philosophy from a "hard" and quasi-mathematical subject into
a "soft" one—a subject in which apodicity was less important than
creativity.[19] With the early Hegel, and with the Kierkegaard of the
"aesthetic" works (who could laugh with Hegel's *Phenomenology* and
at his *Encyclopedia*) philosophy as the free play of this historical consciousness made its first appearance.[20] This was the first period in modern philosophy in which science-vs.-religion and science-vs.-common
sense were less important than the tension between common sense and
what was happening in politics, and in art and poetry. It was the first
in which argument was less important than insight, because (roughly)
what argument in philosophy could do Kant seemed already to have
done. But argument was distrusted precisely because Kant was. Once
empirical inquiry was put aside, all that remained seemed to be "transcendental arguments concerning the conditions of the possibility of
experience." Such arguments presupposed the status quo, for experience
meant experience-and-knowledge-as-we-know-it. Further, such arguments assumed that the mind could know its own limitations, its own
processes of molding and the possible range of such processes, in some
special way that it could know nothing else. But the Kantian claim
that we can understand the possibility of synthetic a priori knowledge
if *we* are its ground, but not if nature is,[21] was based on the old Cartesian notion that "nothing is closer to the mind than itself." Kant, in
the act of saying that nature was made rather than found, transcended
his own methodological limits,[22] and left himself defenseless against
the Romantic insistence that Spirit's self-consciousness is an unending
development, and that no transcendental argument can freeze it in
place.

But this romanticism seemed to English-speaking neo-Hegelians
like T.H. Green and John Dewey to require a new philosophical
"ground." Such men wanted a new theory about the nature of man
and the world (e.g., Absolute Idealism, Evolutionary Nationalism)[23]
which would provide the sort of permanent matrix for empirical inquiry and political change which Kant had envisaged. The realism-
vs.-idealism controversy which agitated the nineteenth and early twentieth centuries, and helped to reharden and reprofessionalize philosophy
after Hegel, arose from the lingering conviction that something specifically philosophical must be said about how coherentist tests for agreement on truth and goodness built into the current practices of our

culture could be joined with the intuition that Truth is One, or that the object of inquiry and social change must be to "correspond" to something "out there." The Kantian attempt to interpret objectivity as intersubjectivity needed to be reconciled with the suspicion that the whole community of subjects might be marching in the wrong direction, a suspicion fostered by the fact that our ancestors had spent so many centuries doing just that. The idealists thought that the only philosophical thing to be said was something speculative and surprising: e.g., that the World-Spirit was leading us (though perhaps in zigzags) toward a unity of Subject and Object. The realists thought that the only philosophical thing to be said was something reductionist: something to show that there was no "mind" or "reason" in any traditional sense, over and above adaptive behavior. The idealists seemed to deify man and the realists, like Darwin, to brutalize him.

The "linguistic turn" marked a return to Kant and the notion of transcendental argumentation. For the objections to a special access to our noumenal mental processes which were decisive against Kant did not seem to apply to our access to the meanings of the words in our language, and these meanings did not (except in a trivial sense) change in the course of empirical inquiry. The analytic movement in philosophy was based on a tacit agreement to pretend that Hegel had never lived. Russell, like Husserl, decided that the task of philosophy was to repeat Kant's achievement in "putting philosophy upon the secure path of a science" by a rediscovery of the formal, but to do so without a theory of the relation between Subject and Object. The discovery of quantificational logic seemed to provide the permanent matrix within which the results of any future empirical inquiry might be placed. The discovery of surprising "analyses" of common-sense statements seemed a satisfactory substitute for the defense of familiar synthetic a priori truths. Such books as *Mind and the World-Order* and *Language, Truth and Logic* suggested that by discretely ignoring "pure intuitions" and relativizing Kant's table of categories we could have both the empiricism of Hume and the purity and formality of Kant.[24] This success in finding something peculiarly philosophical to do without having to take sides on the metaphysical issues raised by Hegel concerning the nature of subject and object led logical empiricists to say that they had discovered idealism-vs.-realism to be a pseudo-problem, capable of being dissolved by a restatement of Kant's phenomenalist position in the *Paralogisms*. Philosophers like Ayer rediscovered what

Austin called "the ontology of the sensible manifold," and thereby saved both the idealist claim that truth could only be a matter of coherence among representations and the realist claim that truth was found rather than made. This account of knowledge required a firm Kantian distinction between questions of fact and questions of right and wrong, as well as a firmly anti-Kantian claim that the latter were merely "emotive." But this was thought a small price to pay for the "overcoming of metaphysics."[25]

In the period since Quine's "Two Dogmas," Wittgenstein's *Philosophical Investigations,* and Sellars' "Empiricism and the Philosophy of Mind" (roughly, the twenty years beginning in 1950) the holistic criticisms which pragmatists and idealists had made of empiricist dogmas were revived, phenomenalism once again fell into disrepute, and the idealism-realism issue arose once again within the context of philosophy of science. The sense of "language" as the formal and unchangeable matrix of inquiry was lost, and philosophers recaptured the Hegelian picture of human inquiry as punctuated by revolutions which made new sorts of experience possible. Philosophy, after becoming still more hardened and professionalized through Russell's return to Kant's program, now softened slightly once again and became receptive to influences from anthropology, history, literary criticism and radical politics—not to speak of Continental philosophers who had remembered Hegel and had stayed aloof from both the analytic movement and Husserlian phenomenology. But this gradual turn from neo-Kantianism to neo-Hegelianism stayed "linguistic," not in the sense that the analysis of meanings remained the philosopher's field of study, but in the sense that philosophical problems were now put in terms of the relation between language and the world, language and culture, language and politics, the language of science and the language of common sense, the language of the natural and that of the behavioral sciences. Much of this talk of language was merely faddist, but the fashionable jargon marked a genuine change in the nature of philosophical reflection. For questions of the nature of reason, of subjectivity and objectivity, of the conditions of the possibility of experience, which had seemed to require metaphysical resolution in the nineteenth century, now seemed to require only sociological or historical description. The topic changed from the relations between Nature and its Mirror to the comparative utilities of different ways of talking. Thus logical empiricism actually *did* help us "overcome metaphysics," not by the "logical analysis of language" but by showing that there could be no such analysis.[26]

The decisive shift was made possible by the adoption of behaviorism in epistemology. To regard the warrant of assertions as given by practice rather than by the nature of the human subject (either as Platonic spectator or Kantian creator) was to give up the idealism-realism controversy along with the rest of epistemology. For the problem created by the tension between the relative, transitory, parochial, coherentist tests of truth provided by various sciences and scientific epochs on the one hand, and our intuition that Truth is One and consists in "correspondence to reality" on the other, cannot be stated without the notion of representations which correspond to something else which is not just one more representation. *The effect of Quine's and Sellars' attack on privileged representations was to trivialize the notion of language-as-representation altogether.* For if there are simply sentences whose assertion is to be judged in terms of the parochial standards of one's own culture, and if these sentences are to be compared neither with "meanings" nor "experiences" which determine their use, then the only thing to compare them with are other sentences — or, more precisely, with other disciplines, epochs, and cultures which permit the assertion of alternative sentences.[27] Without a permanent formal framework of concepts or meanings and a foundation of intuitions or experiences, inquiry cannot be seen as faithful to the source of either general or individual representations. Without the notion of a source of representations (the External World, the Transcendental Ego, the World-Spirit) to which the inquiry must attempt to penetrate, the notion of "correspondence to reality" no longer expresses the nature of Truth. For speech, unlike the mind ("man's glassy essence") does not lend itself to the imagery of Mirror and Object Reflected. It *can*, of course, be described in terms of such images (as, indeed, can anything) but whereas the Cartesian notion of "mind" was built around this imagery, the notion of "speech" was not. Speech is primarily a matter of coping with the people about you, and even when *written* language becomes the important form of language its character as "representation" is parasitic upon viewing it as "the expression of thought " — the Descartes-Locke conception of language as the outward expression of events in an inner arena.[28] Philosophers who have abandoned the idea ideae (except insofar as this idea may be convenient for empirical psychology) no longer think of language as the mirror of a mirror, and thus the temptation to think of it as a collection of representations (as *itself* the Mirror of Nature) is diminished.[29]

Thinking of language as facilitating practice rather than embodying theory produces a pragmatic notion of truth. The notion of correspondence fits the etymological sense of "theory" as *view*. As long as the concept-intuition, or language-experience, model held good, theory had to be seen as distinct from practice — as distinct as looking is from manipulating. James' pragmatic definition of truth as "whatever proves itself to be good in the way of belief"[30] — the true sentence as the sentence asserted by the man who knows how to get what he wants — takes truth to be something inherently relative, inherently temporary. The impact of Quine and Sellars upon philosophy is to make such a pragmatic view respectable by making it impossible to answer the question: how do we know when we have achieved a correct representation? This question only looked answerable as long as there were some representations which were privileged and which thus could serve as fulcra. But once these fulcra are gone, and once justification is thought of holistically and as defined by social practice rather than in terms of a relation to a privileged foundation in the external world or the subject's nature, then the temptation to ask such a question diminishes. As it diminishes, the ability to take James' definition of truth seriously increases.[31]

To sum up, the linguistic turn made it possible for Quine and Sellars to restate the Hegelian criticism of the Kantian notions of concept and intuition in a way which let us see inquiry neither idealistically (as possible only because the object of knowledge as well as its subject was somehow "spiritual in nature") nor reductionistically (as a process which differs only in complexity from adaptive behavior).[32] If we abandon Quine's reductionist notion of "limning the true and ultimate structure of reality" and Sellars' nostalgic vision of inquiry converging to more and more adequate Tractarian "picturings" of the real, then we can admit as many or as few intentions, norms, ghosts, World-Spirits and other explanatory entities as we find convenient. We need neither flee to them as the idealists did, nor from them as naturalists do. By ceasing to think that the vocabulary of physics is automatically more of a "picture of what is out there" than that of politics, religion, anthropology, or literary history, we give up the notion of philosophy as mediating between theory (the representation of the real) and practice (everything else men do) and see it as Dewey saw it — criticism of culture, critical comparison of various possible vocabularies and practices, criticism which allows itself to be continuous with the rest of culture rather than desperately insisting on a transcendental privilege. The "linguistic turn" was (we may hope) the last expression of the attempt at magisterial neutrality which Plato taught us to expect of the philosopher — the last attempt to avoid the pragmatism common to Nietzsche and James,[33] a pragmatism whose chief motive is to de-transcendentalize philosophy. By taking seriously Kant's notion that the Mirror of Nature would always be distorting, and by identifying the distorting element with language, analytic philosophy helped make it possible to put aside the whole dialectic of Subject and Object, of object and representation, and thus all notions of "mirroring," "distorting" and "constituting". Viewing language as an abstraction from linguistic behavior, in the manner of Quine and Sellars, makes it possible to see the making of true statements as of a piece with the rest of human life, rather than as the point at which human life encounters the demands of the Wholly Other.

5. CONCLUDING REMARKS

My contribution to discussion of the question " Does Transcendental Philosophy have a Future?" has consisted almost entirely of the claim that recent developments in analytic philosophy have destroyed the transcendental hopes which were built into the beginnings of that movement. I would like to append a few brief remarks which deal more explicitly with the topic of this volume. The first remark will be very brief: it concerns the often heard suggestion that arguments such as Wittgenstein's so-called Private Language Argument and Strawson's rendition of various Kantian arguments give us new paradigms of transcendental argumentation, argumentation of the sort which might become the basis for a species of transcendental philosophy. I have argued elsewhere that both Wittgenstein's and Strawson's arguments should be taken as having merely negative force against certain concrete suggestions made by their empiricist opponents.[34] More generally, I have argued that transcendental arguments can never be more than *ad hominem* negative arguments, and cannot establish "necessities."[35] I do not want to repeat myself in this paper, so I will simply note that the suggestion that with Strawson analytic philosophy began to turn away from empiricism towards something like a Kantian "metaphysics of experience" seems to me misleading. It is true that there is, in Austin, Strawson, Hampshire, et. al., a turn away from certain (roughly phenomenalistic) assumptions common to Hume and Russell. But this seems to me not a methodological shift, much less one which helps achieve or restore transcendentality. Rather, it is simply the bringing forward once again of certain traditional anti-phenomenalist arguments used by Reid, by Kant, by British Idealists such as Green, by American pragmatists such as Dewey, and by phenomenologists such as Merleau-Ponty. The only thing transcendental about these arguments is that they include some arguments used by Kant in the "Transcendental Deduction." But this is not enough to make them harbingers of a new sort of transcendental philosophy.

The second remark I want to make concerns the suggestion that analytic philosophy is permeated through and through by scientism, and by an animus against reflexion. I mentioned this suggestion in the first sentence of this paper, only to dismiss it and go off into a discussion of the transcendentalizing urge which I claimed to be common to Kant and to Russell. Let me end by taking it up again. This suggestion has recently been fleshed out in detail by Habermas in his "Postscript" to *Knowledge and Human Interests,* and I shall focus on his formulation — though so briefly that I shall do little more than indicate the lines along which I wish to disagree.[36] Habermas sees an opposition between what he calls "self-objectivation" and "self-reflexion," and takes the bankruptcy of the former as shown in what he calls "the self-ironical positions of Sellars and Feyerabend" (p. 164). He urges the needs for "a new and transformed transcendental philosophy" (p. 165) based on self-reflexion. I wish to make two points about this. The first is that "self-objectivation" is an inaccurate description of the thrust of Sellars' and Feyerabend's work. The second is that Habermas' transformed notion of a transcendental standpoint seems to me to differ only slightly from the standpoint which Sellars, and perhaps even Feyerabend, would (or, at least, should) adopt when faced with the challenge Habermas formulates.

On the first point, Habermas thinks of "scientistic" philosophers as follows:

> Scientistic theories of science attribute to the sciences an exclusive claim to knowledge, without being able to share in this exclusive

status of science . . . By their scientistic orientation, its members
are obliged to objectivate themselves. Unable to meet the demand for self-reflexion without simultaneous abandonment of
their theory, they reject that demand by conceiving a programme
for science theory which would make all demands for self-reflexion
immaterial when once that programme will have been carried out.
Some day, they say to themselves, all these metatheoretical discussions will be adequately explained in terms of the categories of
the objectivating sciences. Then all of us will realize that it was
a categorical mistake to be looking for transcendental foundations in an area where all phenomena are empirically explainable.
(p. 161)

In Sellars, the distinction which Habermas draws between self-objectivation and self-reflexion appears as, roughly, the distinction between
describing oneself and justifying oneself (between treating oneself as
a thing and as a person). Sellars has no interest whatever in collapsing
the two. On the contrary, he is concerned, as I have said, to emphasize
that the confusion of the two engendered classical empiricism (and,
indeed, the entire project of gaining a quasi-scientific understanding
of "the nature of human knowledge" which begins with Descartes).
Sellars' own neo-Hegelian social theory (most evident, though still only
sketchily adumbrated, in the final chapter of his *Science and Metaphysics*) is a match for Habermas' in its attention to the transformation of practical imperatives through changes in the self-images of
societies, and to the interaction between such changes and changes
in science's improved descriptions of men. Sellars' view of "transcendental foundations" is not that they should be replaced by empirical explanations, but rather that we should take them to be moral imperatives
rather than quasi-scientific descriptions of our cognitive faculties. The
pragmatic attitude toward knowledge which, I have claimed, arises
naturally out of Sellars' and Quine's work (and which is taken to
rhetorical extremes by Feyerabend) need make no attempt to "arrest
reflexion." On the contrary, it wishes to forestall attempts to *base* new
imperatives upon scientific discoveries, and thus liberate the moral imagination from "scientific" criticism.

Perhaps the simplest formula which will express the relation between Habermas' and Sellars' position is that Habermas wants transcendental philosophy to ground "a theory of the constitution of objects" in a "theory of truth designed as a logic of discourse" (p. 170),

whereas the pragmatism which stems from epistemological behaviorism wants to describe and enlarge the logic of discourse, while abandoning notions of "constitution." It wants to abandon the claim that Kant created, as Habermas claims,

> a type of non-objectivistic foundation of knowledge, which no epistemologically oriented theory of science can afford to ignore without running the risk of arbitrarily arresting reflexion. (p. 164)

Or, one might better say, it can grant this, but would then go on to claim that we do not need, and should stop trying for, an "*epistemologically oriented* theory of science.*" If we have an understanding of our practices of scientific inquiry (which will, as any self-understanding must, owe much to Marx and Freud), then we have all the understanding that philosophy is going to give us— but what it gives us is not clearly distinct from what the history and sociology of science gives us. It is, at any rate, not distinct by virtue of being "foundational."

To turn now to my second point, I find it difficult to see that there is a real difference between Habermas' position and the upshot of the epistemological behaviorism I have been outlining. His "transformed transcendental philosophy" often seems to coincide with what I have been calling "de-transcendentalized analytic philosophy," with the differences being largely sociological ones concerning the predecessors and catch phrases cited. Habermas says, for example, that

> As long as cognitive interests can be identified and analyzed through reflexion upon the logic of inquiry in the natural and cultural sciences, they can legitimately claim a 'transcendental' status. (p. 181)

This seems unexceptionable, but to become dubious as soon as one finds him also saying that

> Every form of transcendental philosophy claims to identify the conditions of the objectivity of experience by analyzing the categorical structure of objects of possible experience. (p. 180)

It is as if Habermas swung to and fro between a looser and novel sense of "transcendental" in which anything counts as transcendental if it puts aside "truthfulness to reality in the sense postulated by philosophical realism (p. 180), and a stricter and older sense of "transcendental" in which to be a transcendental philosopher means doing what

Kant said he was going to do—meeting the conditions I listed in section 1 of this paper. I can bring this doubt about Habermas' sense of "transcendental" together with what I have been saying in section 4 by citing yet another of Habermas' formulations:

> What does it mean for a theory, or for theoretical knowledge as such, to ground itself transcendentally? It means that the theory becomes familiar with the range of inevitable subjective conditions which both make the theory possible *and* place limits on it, for this kind of transcendental corroboration tends always to criticize an overly confident self-understanding the theory may have of itself. (p. 182)

This suggests an interpretation of Habermas' project at which neither Sellars nor Feyerabend would boggle: viz., that being transcendental consists *purely and simply* in shifting focus from "philosophical realism's" view of a certain inquiry to the sort of view which the historian, the sociologist, the Marxist, or the Freudian, takes of that inquiry. Such a shift of focus, for Sellars, would be a shift from, roughly, theoretical to practical reason, from taking society's practices of justification at face-value to looking behind them for their causes and the possibilities they exclude. But this shift of focus is *not*, for Sellars, a shift from content to structure, from the contingent to the necessary, from science to philosophy. In Habermas, however, the passage I just quoted is followed immediately by this:

> In the meantime this mode of reflexion has also taken the shape of a rational reconstruction of generative rules and cognitive schemata. Particularly, the paradigm of language has led to a reframing of the transcendental subject to the system of conditions, categories or rules established by linguistic theory. (p. 182)

If I understand this passage, Habermas is here (as perhaps also in his general project of formulating a universal pragmatic) putting his foot on the same tempting path which was trodden by Russell, C. I. Lewis, Ayer, and others who saw "language" as the name of a new subject-matter of transcendental inquiry. These men, as I have said, thought that shifting from "thought" to "language" would permit the three conditions of transcendentality I listed in section 1 to be fulfilled without having to worry about the relation between the constituting transcendental ego and the subject-matter of empirical psychology. Since I myself do not see anything in, e.g., Chomsky or Searle which could serve to revitalize this hope of the early, transcendental, days of analytic philosophy, it seems to me that Habermas may, by wishing to base a transcendental project on their work (cf. p. 160) be falling into the same trap as that into which the Vienna Circle fell. The logical positivists thought that *Principia Mathematica* had somehow given them the key to the nature of scientific inquiry, and that they could live up to Kant's promises by making use of a result of extra-philosophical inquiry which was unavailable to Kant. If Habermas thinks that linguistics and philosophy of language supply insights which will do for "epistemologically oriented theory of science" what symbolic logic did not, then I suspect he is wrong. His project, I would claim, itself needs de-transcendentalization. But I cannot claim to have grasped his project well enough to be sure that this criticism is to the point.

However it may be with Habermas' project of "universal pragmatics," I think that it would have fruitful consequences for philosophy if the de-transcendentalized, pragmatist, form of analytic philosophy which I have been discussing came into contact with certain discourses which have so far remained outside it, and which are central to Habermas' and others' attempts to formulate a new standpoint for philosophy. These are the discourses, such as Marx's and Freud's, which bring together (though without an attempt at "synthesis") the formulation of moral imperatives with a better grasp of empirical causal processes, thus blurring, in a non-epistemological way, the line between description and justification. These discourses are more easily readable within a tradition which has not forgotten Hegel than within the analytic tradition (which, I have suggested, made itself possible only by repressing Hegel). As Habermas says, in the *Phenomenology* Hegel "embraced a concept of reflexion which contains the idea of an *analytical emancipation* from *objective illusions*" (p. 183); that book, and that model of self-transcendence, have so far been kept beyond the pale by analytic philosophers (with such occasional exceptions as Hampshire, Charles Taylor, and Feyerabend). But the moral of epistemological behaviorism — that justification is not a matter of the set-up of our cognitive faculties, but of what society lets us get away with — obviously needs to be conjoined with an historicist understanding of social practices. It also needs to be conjoined with what Habermas describes as Freud's "removal of this self-critical notion of reflexion from its epistemological context by relating it to the reflexive experience of an empirical subject" (p.

183). If epistemological behaviorism is able to help us resist the urge to imitate Kant (the great father-figure of our profession) then it may help us see more clearly how Marx and Freud can perform philosophical functions without performing transcendental ones.

Another set of discourses with which de-transcendentalized analytic philosophy might profitably be linked up are such historical accounts of the geneses of the Cartesian and Kantian philosophical problematics as Heidegger's and Foucault's. Analytic philosophy might come to see epistemology, and the urge to be transcendental, not simply as impossible of realization (for Sellarsian and Quinean reasons) but as historically determined destinies (as in Heidegger) or brute contingencies (as in Foucault). Such an attitude towards the genesis of modern philosophy lets us see the textbook "problems of philosophy" as requiring neither solution, nor "dissolution" by "conceptual analysis," but as comparable to social or personal problems. All this might help analytic philosophers get some perspective on the history of the analytic movement itself. If this movement is indeed in its latter days—if it is high time for the owl of Minerva to appear—then we might get something quite new and unpredictable and interesting out of its terminal efforts at internal reform.

However this may be, I hope that what I have said about Quine and Sellars will help show that analytic philosophy is not locked into empiricism, nor scientism, nor naive philosophical realism, nor projects of self-objectivation. Behaviorism, oddly enough, can be as productive of self-reflexion as depth psychology, and as emancipatory. It can do this because it does not provide a new self-objectivation, but rather an understanding of the limits of explanation, description, science, and cognition itself. By helping de-transcendentalize our discipline, it helps us take our self-objectivations less seriously and our social hopes more seriously.

NOTES

1. For the phrase from Wittgenstein, see *Philosophical Investigations*, Part I, sec. 89. For Quine's discussion of "first philosophy," see his "Epistemology Naturalized" in *Ontological Relativity and Other Essays* (New York, 1969). For Davidson's distinction between the proper concerns of semantics and the distinctions introduced into philosophy of language by the positivists'

need to give reductionistic analyses of individual expressions, see his "Truth and Meaning," *Synthese*, 1967, p. 316.

2. In his "Philosophy as Rigorous Science" (1910), Husserl analyzed both naturalism and historicism as forms of scepticism and relativism. See the translation of this essay in Husserl, *Phenomenology and the Crisis of Philosophy*, trans. Lauer (New York, 1965), esp. pp. 76–79, 80, 122. He begins his criticism of naturalism by repeating the attack on psychologistic conceptions of logic made in his *Logical Investigations*. (Cf. pp. 80ff. on naturalism's self-refutation through its reduction of norms to fact.)

3. Russell ended the chapter called "Logic as the Essence of Philosophy" in his *Our Knowledge of the External World* (1914) with the claim that "The old logic put thought in fetters, while the new logic gives it wings. It has, in my opinion, introduced the same kind of advance into philosophy as Galileo introduced into physics, making it possible at last to see what kinds of problems may be capable of solution, and what kinds must be abandoned as beyond human powers. And where a solution appears possible, the new logic provides a method which enables us to obtain results that do not merely embody personal idiosyncrasies, but must command the assent of all who are competent to form an opinion." For my present purposes, the standard charge (made, e.g., by Dummett and by Anscombe) that Russell confused the specifically semantical doctrines of Frege and Wittgenstein, which *did* spring from the new logic, with epistemological doctrines which did not, is irrelevant. The charge is fair enough, but without this very confusion the analytic movement would either not have gotten off the ground or would have been quite a different thing. Only in the last two decades has a clear distinction between "linguistic philosophy" and "philosophy of language" begun to be made.

4. See Russell, op. cit. p. 61 (in the American edition [New York, 1924]), and Husserl, op. cit., pp. 110–11.

5. See Herbert Spiegelberg, *The Phenomenological Movement*, 2nd ed. (The Hague, 1965), I: 275–83, and David Carr's "Translator's Introduction" to Husserl, *The Crisis of European Sciences and Transcendental Phenomenology*, pp. xxv-xxxviii.

6. I think that in England and America philosophy has already been displaced by literary criticism in its principal cultural function — as a source for youth's self-description of its own difference from the past. Cf. Harold Bloom, *A Map of Misreading* (New York, 1975), p. 39: "The teacher of literature now in America, far more than the teacher of history or philosophy or religion, is condemned to teach the presentness of the past, because history, philosophy and religion have withdrawn as agents from the Scene of Instruction, leaving the bewildered teacher of literature alone at the altar, *terrifiedly* wondering whether he is to be sacrifice or priest." This is because, roughly, of the Kantian and anti-historicist tenor of Anglo-Saxon philosophy. The

cultural function of teachers of philosophy in countries where Hegel was not forgotten is quite different, and closer to the position of literary critics in America.

7. See Davidson, "On the Very Idea of a Conceptual Scheme," *Proceedings of the American Philosophical Association*, 1973, p. 11.

8. See "The World Well Lost," *Journal of Philosophy* 69 (1972), 649–66.

9. I have attempted to summarize this literature, up to 1965, in the introduction to *The Linquistic Turn*, ed. Rorty (Chicago, 1967).

10. For an interpretation of Quine as attaching the explanatory utility of the "philosophical notion of meaning," see Gilbert Harman, "Quine on Meaning and Existence, I" (*Review of Metaphysics* 21 [1967], 124–51, esp. 125, 135–41).

11. Cf. Sellars, *Science, Perception and Reality* (London and New York, 1963), p. 167.

12. For this sort of criticism of Quine's behaviorism, see Grice and Strawson, "In Defense of a Dogma," *Philosophical Review* 65 (1956), 141–56. For such criticism of Sellars, see Chisholm's criticism of his claims about intentionality, in their correspondence printed in *Minnesota Studies in the Philosophy of Science* II, pp. 521ff.

13. Sellars and Quine themselves, unfortunately, do not always see the matter in this desirably light-minded way. For criticism of Quine's "flight from intensions" and his resulting doctrine of the "indeterminacy of translation," see Hilary Putnam, *Philosophical Papers*, 2: 153–86, and my "Indeterminacy of Translation and of Truth," *Synthese* 23 (1972), 443–62. The same criticism can be applied, *mutatis mutandis*, to Sellars' insistence that "the scientific image" excludes colors and intentions, but this issue is more complicated. On Sellars' treatment of colors, see James Cornman, "Sellars, Scientific Realism, and Sense," *The Review of Metaphysics* 23 (1970) and Sellars' reply, "Science, Sense Impressions and Sensa," *Review of Metaphysics* 24 (1971). Sellars' treatment of intentions is connected with his Tractarian doctrine of picturing. I have criticized this doctrine in "Transcendental Arguments, Self-Reference and Pragmatism" forthcoming in the proceedings of a conference on transcendental arguments held at Bielefeld in 1977, edited by Rolf Horstmann.

14. Unfortunately, both men tend to substitute correspondence to physical entities, and specifically to the "basic entities" of physical sciences (elementary particles, or their successors). Sellars' (and Jay Rosenberg's) attempt to salvage *something* from the Platonic notion of knowledge as accuracy of picturing is criticized in the article cited in the previous footnote. My own attitude is Strawson's (and, incidentally, Heidegger's): "The correspondence theory requires, not purification, but elimination." (P. F. Strawson, "Truth," reprinted in *Truth*, ed. Pitcher [Englewood Cliffs, N.J.,

1964], p. 32)— or, more mildly, it requires separation from epistemology
and relegation to semantics (see Robert Brandom, "Truth and Assertability,"
Journal of Philosophy 73 [1976], 137–49.)

15. Cf. Sellars' claim that "The idea that epistemic facts can be analyzed
without remainder—even 'in principle'—into non-epistemic facts, whether
phenomenal or behavioural, public, or private, with no matter how lavish
a sprinkling of subjunctives and hypotheticals is, I believe, a radical mistake,
a mistake of a piece with the so-called 'naturalistic fallacy' in ethics." The
importance of Sellars' approach to epistemology is that he sees the true and
interesting irreducibility in the area not as between one sort of particular (mental, intentional) and another (physical) but as between descriptions on the
one hand and norms, practices, and values on the other.

16. Sellars, op. cit., p. 170.

17. Quine, *From a Logical Point of View* (Cambridge, Mass., 1953),
p. 42.

18. He can also (as by Heidegger) be viewed as developing the dialectic of being-as-presence begun by Plato through bringing out the subjectivist
(temporalistic) implications of the notion of presentness. Whether or not one
agrees with Heidegger that subjectivism was already inherent in Plato, one
can agree that Kant was a decisive stage in the movement from a "spectator
theory" of knowledge to a pragmatic view.

19. See Husserl "Philosophy as Rigorous Science," p. 75: "a fully conscious will for rigorous science dominated the Socratic-Platonic revolution of
philosophy . . . It renews itself with most radical vigor in Kant's critique of
reason . . . Again and again research is directed toward true beginnings,
decisive formulation of problems, and correct methods. Only with romantic
philosophy does a change occur. However much Hegel insists on the absolute
validity of his method and his doctrine, still his system lacks a critique of
reason, which is the foremost prerequisite for being scientific in philosophy.
In this connection it is clear that this philosophy, like romantic philosophy
in general, acted in the years that followed either to weaken or to adulterate
the impulse toward the constitution of rigorous philosophical science."

20. This historical consciousness is what Stanley Cavell identifies as "the
essential fact of the modern": "the consciousness that history will not go away,
except through our perfect acknowledgement of it (in particular, our
acknowledgement that it is not past) and that one's practice and ambition
can be identified only against the continuous experience of the past" (*Must
We Mean What We Say?* [New York, 1969], p. xix). Compare Harold Bloom:
"Romantic tradition differs vitally from earlier forms of tradition, and I think
this difference can be reduced to a useful formula. Romantic tradition is consciously late, and Romantic literary psychology is therefore necessarily a
psychology of belatedness" (Bloom, op. cit., p. 35).

21. "If intuition must conform to the constitution of the objects, I do

not see how we could know anything of the latter *a priori*; but if the object (as object of the sense) must conform to the constitution of our faculty of intuition, I have no difficulty in conceiving such a possibility" (*KdrV*, B xiii).

22. This problem for Kant is at bottom the same as that diagnosed by Strawson in *The Bounds of Sense* (London, 1966), p. 41: "the resultant transposition [in the Copernican revolution's view of the constitution of sensible objects as appearance] of the terminology of objects 'affecting' the constitution of subjects takes that terminology altogether out of the range of its intelligible employment, viz., the spatio-temporal range." Strawson's point that transcendental idealism depends (*per impossible*) on giving a non-spatiotemporal sense to "affection," "constitution" and "conforming" can be expressed metaphilosophically as the point that Kant has no room for an account of how, limited in the way the *First Critique* describes, we could understand that we are so limited, or, indeed, make sense of the very suggestion.

23. Dewey is an interesting study in vacillation on this point. Half the time he wished to deprofessionalize philosophy by insisting that no such matrix was possible or necessary; the other half of the time he insisted on the need for a "naturalistic metaphysics" of the sort attempted in *Experience and Nature*. I have discussed the abiguities in Dewey's attitude towards the place of philosophy in culture in "Dewey's Metaphysis," in *New Studies in the Philosophy of John Dewey*, ed. Steven M. Cahn (University Press of New England, 1977).

24. "A priori truth is definitive in nature and rises exclusively from the analysis of concepts. That *reality* may be delimited a priori, is due, not to forms of intuition or categories which confine the content of experience, but simply to the fact whatever is denominated 'real' must be something discriminated in experience by criteria which are antecedently determined." (C. I. Lewis, *Mind and the World-Order* [New York, 1929], p. x) See also Ayer's remark that the way to avoid Hume's problem about the status of logic and mathematics "is perhaps already enshrined in Kant's famous dictum that, 'although there can be no doubt that all our knowledge begins with experience, it does not follow that it all arises out of experience'?" (*Language, Truth and Logic* [London, 1936], p. 74).

25. Cf. *KdrV*, A 385.

26. This attitude towards the upshot of the logical empiricist movement is illustrated by Urmson in his *Philosophical Analysis* (Oxford, 1956), esp. chaps. 10–11.

27. See Ian Hacking's description of the replacement of "the heyday of meanings" by "the heyday of sentences" in his *Why Does Language Matter to Philosophy?* (Cambridge, 1975), esp. chaps. 11–13. See also my review of Hacking's book in *Journal of Philosophy*, July 1977.

28. See the polemic against this view of writing in the work of Jacques Derrida.

29. The temptation has not vanished, however, as is shown by Sellars' discussion of "picturing" in his *Science and Metaphysics*, Jay Rosenberg's discussion of "protocorrelation semantics" as necessary for the defense of "realism" (in *Linguistic Representation*) [Dordrecht, 1975], and the notion (in Putnam, Kripke, Boyd, Field, and other) that "realism" demands some sort of relation of "correspondence to reality" which may be assured by developing a "realistic theory of reference." I discuss some of these views in the essay mentioned in n. 13 above.

30. *Pragmatism* (New York, 1907), p. 76.

31. For an example of the sort of epistemology which results once privileged representations are abandoned, see Keith Lehrer's *Knowledge* (Oxford, 1974)—e.g., his defense of that claim that "There is no exit from the circle of one's own beliefs from which one can sally forth to find some exquisite tool to measure the merits of what lies within the circle of subjectivity" (pp. 17–18). Once one adopts this coherentist approach to justification, it is hard to avoid invoking "pragmatic" criteria for choosing among alternative coherent schemes, and thus winding up with a view rather like James'.

32. Taking these criticisms to their limit means, I believe, adopting the view common to Sellars and to Sartre; that the true dualism to be invoked in explaining man's uniqueness is not between abstract and concrete, nor between the mental and the physical, nor between the intensional and the extensional, but rather between norms and descriptions, practice and theory.

33. On Nietzsche as holding a pragmatic theory of truth, see Arthur Danto, *Nietzsche as Philosopher* (New York, 1965), chap. 3..

34. See "Strawson's Objectivity Argument," *Review of Metaphysics* 23 (1970), pp. 27–44 and "Verificationism and Transcendental Arguments," *Nous*, 1971, pp. 3–14.

35. See my essay in the proceedings of the Bielefeld conference, referred to in n. 13 above.

36. This piece has been translated by Christian Lenhardt, and published in English in *Philosophy of the Social Sciences* 3 (1973), 157–89. My quotations will be from that translation, and the page numbers in parentheses refer to it.

5. REASON, SOCIAL PRACTICE, AND SCIENTIFIC REALISM

Frederick L. Will

I

The recent subsidence of empiricism in the theory of knowledge has resulted in some substantial displacement of problems in this subject. Various topics for which empiricist theory, if otherwise successful, seemed capable of providing fairly satisfactory treatment now seem to have become highly problematical. One of the most important of these topics is that of scientific realism, embracing the general question of the possibility of access in knowledge to objects that are independent of any practices of thought and action through which knowledge of them may be achieved. This topic takes on a very different aspect when it is looked at apart from the suppositions about access that were central features and for a long time central attractions of empiricist theory.

Empiricism is a highly individualistic philosophical view, though like most individualistic views in contemporary social philosophy it has not been much aware of itself as individualistic and hence as one of the *possible* alternative views. It has seemed, rather, in this respect, the obviously right view.

Accompanying the subsidence of empiricism — indeed a primary cause of it — has been an increasing emphasis upon the social aspects of knowledge, upon knowledge as essentially a communal institution. Testifying to the extent of this influence has been the penetration of what had hitherto been seemingly impregnable redoubts of individualism as opposed to socialism on these matters, namely, physical science and mathematics, by paradigm theory and other revolution theory, by social evolution theory, and by what may be called "*Lebensformen* theory."

Foundational theory, of which empiricism is one species, has been thoroughly individualistic since its manifesto in the epistemological and metaphysical works of Descartes, an aspect that received hyperbolic expression in the famous *Cogito*. Both the empiricist and rationalist versions of Cartesianism sought to demonstrate that there are certain human resources capable of serving as firm bases for the criticism of social phenomena because they are quite independent of these phenomena. And both professed to find these resources in special acts of intuition that individuals are capable of performing quite independently of social influences, independently of any resources that are theirs only because they are members of communities. What distinguished the empiricists from other adherents of this individualist and foundational philosophy was the special trust invested by them in that sub-set of intuitions that was regarded as being furnished by inner and outer sense. It was primarily through a recourse to these, and what conclusions could be drawn from them by intuitions of the more rationalist kind, that the adherents of empiricist foundationism proposed to follow the ringing injunction of Descartes, that we direct our inquiries "not to what others have thought," but to what the "unclouded and attentive [individual] mind . . . can clearly and perspicuously behold and with certainty deduce" (Descartes 1967).

For generations the empiricist program, which was to account for knowledge by showing that it could be assimilated to this model, had been stalled by the problem of demonstrating how the needed conclusions could be drawn in this manner from the stipulated premises (the so-called Problem of Induction). Now, in consequence of the recognition of the social aspects of knowledge, and indeed, of experience itself, the putative data of sense, hitherto thought to exemplify primitive independent objects of knowledge, were discovered to be in a variety of ways dependent upon, subject to determination by, the very kinds of social artifacts, opinion and practice, of which they were required by the theory to be independent. In American philosophy assimilation of this discovery and the drawing of what seemed to be some profound skeptical consequences of it were accomplished in one short philosophical generation from C. I. Lewis to W. V. Quine and vigorously exemplified by the latter in a variety of writings, including, among the more recent, *Ontological Relativity* (1969).

A recent writer who has been most effective in drawing attention to the social determinants of knowledge has been, of course, T. S. Kuhn. In his very widely read and influential book on scientific revolutions he supported the thesis of the social determination of what actually function in scientific work as observational data with a persuasive array of examples from the history of these disciplines. And one of the conclusions that he tentatively suggested we might draw is that in the domain of science something like ontological relativity, or at least physical relativity, does hold. Granted that there is something in the career of science that can rightly be termed progress, it may be a serious mistake to think that in this progress, in contrast with progress in other fields, say, art, political theory, or philosophy, large-scale changes of patterns of thought (Ptolemy to Copernicus; Newton to Einstein) "carry scientists and those who learn from them closer to the truth" (1964, p. 169). It was thus not incautious exposition but philosophical considerations of an important and unsettling kind that impelled Kuhn, while wishing to maintain that after one of these so-called scientific revolutions, "the scientist . . . is still looking at the same world," also to say that the large-scale patterns of thought that he called paradigms "are constitutive of nature," that "after discovering oxygen Lavoisier worked in a different world," and that "pendulums were brought into existence by something like a paradigm-induced gestalt switch" (pp. 128, 109, 117, 119).

II

A philosophy of science committed to the view that it is possible to succeed in our quest for truth about the physical world is required to provide some acceptable account of how knowledge of this truth can be achieved. It was the distinctive way in which, according to the empiricist philosophy, this is accomplished — in particular, the way in which a coordination between our thoughts and their objects is achieved by an "unclouded and attentive mind" — that was increasingly discredited by the increasing emphasis upon the social determinants of our language, our ways of thinking, our "conceptual schemes." The abandonment of the very feature of the philosophy in which the union of thought and object is to be consummated independently of these determinants resulted in a philosophy unable to talk about the objects with which thought is supposed to be coordinated in exactly the same way that in Kant's theory of knowledge the scientist was held to be unable to speak consistently about things-in-themselves.

It is, furthermore, of great importance for philosophical understanding here that one grasp that the problem of realism in physical science and elsewhere is one particular phase of a much more general problem about the revision and reconstruction of social practice. The more recognition there is of the social aspects of language and thought, the more the roots of our patterns of thought and inquiry are exposed in the forms of life, in social practice, the more pressing becomes the need to understand how thought and inquiry rooted in practice itself can yield valid criticisms and properly grounded clues for the reconstruction of this practice. And when the specific practices concerned are practices of scientific inquiry, one particular, most important matter needing clarification is how and in what circumstances the criticisms and clues for reconstruction yielded by those practices may be taken as proper guides to the truth or falsity of claims concerning the objects with which the practices are employed.

Three essential pieces of the puzzle posed by these matters have now emerged. There is, first, the important shift from individualism to what, were not the term already pre-empted for other uses, might properly be referred to as "socialism" in the theory of knowledge. Incorporated in this shift is a recognition of the extent to which knowledge, as a human institution, is not merely rooted in, but is constituted by social *practices*. Though not the only ingredient, so thoroughly essential and determinative are these practices that what at any given time we have achieved as knowledge is quite inconceivable without them. In consequence of this shift and recognition the focus of the traditional philosophical questions about the criticism, appraisal, etc., of putative items of knowledge likewise shifts. The concerns represented in these questions become largely concerns about the performance of these functions in connection with the practices which these times incorporate.

And given that on such a view, criticism, appraisal, and the other similar functions are recognized to be themselves informed, directed, and, indeed, in good part constituted by social practices, there are now present all the materials for the generation of a philosophical difficulty that has been urged against such a social theory of knowledge in a variety of forms in recent discussion. How can one view the criticism, appraisal, and so on, of practices as being always performed in thorough and essential dependence upon social practices themselves, without entrapping oneself in some sociocentric and in the end fatally skeptical predicament? How, if one views in this way the processes of criticism, appraisal, and so on, including fundamental philosophical forms of these functions, can the results attained be viewed as legitimate or valid ones?[1]

If we now encapsule in the term "governance" all the functions of criticism, appraisal, reform, and reconstruction referred to, and use the more common philosophical term "*rational*" to express the question about the legitimacy or validity of these processes, we may formulate the central question summarily as a question about the rationality of the governance of social practices. Can the governance of practices be performed in thorough dependence upon practices? When the governance of social practices is conceived to be carried out always and necessarily in this practice-informed and hence practice-dependent way, can the processes and the results ever be regarded as rational? These general questions may then be applied to distinctively cognitive practices, to practices in domains like those of the physical sciences, in which the validity or rationality of the practices entails a capacity on the part of the practices to yield reliable information concerning objects of some sort with which they are engaged. So applied, the general questions yield, among others, the question of *realism*.

III

In partial answer to the question of realism a few examples will presently be given of the establishment of the existence and character of independent objects through the practice-informed, practice-directed governance of practices. By themselves, however, such examples are insufficient for elucidating the matter. They meet the questions about the possibility of such establishment only obliquely. For these questions are philosophical questions about possibility, asking not so much for proofs *that* a certain kind of achievement occurs as for an explanation of *how* it occurs. Typically in such situations the questions are the expressions of a difficulty encountered in assimilating the facts of occurrence, however patent they may be, into a background of presumption in accordance with which what seems to be demonstrated to have occurred is by some strongly held principles precluded. One can imagine a skeptical observer at Kitty Hawk being puzzled about how it is possible for such a contraption to fly and needing to have the strong yet controvertible evidence from observation that it did fly vindicated in relation to some deeply entrenched principles ensuring that it could not. Similarly, many philosophical observers of the effectiveness of governance need, for the satisfactory assimilation of their own observation, to have it vindicated in the face of some profound philosophical preconceptions that obstruct its being recognized as what it is.

The philosophical difficulties addressed here about governance and realism concern, not governance as it may be conceived in general, but governance as conceived in a social theory of knowledge and of reason, i.e., governance that is itself viewed as carried on in thorough dependence upon practices themselves. Such governance was characterized above as dependent upon practices for its constitution, form, and direction. Henceforth in this essay, purely for reasons of stylistic convenience, these qualifications of the term "governance" will ordinarily not be repeated when the context indicates sufficiently clearly that governance of this kind is intended. Exceptions will be made in those cases in which some special emphasis or reminder seems desirable.

In thinking of such governance one must guard against a pair of related intellectual stereotypes, powerful but illusory Idols of the Theatre. Both of these misleadingly neglect features of practices and their governance that are essential to them. The first of these, which may be called the "Relativist Illusion," seriously underestimates the plurality of types of practice and the liberating effect of this upon the process of governance. The second, which may be called the "Coherence Illusion," seriously underestimates other external components of the existential situations in which practices are engaged in.

It is characteristic of practices that they cohere with other related practices in systems, wholes, *Gestalten*, "conceptual schemes" or "frameworks." These vary widely in both magnitude and in the tightness with which the components are bound together. The recognition of the capacity of large and tightly organized collectives of practices in everyday life, science, and other domains to determine the character of thought and action, and therewith the consciousness, experience, and life of the individuals who participate in them, has had the effect of intellectual shock upon those whose philosophical expectations were molded by individualistic empiricism. The momentum of a sharp reversal in the estimation of the effect of social practice in the development of knowledge has led many of these mistakenly to overestimate the monopolistic effect in methodology, judgment, and opinion that a single system of practices may have. Viewing the thought and action of an individual brought up in and participating in such a system as determined exclusively by that one system, they have concluded that what can be effected by thought and action guided by practices, and hence also what can be effected by similarly guided governance of practices, is necessarily restricted to internal refinements in this system, fleshing out its details, leaving the essential character of the system unaltered. By means of the kind of governance of practices that is under examination here, applied to practices assumed to cohere in one overarching and dominating system, it appears that it is possible to produce only effects that are in conformity with accepted practices, and thus of course never effects the cumulative consequence of which would be the displacement of one system of practices by another. Changes of the latter sort, changes of systems themselves, when they occur, must be effected by other means, by some other form, or forms, of determination, which, if the term "rational" is reserved for practice-informed and hence practice-dependent governance, must be judged to be other than rational.

This view is provocative, but extremely unrealistic in its totalitarian model of the way in which systems of practices influence, direct, and give form to the thought and action of those who participate in them. The relation between a system of practices and participants in it is conceived to be like that between an absolute sovereign and a community of subjects, subjects who can be released from their servitude to one sovereign only when somehow that one is overthrown by another, whose utter subjects they in turn now become. But systems of practices in science, politics, religion, education or other domains need not be and are not ordinarily, if ever, like this in their determining effects in the communities that participate in them. Rather they coexist in these communities with other systems, with which they both cooperate and compete in their effects upon their participants. These other systems are part of the existential situation in which any system of practices occurs: no less a part than the nature of the human beings engaged in the practices or the physical environment in which the practices are followed.

There are, to be sure, great differences from individual to individual, from group to group, and from one system of practices to another, in respect to the dominance exerted by a given system of practices in the determination of the thought and action of the members of the group. But what one does not find, even in extreme cases, is a state of complete hegemony maintained over a group of individuals by one all-embracing system of practices. A feature of any moderately civilized society that helps to dissipate the danger that the members of the society will become the captives of one such system is that they are simultaneously the participants in many: of many and various frameworks, conceptual schemes, linguistic and thought structures, systems of categories. As a plurality of communities has been one source of freedom in modern democratic states; as checks and balances, despite their logical untidiness, have proved to be elements of a workable system of political self-governance; so to some considerable extent the possibility of rational governance of practice, in individuals and groups, lies in the plurality of accepted systems of practices.

The strength of the totalitarian view of the determination of thought and action by accepted systems of practice derives in good measure from the confluence of two streams of thought. One of these is the increasing recognition of the social determinants of thought and action; the other a highly restrictive, narrow view of human reason. Without the latter, without certain preconceptions about the limited processes which could be recognized as being rational, what might have emerged from the recognition of the social determinants of thought and action was a view of the social character of reason itself. Athwart this avenue of philosophical development lay a deeply entrenched view of the processes of reason as *essentially calculative* ones participated in by individuals in their capacity as individuals; thus as essentially *individual* processes rather than as group or communal ones. Rational results, upon such a view, are only those which can be shown to be derivable by a process that begins with grounds having a certain form, namely, that of symbolic formulae, and proceeds by performing similarly symbolic transformations upon these grounds, transformations sometimes discriminated into two sub-species, deduction and induction.

Little reflection is required to see that what can be achieved by rational processes as so conceived is severely limited. There is no provision, in this conception, for procedures for the revision, radical or moderate, of the canonical forms of formulation of grounds or the canonical procedures of eliciting consequences. And, equally striking, there is no provision in what are conceived to be rational processes for the revisionary effect, both with respect to grounds and the processes of proceeding from them to consequences, of communal, inter-personal relations. All those real processes by which our grasp of grounds and recognition of consequences are molded and remolded by communal life and thought proceeding from generation to generation are extruded from the conception of rational processes. It is a strange prejudice that precludes the classification as rational of any processes of development, in science, morals or whatever, that cannot be managed in one single generation and therefore require transgenerational mutational processes of intellectual reproduction. It is a strange prejudice that restricts the dimension of rational results to those that could be encompassed, beginning with accepted procedures, by one person in one lifetime. The transitions from introspectionism to a more functional psychology, from absolute space and time to relativity, or from deterministic to statistical mechanics, are not proved to have been non-rational by the fact that they required too great a reconstruction of settled habits of thought to be managed by many, especially in the older generations of investigators in these domains, to whom they were offered. Similar comments apply to the reconstruction of habits of thought with respect to the Commerce Clause of the Constitution signalled by the historic decisions of the Supreme Court expanding the scope of constitutional federal regulation of interstate commerce at the end of the fourth decade in this century. They apply also to the similar historic decisions concerning *de jure* segregation handed down in the sixth decade, and, to add but one further example from a very different domain, to the transition in the interpretation of the Scriptures slowly made in Protestant Christian thought in the past hundred years.

IV

In the Relativist Illusion the predicament seen to be confronting the participant in a system of practices is one of incapacity of governance. Systems of practices, or conglomerates of such systems, are conceived to determine the main features of a participant's thought and action so completely that he is rendered incapable of any fundamental criticism of or dissociation from the system or systems involved. Any activity pretending to be governance in any important, constitutional respect is a sham. The predicament contemplated in the Coherence Illusion is of a different kind. It is not that effective criticism and judgment is in general impossible, but rather that in one cardinal respect it is inutile. Whatever discriminable differences there may be between systems of cognitive practices, in one respect they are all the same. This is in respect to their preclusion of the access of participants in systems of practices to independent objects of knowledge. One and all, in an irremediable way, systems of practices deceptively interpose themselves between objects and aspiring knowers, proffering to the latter artifacts of practice in place of the aspired-to independent objects.

There is indeed a danger that in emphasizing the role of systems of practices, frameworks, or institutions in the pursuit of knowledge one will generate this illusion. For in spite of great efforts to forestall this effect, it remains difficult to prevent many who are stimulated to think of these matters from neglecting one of the very things that the terms "practice" and "practices" were intended to emphasize, which is that the modes of proceeding denoted by these terms are in a variety of ways affected by, controlled by, or more exactly, constituted in part by determinants external to, independent of, the individuals engaged in them. Practices are modes of proceeding, forms of activity, that are themselves realized in certain kinds of existential situations. They require certain kinds of situations for their realization, and are guided by features of these situations in the specific manner in which they are realized. A human practice thus incorporates within itself, besides the human beings engaged in the practices, other components of the existential situation. The determining or constitutive effect in this regard that is of special relevance to the topic of realism is that produced in our cognitive practices by the objects of investigation: objects which, if revealed with sufficient clarity and certainty by the investigation, become objects of knowledge, Keeping this effect firmly in mind is most helpful in devising an acceptable answer to the primary question about realism that is posed by a view of rational governance as necessarily practice-informed and practice-dependent, namely, of how it is possible by means of such governance to acquire knowledge of objects that are not dependent in their existence and character upon practices.

A good part of the deceptive power of the Coherence Illusion associated with this question lies in a neglect of the roots that practices have in independent objects. Recognizing the thoroughly social character of most of our practices, including our cognitive ones, but neglecting the independent roots or components of such practices, one seems to become again a captive of practices. Practices are thought of as having their existence and careers independent of objects; governance is correspondingly conceived to be a process that takes place quite independently of objects, and is thus incapable of yielding as a product genuine knowledge of such objects.

The obvious place to begin in dispelling such an illusion is at this metaphysical source. The case that governance is a process impotent with respect to objects stands or falls with whatever case there is that, conversely, objects are impotent with respect to governance itself. And this latter case, in turn, stands or falls with the case that practices and objects are impotent with respect to each other. If independent objects can affect thought and action in and through cognitive practices, and if in consequence thought and action according to these practices are competent to acquire knowledge of such objects, then *governance* of these practices, itself a phase of this thought and action, is likewise competent with respect to knowledge. One point central to the case about governance here deserves emphasis, though it cannot be dilated upon. It is that governance, as an activity directed to the control of practices, is continuous with activity according to practices directed primarily to more direct, non-governantial ends. Control, modification of, as well as stabilizing of practices, is a natural concomitant of the conduct of the affairs of life according to these practices. That is why, to use a piece of formal terminology, the competence of governance of practices to acquire knowledge of independent objects is but a lemma, once the proposition is established that activity in accordance with practices is competent for this purpose.

A major source of the Coherence Illusion, as it arises with respect to practices and their governance, is thus an unrealistic view of practices, a view of them that neglects the effects that objects independent of both practices and their governance have upon both of these. When these latter effects are neglected, talk about governance of practices by means of practices easily suggests a procedure that might be engaged in independently of the external existential situation in which practices are realized and by which they are in part controlled. One thinks of an individual or group arranging, re-ordering practices, much in the way that someone might in some private retreat sort out and compose his feelings after some disconcerting emotional episode. But practices are not private entities like feelings, and governance not such an autonomous procedure.

To the credit of the empiricists in modern philosophy was their recognition, which they tried to articulate in their theories of impressions, sense-data and the rest, of this limitation upon the autonomy of cognitive practices imposed both for individuals and groups by the existential situations in which the practices have their roots. Although these existential situations may be internal to the individuals following the practices as well as external to them, the empiricists, who in contrast with the rationalists emphasized the role of the environment in human knowledge, tended to neglect the internal determinants of cognitive practices. Implicit also in the empiricist program was a sound presupposition that there is a great deal of variation among our practices in the degree of determination that external situations impose upon them, that in this respect there are levels of determination effected by the environment upon practices of a cognitive kind. At the basal levels of common sense practices dealing with molar objects and with other living creatures, including our fellow human beings, the degree of determination in which features of the existential situations, both external and internal, limit the kind of practices that may be followed, is very great. How much of the determination at this level is external, exerted by the objects, states, or whatever with which the practices are engaged, and how much is internal, itself the product of millions of years of evolutionary contrivance, it is difficult to say, or even to ask. So complex and ill-defined at the present time remain the factors whose effects have to be accounted for, that it is difficult for us to know, when we set out to ask, just what it is we are asking.

If it is true, as was said above, that activity in the governance of practices is continuous with activity in accordance with these practices, it is likewise true that the mixture of these activities at different levels varies widely. Those writers in the theory of knowledge and philosophy of science who have recently called attention to the effects of social determinants in the development of perceptual discriminations have helped us to discern aspects of tractability to governance at a level of practice in which determination of another kind, and hence intractability to governance, is a much more dominant feature. These variations of degree of determination by existential situations, and of consequent degrees of intractability to governance, added to the sometimes deeply entrenched effects of learning, help to make understandable the high degree of directness, obviousness, and determination *for us* exhibited by results obtained by cognitive practices at some levels, like those of ordinary perception and perceptual observation, in contrast with the equally high degree of indirectness, implicitness, and discrimination *by us*, exhibited at other levels, like those of the construction of models and the development of theories.

V

The history of scientific knowledge is rich with episodes illustrating in striking ways the efficacy of activities following practices in achieving knowledge of objects other than the practices themselves. One of the lessons to be learned from an exploration of this history is that in following the general formula, *per usus ad astra*, through these various new institutions, allowances must be made for the peculiar characteristics of the institutions. The practices of physical science, for example, are not to be assimilated to those of apothecaries or gardeners, as Hobbes rightly said while mistakenly deprecating Boyle's experiments with the air-pump. For one thing, the goals of these contrasting activities are very different. The practices of science are practices developed for the exploration of nature; they are the gears and levers of a great engine that has been fashioned over the years for the purpose of expanding knowledge of a certain kind, of using achieved knowledge to generate further knowledge, much in the way in which in capital investment wealth is employed to produce more wealth. The primary crop that Mendel was interested in harvesting from his garden was not peas, but information about the transmission of inherited characters from one generation to another in these plants. This was a difference in practices that some of the more enthusiastic exponents of pragmatism, most notoriously William James, tended to neglect and were roundly rebuked by their critics for neglecting. Not all "working," to use one of the controversial terms in the disputes over pragmatism, is the same; not all practices are devoted to the same ends; "leading prosperously," to pick out another phrase, in the natural sciences is to be construed in science in the context of the problems and goals of these institutions. It is badly understood if it is construed in science primarily in ways that are appropriate to economic, moral, or even religious institutions. A similar lesson applies, though not so strikingly, to the relationship, so important in our own day, between the institutions of science and of technology. Close as this relationship is, understanding of technology is not well served when it is conceived to be merely the transplantation of scientific practices, the exploitation of these practices for wider human ends. It is this, but not merely this, if for no other reason than that in the transplantation of practices from one institution to another devoted to very different primary ends, mutations, sometimes small and sometimes great, must be expected in the practices themselves.

All this may seem to be little more than redescribing certain obvious features of the development of knowledge in a special terminology, and to have little bearing upon the question of how knowledge about independent objects may be achieved by means of practice-informed, practice-directed governance. The terminology, however, is important, because what it is intended to convey, beyond the painfully familiar truism that our thoughts, opinions, hypotheses, etc., are altered by "experience," is that one of the ways in which experience influences the suppositions we make about the existence and character of independent objects of knowledge is through altering our practices. Recognizing this is a first step in dispelling whatever incredulity may be aroused in our minds by the suggestion that, in both individuals and groups, clarification or grasp of hitherto unappreciated or unrecognized relations of practices may yield new knowledge of objects.

VI

Simple practical examples of objects of knowledge that were thoroughly independent of the practices through which they were discovered were various gross features of the earth that came to be known through the practices of navigation and exploration that were developed and followed in the fifteenth century. Columbus did not succeed in answering the chief question that motivated him in his western voyages, that of whether there was a practical direct route to the Orient across the Ocean Sea. After a long period of time, Western Europe, through various emissaries engaged in a variety of activities, military and naval, commercial, religious, and scientific, and following a corresponding variety of practices did finally reach an answer to Columbus's question. By the time the answer was reached the question itself had undergone great change, chiefly as a result of activities engaged in and practices followed in arriving at an answer to it.

The effectiveness of activities following practices in achieving knowledge of objects other than and independent of the practices is illustrated in the early discovery by Galileo of four of the moons of Jupiter. Similarly illustrated, through to lesser extent, is the effectiveness of the governance of practices in the same regard.

In that discovery, as we would say now, signals coming from Jupiter and those moons played an important role. How did they play this role? By impinging upon Galileo, who, in addition to having a telescope to help gather and transmit these signals, was a well trained and experienced natural philosopher, or, as we should say now, scientist. As such this man at the small end of the telescope was expert in a complex set of cognitive practices designed to exploit effects like this in cognitively rewarding ways. Galileo did not simply stare at those oddly moving lights, never before reported, like a child marvelling at the shifting sights in a kaleidoscope. He tried to understand these lights from the point of view of the astronomy and physics available at his time, following a complex set of technical practices of thought and action available in or appropriate to these branches of learning: practices of observation, calculation, and instrument construction, and practices embodied in a complex technical language. Proceeding thus he translated the signals into messages from Jupiter to the effect that it was not alone in its movements in the heavens, but was accompanied in both its retrograde and direct movements by other bodies or stars revolving about it. Since these stars, like Jupiter, Venus, and others, did shift their positions relative to the fixed stars, he classified them with the other long-recognized wandering stars or planets. There was not yet (Newton's *Principia* being still over fifty years away) an explanation in the Copernican "system of the world" of how the earth could move in an orbit about the sun without losing its moon, and this, as Galileo commented in the *Sidereal Messenger*, was regarded by some people as a decisive objection to that system. That Jupiter, recognized in *both* the Ptolemaic and Copernican system to be moving in some kind of orbit, could do so without losing its own accompanying bodies now appeared to dissipate much of the force of this objection.

The transition from Ptolemaic to Copernican astronomy exemplifies more than the preceding example the acquisition of new knowledge by means of the governance of practices. In the end Copernican theory effectively supplanted Ptolemaic theory in spite of the

fact that there were no crucial experiments to dictate the decision between the two theories, and in spite of the fact that, Kepler's ellipses
having not yet been discovered, there remained in the Copernican view
a large number of insuppressible epicycles. The Copernican theory was,
as it is commonly said, a simpler theory than its older rival. More precisely, as Dudley Shapere has put the matter, although it had no distinct
advantage over sophisticated versions of the Ptolemaic theory with
respect to observational adequacy, predictive accuracy, or number of
epicycles, "it did, in its details, provide a far more unified account
of solar system astronomy." A variety of items that on the Ptolemaic
view were arbitrary assumptions or mere coincidences followed naturally
from the Copernican theory.

  Yet, as Shapere emphasizes, these items of disunity were not *problems* recognized as existing for the Ptolemaic theories. So long as "astronomical theories were considered [as in much of the tradition they
had been] as mere collections of devices, to be applied to different
cases in different ways according to need, for the sake of prediction . . .
[as] mere predictive devices, constructed to 'save the phenomena,' "
the items cited were not and certainly did not need to be recognized
as problems. However, these items were and did need to be recognized as problems when each of the rival astronomical theories was
taken, as Copernicus seems to have taken his theory, as not merely
an instrument of calculation or prediction, but "as a realistic representation of the structure of the solar system." It was indeed largely because
of the high degree of unity achieved with respect to these items by
the Copernican theory that it became easier at this time to view astronomical theory as realistic and representational, rather than merely a
predictive, fictional device. But when the Copernican theory itself was
so viewed, it came into conflict with certain portions of Aristotelian
physics, so that the acceptance of this theory, realistically interpreted,
was in turn a beginning, important step in the transition to the new
physics that culminated in the next century in the work of Newton
(1975, pp. 101, 103).

  One begins to appreciate some of the logical momentum at work
in this rich and fascinating episode of theory change in astronomy when
one begins to look upon the rival theories in question, not as sentences
to be parsed, or logical propositions to be analyzed, but more importantly, as rival programs for the governance of practices and of the intellectual institution of which these practices are features; when one

thinks of what sort of institution astronomy had been in the centuries preceding Copernicus, and of what sort of institution, according to certain tendencies in it, it might become. If astronomy, hitherto primarily an institution for celestial calculation, was in the process of giving increased emphasis to another mission, that of developing an acceptable cosmology, and was therefore in the process achieving a new identity among the cognitive and other institutions of the time, then there was strong logical impetus to the change, rooted in the inner dynamics of the governance of practices in these institutions. "Simplicity," then, suggesting as it does, a somewhat subjective quality discriminated by a kind of refined logical taste, appears to be a questionable, pale misnomer for the kind of strong dynamic that is not peculiar to this case, but rather is characteristic of any large-scale scientific change.

Commenting upon the synthetic unity that is easier to recognize in the Copernican theory than to analyze, Shapere observes that "nothing is to be gained in illumination, and much is lost because of highly misleading associations, by referring to such considerations as 'aesthetic' " (p. 102, n. 4). Yet such was the kind of extremity to which the philosophy of science was driven when it set out to understand this particular episode of scientific change, after having first resolutely blinded itself to some of the aspects of these considerations that are most important for their illumination.

A now familiar story from recent physics that exemplifies strikingly discovery by means of governance deserves brief mention. Without changes in the governance of practices of thought and action ("conceptual change") in the field of atomic physics the discovery of nuclear fission could not have been achieved in the way it was. Indeed it now appears that it had already been achieved earlier than its more celebrated discovery, for example, by Fermi in Italy, but was not recognized as such. Similarly when Hahn and Strassmann in Berlin during the fall of 1938 had bombarded uranium salts with neutrons, producing nuclear disintegration and its products, they were informed of this by one set of firmly entrenched practices that told them that they had derived barium in this process, while another set led them as strongly to suppose that such a result, by the means they had employed, was not possible. So Hahn, an outstanding nuclear chemist, proceeding with the greatest care in the identification of the materials produced in the experiment, found his test declaring for barium but, with his assistant,

Strassmann, in reporting the results of their experiment to the German scientific periodical, *Naturwissenschaften*, was led to say "as chemists we are bound to affirm that the new bodies are barium . . . [but] as nuclear physicists we cannot decide to take this step in contradiction to all previous experience in nuclear physics." It was left to Lisa Meitner, a long-time associate of Hahn, at the time a fugitive of the Hitler government in Sweden, to see first the way to solve the apparent dilemma. Within a few weeks of learning the results of the experiments in a letter from Hahn, she was able to suggest a way in which, by a suitable alteration in the way the results of the experiments were construed, they could be satisfactorily and very excitingly explained.

These and a multitude of similar examples that may easily be drawn from the history of knowledge, and particularly scientific knowledge, attest the capacity of practice-directed governance of practices to make valid determinations of the existence and character of objects. Of the general effectiveness of this procedure in generating valid determinations of objective matters, the corporate project of theoretical physics is a paradigm exemplification, as are to a lesser extent similar projects in other domains of the physical sciences. There is some irony in the present phenomenon in philosophy that at a time when such governance has most spectacularly demonstrated its effectiveness in this regard in scientific domains, among philosophers sensitive to developments in science this success has generated little confidence in the capacity of similar governance to achieve similarly valid results in corresponding projects in their own domains. Rather, some of the most acute and distinguished contemporary philosophical writers in the United States, when they don their ontology hats, or seat themselves in their ontology chairs, find themselves persuaded of profound skepticism concerning the capacity of governantial processes in this regard.[2]

In this connection it may be desirable here to append a few words upon a point that is implicit in the preceding pages but which it has not been possible to develop. It is that just as human practices are primarily social or communal features of our lives, generated and formed in us and engaged in by us as members of communities, so it is with practice-informed, practice-directed governance. This is not to deny that some valid determinations of governance are effected by private, individual conscious reflection. It is rather to emphasize that even these determinations are indirectly social in character, and, further, that the thesis of the competence of such governance to make valid determinations of existence and character leaves open the question of the relative effectiveness of these more individual modes of determination in comparison with the more overtly social and impersonal ones. Without doubt one effect of a transition from the traditional and received views of reason and knowledge to a more social view of these matters is a marked alteration in some very common though highly implicit presumptions in much contemporary philosophical thought concerning the capacity of individuals to make rational determinations and achieve knowledge on their own, without reliance upon group and institutional resources. Just how much in the way of valid determination by governance is possible by means of individual reflection, whether in the forms of calculation or armchair philosophizing, is another matter, and not something that can be discovered *a priori* by Cartesian meditation. Rather it remains a topic to be explored in the development of the social view of reason and knowledge, in conjunction with related inquiry in a wide range of relevant fields of study, including psychology, sociology, anthropology, the history of science, and the philosophy of that history generally.

VII

To recognize the role that practices and their governance play in the conduct of investigation is by no means to depreciate the role that the objects of investigation themselves play, in particular cases, in determining the course of investigation and, eventually, its results. It is to facilitate the effectiveness of objects in this regard that practices in the cognitive domains of our lives are developed, revised, and refined. Recognition that knowledge of objects is gained through practices has led some philosophers to conclude that objects thus known are produced by the practices and are thus artifacts somehow dependent for their existence and character upon the practices themselves. Judged in the context of the history of human knowledge, and in particular the fabulous development of physical science in the past four centuries, this is perverse. Cognitive practices are designed to discover and disclose objects, not to produce them, and not to obscure them by interposing between us and them surrogate objects, "phenomenal objects," objects-as-known, as distinguished from independently real ones. Of course not all cognitive practices are *well* designed for the purpose; but as is indeed obvious to us when we are not bemused by some potent philosophical illusion, they are not all *ill* designed. And the same may be said of the kind of governance of practice that is constitutionally dependent in existence and character upon practice, that does not need to be imported from without *for* practice, because it is, in varying degrees and various ways, a natural development of practice itself.

NOTES

1. Asks Q. Skinner in his review of R. Bernstein's *The Restructuring of Social and Political Theory* (1978, p 28): "How can we possibly hope, by using (as we are bound to) our own local assumptions and canons of evidence, to construct a theory which is then employed to criticize these precise assumptions and canons of evidence? Doesn't it begin to look as if the project of 'critical theory' amounts to little more than a version of the Indian rope-trick?"

Over seventy-five years ago Peirce gave this answer: "In studying logic, you hope to correct your present ideas of what reasoning is good, what bad. This, of course, must be done by reasoning. . . . Some writers fancy that they see some absurdity in this. . . . They say it would be a *'petitio principii.'* . . . Let us rather state the case thus. At present you are in possession of a *logica utens* which seems to be unsatisfactory. The question is whether, using this unsatisfactory *logica utens*, you can make out wherein it must be modified, and can attain to a better system. This is a truer way of stating the question; and so stated, it appears to present no such insuperable difficulty, as is pretended" (*Collected Papers* 2:191).

2. In point are the doctrines advanced in W. V. Quine, *Ontological Relativity* (1969); Richard Rorty, "The World Well Lost," *Journal of Philosophy* 69 (1972): 649–65; Nelson Goodman, *Ways of World-making* (1978); and Quine, Review of Goodman, *New York Review of Books*, November 23, 1978, p. 25.

REFERENCES

Descartes, R. 1967. "Rules for the Direction of the Mind." In *The Philosophical Works of Descartes*, orig. published 1911, trans. by Haldane and Ross. Cambridge: Cambridge University Press.

Kuhn. T. S. 1964. *The Structure of Scientific Revolutions*. Chicago: Phoenix
   Books edition.
Peirce, C. S. 1931–1935, 1958. *Collected Papers*. Cambridge, Mass.: Har-
   vard University Press.
Shapere, D. 1975. "Copernicism as a Scientific Revolution." In A. Beer and
   K. Aa. Strand, *Copernicus* (*Vistas in Astronomy*, vol. 17), pp. 97–104.
Skinner, Q. 1978. "The Flight from Positivism." *New York Review of Books*,
   June 15, pp. 26–28.

6. ON GADAMER'S HERMENEUTICS

Dieter Misgeld

Ever since the *Verstehen* approach toward the study of culture and society has been considered, reference has been made to hermeneutics, the theory of interpretive understanding, as a method peculiar to these fields of study. Since Schleiermacher and Dilthey hermeneutics is a general theory of *Verstehen* as the access to all expressions of human individual, cultural, and historical life. In the case of Dilthey in particular, such a general theory would be the basis of *Geisteswissenschaften*.[1] Yet it is an achievement of Hans-Georg Gadamer's *Wahreit und Methode*,[2] the most important work on hermeneutics to have appeared since Dilthey, to make us appreciate that the tradition of hermeneutics predates systematic reflection on the logical and epistemological status of *Geisteswissenschaften* carried out under the title of 'Hermeneutics' by Schleiermacher and Dilthey, and the *Verstehen* problematic. Gadamer makes clear that this history reaches further than even Dilthey thought when he wrote the first history of hermeneutics, for Dilthey claimed that "the science of hermeneutics only begins with Protestantism" (Dilthey, 1966, p. 597).[3]

Gadamer attempts to show, as Dilthey and others in the hermeneutical tradition already acknowledged, that a theory of the rules to be followed in the interpretation of texts has affinity to the ancient discipline of rhetoric. It is conceivable, Gadamer claims, that the notion of method derived from the natural science, is altogether unsuitable for the interpretation of historical traditions, works of art, and for our accounting even of the understanding we have of language. Rhetoric, Gadamer argues, "from oldest tradition has been the only advocate of a claim to truth that defends the probable, and that which is convincing to the ordinary reason, against the claim of science to accept as true only what can be demonstrated and tested" (1976a, p. 26.)[4] Rhetoric also places the element of critical distance in the understanding of what is said second to an appreciative subordination of understanding to the course of ongoing speech. It denies that there is a purely

143

cognitive argument. Gadamer's reference to rhetoric as a paradigm for hermeneutics is meant to show that interpretive understanding differs from theoretical knowledge. Our knowledge of historical tradition, for example, is basically quite similar to how we understand arguments in the context of interaction situations. Therefore, rhetoric and the humanist tradition since the Renaissance are two of the historical clues one can use in order to liberate the humanities from the restrictive role of the ideal of scientific method.

It may seem, however, that Gadamer, apart from the reference to forgotten traditions such as that of rhetoric, pursues the easiest line of criticism available, when he attempts to limit the claims to knowledge derived from the standards of inquiry most systematically tested in the natural sciences. He may challenge beliefs hardly anyone since the early days of logical positivism would still entertain. Yet the matter is not quite so obvious. Gadamer proposes to use the notions of truth and method disjunctively, as if the one had no relation to the other. In a reversal of the usual conception, he seems to claim that truth can be found only if it is argued that "the hermeneutic phenomenon is basically not a problem of method at all" (1975, p.xi).' One should not construe this to mean that hermeneutics rejects science. There is a claim that the idea of science, at least as present in the context of *Geisteswissenschaften,* is not fully exhausted by the ensemble of scientific methods. Gadamer attempts to build on a resistance "within modern science against the universal claims of scientific methods" (1975, p. xii). Although he is not interested in documenting this fully, he addresses indirect evidence in his examination of the hermeneutical tradition (1975, pp. 153–235).

One does not only find that hermeneutics has a close relationship to rhetoric; one also discovers that an appeal to authoritative examples and precedents or to what has been found to be a fitting, proper, and effective mode of speech, and is recognized as such according to customary standards of evaluation, is not restricted to a theory of argumentation in rhetoric. It is also found in the disciplines of law and theology (1975, pp. 289–305, 1976*a*, pp. 198–212). Both disciplines have their own tradition of hermeneutics. Their mode of proceeding cannot be altogether uninteresting to the study of historical and cultural documents, which frequently have the status of singularly important texts, for they recognize such texts themselves. The cultural importance attributed to them cannot be appreciated by merely applying historical critical methods and then noting that a text has been found that has been considered singularly important in a culture or epoch. This procedure can only apply to cultures with which we have nothing in common. When this is not the case, some other way has to be found of making out why a text lays a particular claim on those interpreting it. It cannot be a question of finding the 'objective' evidence. Dilthey's proposal was that historical scholars are somehow to transpose themselves into the situation of the culture, so that they can regenerate for themselves the sense of importance such a text possessed. Here Gadamer certainly finds a basis for a resistance to scientific method, if it requires the complete suppression of subjectivity, of empathetic and intuitive finesse which is a consequence of erudition.[5] But this is not all for him: Dilthey's justification of empathy does not sufficiently upset the paradigmatic role of scientific method connected with Mill's claim that the subject matter of the "moral sciences falls within the scope of inductive logic."[6] The historical scholar can still treat what he studies as merely an object of study, or of a distantiated and distantiating interest, be it a scholarly or an aesthetic interest. Gadamer suggests that inquiry in *Geisteswissenschaften* has greater proximity to a mode of discursive reflection than Dilthey thought. The study of the past may be likened to a form of self-examination. A situation of dialogue is the paradigm not for what normally goes on in these studies, but for what may, and ought to happen, for in dialogue, self-examination and the probing of what others say are closely intertwined. Both are always the accomplishment of a reciprocal relationship.

If truth is to be found in a dialogical mode of inquiry, it cannot be found by the application of scientific method. Yet Gadamer goes even further in order to legitimate his refusal to grant the title of 'truth' to what results from scientific method. He also claims that hermeneutical understanding can be something like an event, the unexpected and not planned for recognition of a truth, which has an overpowering reality for us. Discursive reasoning would always come too late, so to speak, if it was to provide exclusively analytical grounds for this recognition of truth.

Nothing puts Gadamer at a greater distance from Dilthey's hermeneutics than such claims; and Gadamer is well aware of it. A critical reader faces the task of separating what seems to be a reasonable claim, illustrated by reference to the theory of the rhetorical arts, the role of discursive reflection, the interdependence of self-examination and of what a document of the past may have to say to us, from the farther reaching claim that truth is beyond discursive redemption. I shall turn to this once more.

Yet on this basis Gadamer's hermeneutics cannot just be the continuation of Dilthey's enterprise. For Dilthey, the general theory of *Verstehen* was to legitimate *Geisteswissenschaften* as an independent field of inquiry. It is shown as possessing distinct procedures derived from some type of identity between the inquirer and the subject matter studied. Here mind understands itself, and this is not just meant as a psychological thesis. Dilthey remains an Hegelian in the sense of recognizing something like 'objective mind'. Yet he also subscribed to the aim of an objectively valid reconstruction of historical events and psychological states, to a concept of science consisting of a set of descriptive and theoretical propositions. Therefore, Gadamer claims that for Dilthey "what is method in modern science, remains everywhere the same and is seen only in an especially exemplary form in the natural sciences" (1975, p. 8).

Gadamer's position is to uphold Dilthey's claims with regard to the distinctiveness of the historical and cultural sciences, while providing a different rationale and at the same time using it to undermine claims of the superiority of scientific knowledge. Dilthey attempted to establish a correlation between the distinct subject matter of *Geisteswissenschaft* and its methods. He proposed a problem-centred methodology. Gadamer takes this seriously, yet goes further in proposing that the subject matter of *Geisteswissenschaft*, while distinct from that of the natural sciences, is at the same time linked to areas outside the range of science, no matter how it proceeds and what it selects as its area of inquiry. Thus the historical and cultural studies actually open up areas of inquiry not available to 'science'. They become linked to the historical experience of life and to communication in natural language which always precedes and is subsequent to scientific study of phenomena and events, no matter what their distinct procedures and topics are. This is the point of Gadamer's insistence that hermeneutics predates the *Verstehen* method: "From its historical origin, the problem of hermeneutics goes beyond the limits that the concept of method sets to modern science" (1975, p. xi). A recovery of the older tradition in hermeneutics, such as legal and theological hermeneutics, and of the connections with the traditions of rhetoric and of humanist erudition permits Gadamer to break out of the framework of the methodological considerations that Dilthey established. Gadamer's inquiry joins the human sciences with "modes of experience which lie outside science: with the experiences of philosophy, of art, and of history itself" (1975, p. xii).

Heidegger's analysis in *Being and Time* of hermeneutical (projective) understanding as the basic feature of human existence can be called upon by Gadamer: for whatever method there may be to the thoroughly practical understanding achieved by human beings as a consequence of the interpretive generation of possibilities for leading their lives, it precedes the methods of any science, in Heidegger's view. (Heidegger, 1962, paragraphs 31–34, 41, 68, 74). The preontological self-explication of human beings in their life experience opens the door toward foundational ontology.

It is an ontological orientation of hermeneutics (1975, pp. 345–449) which Gadamer pursues in analyses saturated with the older, as well as the Diltheyan concerns of hermeneutics and with reflections on the guiding concepts of the humanities, which link their disciplinary tasks with their educational, and cultural role. Concepts such as those of good sense, *Bildung, sensus communis* (1975, pp. 5–39) and taste are explored *via* the toilsome route of a reconstruction of their history in order to show that claims to truth were connected with them which are not those of scientific concepts and propositions. These are concepts that have a normative sense; and when they were still taken seriously, they conveyed a practical meaning of truth in the sense of what it is reasonable to say or do, especially when such insight was measured in terms of the continuity of a tradition, of unshaken customary standards of evaluation.

Yet the hermeneutical problem, which Gadamer places wherever misunderstanding occurs, affects hermeneutics as a disciplined mode of philosophical reflection itself. The very continuity of traditions predating a scientific culture is no longer readily available. This is so, even if hermeneutics reminds us of them in order to make a case for the concept of experiences of truth that transcend the sphere of control of science. This situation is, in Gadamer's view, the very motive for the renewal of hermeneutical inquiry.

Gadamer attempts to show that the continuity of traditions is much less shaken than is frequently presumed. The traditions he has in mind are processes initiating us into the way of life of a culture.

This happens in such a way that we could not conceive of ourselves and the culture without depending on them. "Long before we understand ourselves through the process of self-examination, we understand ourselves in a self-evident way in the family, society, and state in which we live" (1975, p. 245).

Traditions, customs, and mores manifest their superiority over our insistence that they need to be redesigned in an unobtrusive fashion. Their authority asserts itself rather like the authority of an expert when consulted. Gadamer claims: "we always stand within traditions — and this is no objectifying process, i.e. we do not conceive of what the tradition says as something other, something alien" (1975, p. 250). This does not turn Gadamer into an ultra-conservative. For while Gadamer claims that, for example, the development of science will meet a limit, he also says that the limit is unknowable at present (Gadamer, 1967). Nor does Gadamer give his notion of tradition firm substantive content. He does not argue that monogamous or patriarchal family structures will survive no matter what. In his own domain of philosophical scholarship, the study of Greek philosophy and German Idealism (1976b) in particular, there can be no question that he takes a critical attitude toward central concepts.

It is also not the case that Gadamer simply ignores traditions of criticism in the sciences. While he certainly has not taken much notice of those studies interpreting the development of scientific method and theory in terms of the traditions of criticism immanent to the development of natural science, he has traced such developments in his own domain of literary and historical scholarship.[7]

Yet we must take Gadamer's emphasis on the unobtrusive presence of traditions in historical understanding to entail a claim that there are limits to a critical attitude which builds on the antithetical relation between 'historical truths' and historically invariant principles of rationality. Gadamer also seems to suggest that the tradition of criticism accumulated in the development of scientific theory as a tradition of the critical review of such theories is not the paradigm case for an assessment of an understanding relation to the historical past and its most eminent documents. His point, however, is more fundamental. It is a basic conceptual point. Even the tradition of criticism in the development of science remains incomprehensible, unless one entertains a concept of tradition that cannot be explicated in terms of the criteria of adequate knowledge available in this tradition itself. For it is part and parcel of any explication of the concept of tradition to show that traditions are known even in the absence of clear and distinct concepts. One may adhere to traditions without knowing clearly and distinctly that one does, but adhering to a tradition in this way is itself a mode of knowing. If one does know a tradition clearly and distinctly, one can only do so on the basis of a tradition one does not know about in just this fashion. Traditions cannot be changed as the clothes one wears: they would then no longer be traditions. It is part of the concept of tradition, hence, that we must characterize tradition as something we depend on. The concept is not compatible with a concept of an inquirer who is free to choose it or not to choose it in terms of criteria that place him outside any historical context.

Gadamer has not examined the peculiar status of traditions of inquiry present in the development of natural science. One can surmise, however, that he would characterize it in terms similar to those which he applies when assessing the relationship between historical and cultural studies as traditions of learning and the competency of members of a culture to communicate about their historical situation. In both cases a critical elaboration and application of standards of inquiry depends on the prior recognition that it makes sense to do so.

This recognition itself cannot be derived from the criteria inherent in the traditions of specialized inquiry themselves. The grounds for the reasonableness of the inquiry are to be found in communicating about it in other than the terms applied once it is on its way. Also criticism of a tradition of inquiry requires its prior acceptance. Yet criticism and modification of a tradition may also be found to have discovered its 'real' sense, in that there is no objective sense, definitely attainable once and for all, to a tradition. Thus Gadamer argues for a thoroughly historical notion of inquiry. Traditions are open to modification, yet every modification contributes to their continuation. He is antagonistic to concepts of inquiry that postulate the possibility of a complete emancipation from tradition.[8]

The notions of truth and hermeneutical understanding are to be contrasted with scientific method in order to formulate a corrective in a particular historical situation.[9] This is a situation where the application of scientific methods is generally believed to guarantee the progressively successful and cumulatively effective growth of knowledge liberating from past ignorance. Here one is to remember that a translation of the discoveries of science into the context of historical life experience is unavoidable under all historically known circumstances. When it occurs, traditions come into play in the assessment of science which are not those of scientific inquiry itself. The encounter between science, in the form of its 'results' considered in general 'public' discourse, and cultural traditions interpreted in the horizons of life-historical experience and communication in natural language is the only guarantee that a mode of socialization proceeding through the learning of natural language and the encounter with cultural tradition will not be replaced by a mode of social control which does not appeal to the identity of social members formed in the encounter with cultural tradition.[10] It is questionable, if under such circumstances, that one could still speak of members of society as possessing an identity. Thus the continuity of traditions outside that of scientific inquiry balances the claims of scientific knowledge with insights gained from and procedures operative in the communicative experience of cultural tradition.

Yet one may argue that Gadamer has not shown how a mode of inquiry requiring the incessant systematic re-examination of previous truth claims can be reconciled with the continuous, apparently unmethodical, and 'precritical' elaboration of tradition in the interpretation of culture and human conduct. For, after all, his inquiries have their strongest critical focus in noting and analysing an imbalance between the criteria judged to be adequate for the development of science (such as continual criticism) and those 'naturally' adhered to in the course of the development of cultural tradition, which does not require, and may not even be compatible with, such incessant criticism.

Gadamer thus seems to face a dilemma. It is best explicated with reference to the notion of historical consciousness, which is of central importance in his own work. The emergence of historical consciousness provides the most convincing legitimation for a comprehensive reflection on what is involved in understanding the historical past, but seems to render this hermeneutical task superfluous. Thus there is, on the one hand, a consciousness of distance to the historical past in a culture in which historical consciousness is highly developed. Historical consciousness, as in Dilthey's case, actually praises itself for being a very advanced form of modernity. An interest in historical knowledge, far from being typical of cultures where science plays an insignificant role, is characteristic and belongs to a worldview in which the advancement of science plays a dominant role. Historical consciousness is, therefore, the intrusion of the enlightenment into the area of cultural and historical studies. On the other hand, hermeneutics is searching for a continuity of tradition beyond the evolutionary history of historical consciousness and the development of historical critical studies. Gadamer, it seems, must either side with a naive belief in the persistent continuity of prescientific traditions of historical understanding or with a historical-critical consciousness. He in fact, does neither; rather, he believes that continuity of tradition, understood in a specific sense, can be reconciled with a historical critical attitude. How is this accomplished? Hermeneutics is to recognize the legitimacy of motives for a critical, or distantiated disposition toward the heritage of a culture that possesses highly developed forms of historical consciousness. They gain their legitimacy from the very sense of historical discontinuity, which historical consciousness itself generates. To the extent to which hermeneutics does not deny, but is itself an awareness of discontinuity, the whole critical apparatus assembled in the humanities should be put to use.

Motives, however, for taking an interest at all in the study of the historical past cannot be generated out of the body of historical-critical methods. Rather, here one has to recur to a feature of the situation of those studying history and historical texts. Their situation is itself historical. Understanding the historical past is a feature of the activity of life itself preceding the deliberate reconstruction of the historical past. Here Gadamer resumes Dilthey's deliberations.[11] Yet he goes beyond Dilthey when he argues that we are implicated in the historical past through communication in language. Natural languages are historical languages. Reflection on what is said, the explication of language through speech in conversation and discourse is always a historically situated accomplishment.

By exploring the analogy between understanding a text representing a tradition of inquiry, or of literature and art, and a conversation, one can notice how understanding historically is not equal to assuming the role of a distantiated and distantiating observer just noting the facts. Rather, one is assuming the role of a partner in an interaction situation. One acts communicatively, to use Habermas' phrase. Gadamer speaks of a participatory understanding.[12] Participatory understanding cannot bring the object of its knowledge before itself in an objectivating fashion. Here one knows as one knows in speaking that what one says opens up a variety of possibilities of reformulation. What is said, stands in a definite, yet never quite predictable relationship to what is not said. There is no theory of definite descriptions here or of the possibility of finding a finite set of propositions exhausting the meaning of a text. The understanding of texts and of cultural traditions through them is the very paradigm case for a conception of philosophy that views itself as merely a more discursive form of daily communication. Philosophy is not to establish modes of discourse that can replace the possibilities of discourse implicit in daily communicative experience: it is merely to develop them. As such it has a general cultural, not a scientific task. It does not adopt standards of proof derived from formal logic as its norm. Hermeneutics does not, however, merely point to communicative experience as underlying the effort to reconstruct past historical events and cultural meanings as something objective; it also claims that the objectivating application of historical reflection is always surpassed and thus contained in an understanding that knows about historical events in appreciating their action-orienting sense,[13] as well as the possibilities of self-understanding to be derived from them. The way the past is present in the communicative interaction of subjects deliberating and acting under historical circumstances can never be assimilated to the knowledge of the past accumulated in the sciences of history and culture. Therefore, a philosophical reflection on the humanities will not look for invariant standards determining when an interpretation is really 'correct', whether it be by pointing to what the author meant or by searching for the understanding a first readership had of a particular text.[14] It attempts to show that "a text is understood only if it is understood in a different way everytime" (1975, p. 276). The more of what a cultural tradition says is applied to the interpreter himself, such that the truth of his own preconceptions comes into play and into question and he can see a text representing a tradition containing a claim to truth, the better the understanding. Hermeneutical understanding is thoroughly self-applicative.

This means that one learns, that one only understands a philosophical text of the part for example, if and when one learns that the truth about a particular issue addressed by it cannot be found without appreciating what it says. When this no longer occurs, there is no reason for preserving it by means of the employment of historical-critical methods.

Gadamer is confident that the great texts of the philosophical tradition will survive those forms of philosophical consciousness which claim that nothing was done properly in philosophy before the development of philosophy as a rigorous science (Husserl) or conceptual and linguistic analysis in the twentieth century. But this is not very important. It is more important to note that Gadamer adopts and recommends a very open and not at all traditionalist attitude for the study of major cultural traditions. They are of interest as long as we can find truth in them. We are only to make certain that we are open to such claims to truth by avoiding commitments to apparently rigorous methodological standards. Rather than guaranteeing more certain knowledge, they permit us one kind of knowledge only and commit us prematurely to the assumption that the standards in question no longer need to be examined. Beyond the openness mentioned, there is no methodological device for hermeneutics to guarantee one the right attitude.

It is indeed the description of an attitude, rather than the analysis of conditions for the verifiability of truth claims or the falsification of theories which Gadamer pursues in the central sections of *Truth and Method* beginning with "foundations for a theory of hermeneutical experience" (1975, pp. 235–45) and leading to the final part of *Truth and Method* which discusses language (1975, p. 345).

When speaking of someone as hermeneutically experienced, Gadamer really thinks of a person who has "learned to learn," who is committed to self-examination and the examination of his historical situation. The truths to be examined have a practical point. They concern the conduct of our lives. This is why Gadamer favours the example of a carefully conducted conversation as best illustrating what hermeneutical experience is about:

> Reaching an understanding in conversation presupposes that both partners are ready for it and are trying to recognize the full value of what is alien and opposed to them. If this happens mutually and each of the partners, while simultaneously holding onto his own arguments, weighs the counter-arguments, it is finally possible to achieve, in an imperceptible but not arbitrary reciprocal translation of the other's position, a common language and a common statement. (1975, p. 348)

Both in the case of the interpretation of historical texts and in conducting a careful conversation as just described by Gadamer, claims to truth are examined discursively, while the interest of the examination is practical. In both cases as well, the criteria for the suitability, adequacy, convincingness of arguments are developed in the course of conversation's development. There is a "fusion of horizons" (1975, p. 273) such that in the end one no longer knows or cares to know what one's own original point of view was and what the other's, or, what contemporary opinions and thoughts are, rather than the historical ones studied. Historical-critical methods too easily insulate contemporary consciousness from possibilities of self-examination arising out of a confrontation with the past.

A conversation, in which a discursive examination of arguments occurs, is also a good example for the interplay of critical consciousness and of what Gadamer calls participatory understanding. It becomes apparent how hermeneutics has a dialogical situation of inquiry in mind. In it the examination of truth claims is intertwined with a form of interpersonal recognition. The truth of propositions is at stake just as much as the sincerity of dialogue partners is.[15] Here one can find the basis for the hermeneutical claim that being critical is a feature of coming to understand and reaching an agreement. A further examination of the logic of conversations could also show that critical standards can only develop in discursive conversation situations in the course of their realization.[16] Delineation of subject matter, procedures of argumentation and the like are topical only if and when the relationship between those participating in the conversation is thematic as well. Inquiry proceeds with the realization of a reciprocal recognition of the respective identities of interlocutors and with the examination of claims to knowledge and truth, which are formulated without reference to the individuality of those making them.

An analysis of discourse situations, as situations of dialogical inquiry, can therefore also be turned into an analysis of the conditions for the possible genesis of the identity of speakers. Understood in this sense, hermeneutics can contribute to the debate about rationality by developing a concept of rationality derived from the communicative and discursive competence of speakers of natural language. However, it should at least be apparent that hermeneutics considers participants in conversations to be rational only to the extent that they are committed to a search for truth which will make them adopt certain attitudes toward each other. Theoretical and practical concerns cannot be kept separate.

Yet one should mention that an interpretation of Gadamer that considers hermeneutics to have contributed to a theory of discourse, and that builds on Habermas' suggestions for a theory of discourse as foundational for a communication theory of society (Habermas, 1971c), cannot easily be maintained in the face of the interest in the "ontological turn of hermeneutical reflection," which Gadamer attempts to justify. The "ontological turn of hermeneutics," in fact, is usually interpreted as what distinguishes Gadamer most clearly from Dilthey (Palmer, 1969, p. 163). With it are connected ambiguities in his concept of truth, too global and vague a notion of scientific method, and the lack of a clarification of features distinguishing a discursively conducted conversation (*Gespraech*) from routinely engaged in conversational exchanges.

I shall only comment on the concept of truth. Gadamer in one case employs the phrase that in hermeneutical understanding the "truth of our own being" is at issue. This is to say first of all that we cannot give a philosophical text, for example, an 'objectivist' reading: even if and especially if it is not a contemporary text; instead, we must interpret it so it can be seen to have something to say. Otherwise we can only treat it as an object of antiquarian historical scholarship in Nietzsche's (1874) sense. The text, however, is to have something to say to those interpreting it in a particular way. They are to bring their own anticipations of its meaning, their expectation of its making sense in particular ways into play, such that what the text says can emerge as different. Thus Gadamer recommends that one not adopt "an arbitrary procedure that we undertake on our own initiative, but one that, as a question, is related to the answer that is expected in the text," in that "the anticipation of an answer itself presumes that the person asking it is part of the tradition and regards himself as addressed by it. This is truth of the effective historical consciousness" (1975, p. 340). The truth of our being which comes into play in hermeneutical understanding is that we cannot vindicate to ourselves a superiority over what we try to understand and understand it at the same time. Hermeneutical understanding is not compatible, in this conception, with either explaining or fully grasping conceptually what is said, such that no further questions can arise.

Gadamer speaks of truth almost as if it were something extra-linguistic and non-propositional. Yet he also does not believe it to be ineffable. He seems to want to argue for a procedure of open argumentation and reflective examination which proceeds on the basis of a consent, embedded in a shared tradition, and develops toward a further explication of this consent. Yet he is concerned with the idea that the concept of method in science, if transferred to the understanding of culture, gives those who try to account for cultures and traditions a false superiority over their 'object'. He does not argue that traditions, for example, should never be 'explained', but only understood. Instead, he argues that with regard to certain traditions, such as the tradition of philosophical inquiry itself, attempting to explain it would not be compatible with continuing it. Thus, a sense of certainty and assurance emanating from the 'possession' of a method is to be undermined in order to make us recognize our dependency on traditions. This is why he sometimes can be read as recommending the "nonscientificity" of a statement as a criterion of its truth and why he even speaks of "experiences of truth," as if finding out what is true is not a matter of examining utterances and statements. The "ontological turn" of hermeneutics is a bias because it makes it appear as if there were no continuum between hermeneutical reflection and other forms of epistemological, logical or methodological reflection, as if in fact, hermeneutical reflection might not frequently be developed in the context of the latter. It also makes Gadamer neglect the analysis of distinct procedures and criteria of truth connected with various modes of speech, speech acts and discourse, or distinguish conditions for truth from those for the comprehensibility, adequacy, sincerity, of utterances.[17] Thus it may at times appear as if truth in a strong sense were the quality of an experience, never quite to be laid out in words (and as if no proposition in science could ever be true in this sense of true). For in his wanting to deny legitimacy to the view that language is best understood in terms of its objectivating and monological use which concentrates on the delineation of the properties of fact-asserting declarative statements (constative utterances), and justifies their supreme status in knowledge, Gadamer seems to intimate that truth is somewhere beyond utterances. He does not proceed to examine at this point various kinds of language use as Austin or Wittgenstein did.[18] Yet at the same time he very emphatically connects truth with language, in claiming that "being is language" (1975, p. 443). The unresolved ambiguity in his notion of truth results, I think, from his effort to understand language both in terms of the "occasionality of human speech" and in terms of a "totality of meaning" (1975, p. 416) coming into play in speech. Not content with analyzing how language is used in particular occasions and how, whatever the totality of meaning may be, it comes to be noticed in the ongoing activity of speaking, Gadamer only has recourse to notions of an "event of speech," of an "event of truth," some unanalyzable experience.

Yet he has also clearly linked his notion of truth with the development of argumentation and discourse, as I have discussed. This aspect of hermeneutics is relevant in the context of the social sciences and in conjunction with the claim that the basis for philosophy of language lies in the analysis of conversation situations. For Gadamer's strong assertion that "language forms its own reality in the performance of coming to an understanding" (1975, p. 422) contrasts nicely, after all, with most conceptions of language in ordinary language philosophy which emphasize the rule-following aspect of language use rather than its "creative" employment.[19]

Hermeneutics can mediate between phenomenology and ordinary language analysis which both play a role at present in sociology.[20] Hermeneutics does not so much analyze the rule-guided convention-dependent character of speech as the open-endedness of talk, the possibility of taking what is said to some point of completion; rather, it thinks of speaking as a discursive activity, because it can see intentions to make sense of something at work in it.

This sense is to be brought forth in proceeding discursively by addressing what is at issue in a discourse, rather than attending to rules to be followed. Gadamer does not identify the mere performance of speaking — the "mastery of natural language"[21] defined in terms of a competence to follow rules providing for the grammaticalness of speech — as the real issue of the competence to speak. Such competence is just a precondition for the competence to think, in and with language, and formulate, what is worth saying: "The hermeneutical problem is not one of the correct mastery of language, but of the proper understanding of that which takes place through the medium of language" (1975, pp. 346–47). In speaking discursively, we still deal with concepts.

What is said and what is spoken about is still an issue. The rejection of copy and correspondence theories of truth, and of nominalist theories of concept formation (1975, p. 366–78) does not preclude thinking about language in terms of a concept of reason and notions of intelligibility (1975, p. 363). Rather, standards for the adequacy and appropriateness of what one says and what one attempts to express in speaking are internal to the language itself. Adherence to the standards is not reflex-like, and amounts to more than obeying the relevant conventions. The adequacy of these conventions themselves can be seen in terms of what they permit to be communicated, what can be said about an object. Given that language is not a "mere means of communication," but "acquires its own reality only in the process of communicating" (Gadamer, 1975, p. 404), standards for the adequacy of what is said about an object, a topic are as variable as the communication situations we may encounter. Since moving from one to the other communication situation may be a requirement for saying something adequately, they at least entail the openness of one particular language game for translation into another.[22] Hermeneutics rejects the concept of an ideal language, or a normative concept of discourse just as much as the idea that language is a multiplicity of speaking practices which all have their own, disconnected criteria for the adequacy of what is said. Just as Husserl thought that some sort of eidetic unity could be found among the multiplicity of intentional experiences in the noema the intentional object, so hermeneutics finds reason in some overall cohering sense of rationality to be present in the variety of ordinary language speaking practices and of natural languages. Reason is present to the extent that interpretation and translation are possible, to the extent that language games are permeable. 'Reason' is present as a normative dimension of speech as long as we make an effort to translate, to argue, to interpret. Yet this is all that can be said about 'reason', short of bringing the totality of language before us. This would only be possible if we could think of communication as having come to an end. Hermeneutics makes us take note of a dialectical tension between reason and speech, which those forms of sociology closest to it (ethnomethodological sociology) have tended to ignore in wedding the equally descriptive orientations of phenomenology and ordinary language philosophy and, thereby, losing themselves in the variety of empirically discoverable speaking practices and situational understandings.[23]

Yet hermeneutics equally takes exception to naively normative concepts of language and tradition, one example of which is Parsons' concept. He (1951, p. 11) decrees that "a shared order of symbolic meanings," a "cultural tradition" underlies the possibility of "normative orientation" in social action and communication as an "imposed" order which is present independently of the actors' and communicating persons' recognition of its presence. This entails the claim that Parsons knows how to explain why there is order and complexity in human action systems. By introducing the shared order of symbolic meanings as a concept, Parsons intends to explain how there can be stability in human action systems. Cultural tradition and language become "functional prerequisites" of a social system. Hermeneutics does not know of any tradition available in just this way; it knows, rather, that tradition is never available in just this way to those who live in and with traditions. When one reflects on, for example, the interpretation of tradition, one knows that one eventually will come to participate in a shared meaning: but only when one has come to understand what is to be shared. Short of the truism that there are no cultures unless there are languages and traditions that are shared, Parsons does not tell hermeneutics anything of interest. The interest of hermeneutics on the contrary, lies in investigating how, in what sense, under what conditions, something said—be it by a tradition or by contemporary speakers, texts, etc.—can make sense such that it comes to be recognized as a tradition, a text, something said. Furthermore, hermeneutics is also interested in examining the reasons why a tradition, something said, etc., are found to be true. That is, the basis for the recognition of the sense and sensibility of a tradition, for example, is found in what is true about it. Hermeneutics proposes as an analytical task the reflection on how we come to find and what we come to find as true about a tradition, about something said. Traditions can only be defined as traditions when they have the sense of something that can be shared. Traditions are not traditions unless they come to be accounted for as something held in common by those who find and consider themselves to be addressed by them. Yet this sense of "something held in common" must be affirmed, accomplished again and again. It is what is in question. The very conception of how traditions are to be understood on the model of an object to be studied by an observer for example, or a person living through another person's subjective intentional life, or on the model of a conversation—affects the understanding of tradition and how one conducts oneself toward the historical past as something no longer present in one sense, as more present than what is contemporaneous, in another.

Traditions are not physical things. Just as one cannot account for speech performance by merely referring to the vocalization of sounds, so one cannot account for the presence of traditions as "shared symbol systems" by making reference to them as if they were external to the manner in which they are kept alive or buried in their interpretive assimilation to one's own or the culture's self-interpretation. Gadamer analyses the dilemma of the issue of the continuity of tradition in historical consciousness while Parsons obscures the issue with his structural functionalist bias and his interest in the explanation of the genesis of whole social systems. Historical consciousness itself is a cultural phenomenon, ignored by Parsons, open to reflection on its relation to the historical past. Ordinarily, the historical past is available to conduct and speech before it has been filtered through a consciousness explicitly thinking in historical terms. This is one of the avenues Gadamer explores for showing how tradition continues to be present, in spite of and alongside with historical consciousness as a product of cultural modernity.

It follows that the situation of those interpreting tradition either professionally or in their lives has to be taken into account before one can decree that the normative content of culture has the "function" of providing stability for it. In this sense hermeneutics is closer to sociologists who investigate social structure in terms of an analysis of those practices members of a culture and language tradition employ in order to make its organization available to themselves. Hermeneutics, however, unlike ethnomethodology, still has a normative concern. It wants us to recognize that we are to acknowledge our dependency on the availability of a cultural heritage in order to make sense of the present. It does not, however, legislate that, nor how we are to do so: it recommends, least of all, that we must respect traditions in order to have stable social systems. This is, after all, a practical conclusion one can draw from Parsons' analysis. Hermeneutics just argues that we are usually wrong when we claim an independence from the historical past that would make further deliberation over what its documents, for example, have to say superfluous. Hermeneutics claims that we then simply ignore how even the idea of such independence is generated out of an encounter, a confrontation perhaps, with the historical past.

For an understanding of social institutions hermeneutics clearly pursues the course of understanding a society from within (Turner, 1970, p. 177). As such it has affinity to both Winch's analysis of the concept of a social science and to ethnomethodology. Hermeneutics, therefore, is opposed to all notions of social engineering, conceptions for the redesign of social institutions which are not tested and examined with reference to the self-understanding of social actors whose lives are to be reorganized in redesigning social institutions. In fact, hermeneutics claims that institutions cannot be designed analogous to the manner in which an engineer having technical knowledge of the requirements for the construction of machines might approach designing them.[24] Institutions cannot and ought not to be redesigned, for they cannot be accounted for separately from the interpretive understanding which those possess who in some sense belong to them. Yet they can be, through an examination of social norms and roles, discursively examined and communicatively explored, and usually are. Here lies a basis for a theory of institutional change. Hermeneutics does not share the confidence of those who believe that there can be a social science of practical import that will at all resemble natural science.

Gadamer's work, however, is inconclusive when one considers the state of social science. Partially this is due to his undifferentiated concept of scientific method, his analytically inadequate notion of truth and to similar deficiencies in his account of tradition. He never analyses scientific method in terms of a plurality of methods or the relation between theories and methods. He does not clearly distinguish theoretical from "practical" truths, that is, he does not examine the logic of different types of discourse in which these claims might occur. When he employs the concept of tradition, he too frequently speaks of "tradition" writ large, as if the hermeneutical case would not have to be made differently every time with regard to different concepts of traditions, covering different cases such as "traditions of inquiry" and "cultural traditions." Hermeneutics should be a discipline appreciative of these very differences. It should take an interest in the differences between traditions of inquiry in science and outside it. It ought to examine differences and similarities between the interpretive understanding of one's own cultural tradition and that of foreign cultures.

Yet while all these are legitimate complaints, there can hardly be any doubt that hermeneutics, in the form Gadamer gives it, deserves a place in debates about the state of the social sciences. It goes beyond the phenomenolgcial tradition in having an explicit concept of language. Habermas (1970) has attempted to show how it can contribute to a clarification of a "communicative access to the data of social science" beyond phenomenology (Habermas, 1970, Misgeld, 1976, pp. 164–84). Its similarity to examinations of the "logic of conversation" (Grice),[25] ethnomethodological sociology as the study of conversational accomplishments[26] (Garfinkel, Sacks, 1970, p. 361), and generally, to the study of "the inexact logic of ordinary language communication" (Strawson, 1971, p. 27) deserves further attention. Hermeneutics, seen in the perspective of the interest in language which has recently come to the fore in ethnomethodology, may help come to terms both with the tradition of phenomenology and of ordinary language analysis emanating from Wittgenstein and Austin.[27] Neither of these traditions, nor ethnomethodological sociology, have yet developed a notion of inquiry that requires something other than an analytical and descriptive interest only. Hermeneutics, however, is a mode of inquiry that refuses to legitimate any disposition on the side of those inquiring to exempt themselves from what is topical in the inquiry. It is not a matter of merely being reflective about the theoretical work one does, to know, as ethnomethodologists say, that sociological reasoning, including ethnomethodology, is a situated accomplishment. Rather, if inquiry is itself a situated activity, just as much as what one studies, the conduct of life of those inquiring comes to be an issue as does the relation of inquiry to their lives.

Hermeneutics recommends a practically motivated inquiry. Yet in any case, it should be considered in conjunction with all those contemporary efforts that concentrate on a clarification of practical discourse and practical reasoning. In that case, Gadamer's strict disjunction of truth dependent on scientific method and truths to be found in communicative experience can no longer be maintained. Scientific method could come to be seen as a specific case of a variety of methodological accomplishments to be found in the organization of practical reasoning, if the case can be made that practical reasoning is the mode of reasoning on which all other modes are dependent. Gadamer indirectly gives too much weight to scientific method by leaving its dependency on method-like accomplishments of practical reasoning, the rule-dependent character of natural language communication, unexamined, thus leaving himself open to the objection that in his conception reaching agreement in natural language communication has nothing at all to do with method (understood in the above sense). I have tried to show that this would be a one-sided, although not unwarranted account. One can best learn from Gadamer, I suggest, if one reads him to have contributed to the defense of the claim that natural language communication gives priority to practical discourses and that the understanding of claims to theoretical knowledge is dependent upon a process of translation, linking them with discourses orienting action through such communication. In this sense only, it seems, the claim to universality of hermeneutical reflection may be upheld and sense can be made of the provocative and interesting assertion "that the hermeneutical phenomenon is not a problem of method at all."

NOTES

1. Vide vol. VII of Dilthey's *Collected Works* (1914, ff.), so far untranslated. For further sources on Dilthey's work in the logic of *Geisteswissenschaften* in addition to Gadamer's own, vide J. Habermas (1971) and also H. P. Rickman (1962): (the book contains a selection of Dilthey texts in translation, translator unacknowledged). For full bibliographical information and a comprehensive account of Dilthey's philosophy, vide R. A. Makkreel (1975). J. Shapiro, the translator of Habermas' book mentioned above, has recommended the translation "cultural sciences" for the German *Geisteswissenschaften*. While I find this plausible, I have preferred to use either the German word or to operate with circumscriptions alluding to the wide variety of types of study covered. I am not adhering to one fixed use. But it should be clear that *Geisteswissenschaften*, understood in the narrower sense, alludes to historical and literary studies, while Dilthey uses it in a wider sense to make it apply to what Habermas calls the "systematic sciences of culture," which may include all the social sciences (Habermas, 1971, p. 337).

2. German 1st ed.: Tübingen: J. C. B. Mohr, 1960; 4th ed.: Tübingen: J. C. B. Mohr, 1975. All citations are from the translation (*Truth and Method* [Seabury, 1975]). For one of the most important recent philosophical works to have been translated into English, this book has encountered a strange fate. No translator is mentioned, merely the name of two editors of a translation. There are no translator's notes found anywhere in the book, although they are badly needed. Terms such as 'prejudice' introduced to translate *Vorurteil* require justification, particularly since Gadamer himself discusses the history of the word and refers to its French and Latin equivalents. He makes clear that the meaning of the French and Latin word may be closer to 'prejudgement' than to what we normally mean by prejudice. A whole theory is at issue here, not just the translation of one word.

Similarly, a thorough explanation is needed for the concept of *Wirkungsgeschichtliches Bewusstsein*. Historically effective 'consciousness' is a misleading translation of an admittedly difficult novel concept, introduced by Gadamer (1975, p. 267). T. McCarthy, in his translation of Habermas' review of Gadamer, proposes 'consciousness of historical influence.' The advantage of this translation is that it does not prejudge the outcome of philosophical analysis of the concept (F. Dallmayr and T. McCarthy, 1977); for further suggestions, R. Palmer, 1969, p. 191. Here a note explaining and justifying the translation is needed. This applies as well to the concept of *Verstehen* which is frequently modified by Gadamer, or translated into noun phrases, such as *Verstaendigtsein, Einverstaendnis, Verstaendigung, Such verstaendigen*, etc. Gadamer also does not strictly separate the concepts of *Einverstaendnis* (an understanding) and *Uebereinstimmung* (agreement), again a point of considerable importance for an appropriate reading. And there are some downright errors in the translation. In my discussion of Gadamer's hermeneutics I have avoided making reference to or explicating central concepts of his such as 'the hermeneutical circle' or 'historically effective consciousness' (consciousness of historical influences). Their discussion would take too long and is not necessary, I believe, in order to say what they are meant to designate. This is not to say that the essay would not do better justice to Gadamer if there were a detailed examination of such concepts. But that would require a highly specialized investigation of the contexts in which they occur.

3. He specifies that he really means the Lutheran response to Catholic criticism of the *sola scriptura* principle of faith. Vide the Dilthey text quotes on p. 9 of Gadamer/Boehm (1976). This book is an anthology of texts from the history of hermeneutics.

4. This volume contains selections in translation from Gadamer's three volumes of essays (1967) with an introduction by David E. Linge, the translator. The selections are what one would wish. The introduction and the translations are good. Unfortunately one does not find the important "Nachwort" to *Wahrheit und Method* (3rd ed. 1975) in the translation of the book or in this collection of essays. Lacking this, the reader of *Truth and Method* should turn to "Hermeneutics and Historicism," Supplement I in *Truth and Method*. It contains some replies to Gadamer's critics, as does the "Nachwort." Gadamer discusses rhetoric in the essay, from which I quoted (as above), and when he examines Vico (1975, pp. 19–21) and Greek philosophy. Gadamer has written one book and numerous essays on Greek philosophy. Note also, for a discussion of Greek dialectic philosophy, "Hegel and the Dialectic of the Ancient Philosophers" in Gadamer (1976b).

5. Note that the older tradition of hermeneutics, which predates its romantic and post-romantic scientific period, knew of the importance of such factors. When distinguishing between a *Subtilitas intelligyndi* and *subtilitas explicandi* it did not "so much consider methods . . . as a talent that requires particularly finesse of mind" (Gadamer, 1975, p. 274). In this sense, hermeneutics is the theory of the art of interpretation.

6. Habermas (1971a, p. 180) makes very clear how the 'empathy model of understanding' is connected with the adherence to scientific method. Empathy "is . . . the equivalent of observation." Gadamer (1975, p. 460) em-

phasizes that Dilthey never gave up the epistemological foundation which he had sought for in a descriptive psychology that would concentrate on the flow of inner awareness. Habermas and Gadamer can agree, I believe, that Dilthey sought objective knowledge of inner states in their empathetic reproduction. Dilthey did not link understanding with structures of communication or coherences of meaning going beyond the individual's 'solitary' (Habermas) consciousness, as Gadamer and Habermas hold. With reference to Mill, Gadamer claims that Dilthey found himself in a constant debate with the final chapter of Mill's *Logic* (1975, p. 8).

7. Note the examinations of the development of hermeneutics from its biblical to its romantic and then to its methodological stage throughout part II of *Truth and Method*. On the concept of *Bildung* see pp. 19–29.

8. This is the general point of his critique of the Enlightenment. It is also applied to Habermas in "The Scope and Function of Hermeneutical Reflection" (1976a).

9. In the "Nachwort" to the 3rd edition Gadamer observes that he may have exaggerated the independence of the discovery of truth from the employment of method, because he feels that under contemporary circumstances the contrary conception is too prevalent. Part of the hermeneutical enterprise seems to be to salvage the autonomy of philosophical inquiry and to do so by speaking to a particular historical situation and saying what is needed in it, rather than to pursue insights into eternal verities.

10. This is a central theme of Habermas' critique of the systems theoretical approach in sociology and political science developed by N. Luhmann. Cf. J. Habermas, N. Luhmann (1971), also F. W. Sixel, (1976, pp. 184–205). Luhmann's theory of social systems seems to imply that political socialization processes are rational, even if they no longer depend on the citizen's conviction that they are open to discursive examination. If the systems theoretical analysis is correct, a mode of socialization based on the reflective appropriation of tradition is slowly disappearing. It will no longer frequently be the case that the reality of democratic societies is seriously examined in terms of their central normative ideals. The capacity to examine the legitimacy of political norms would wither. The identity of societal subjects *qua* citizens would no longer be rationally grounded or connected with the idea of autonomous critical insight. At this point, Habermas argues, it becomes meaningless to speak of societal members as possessing an individual identity.

11. Dilthey says: "life, experience of life and the human studies are constantly related and interacting. . . . Here life grasps life . . . " (Rickman, 1962, p. 79).

12. Although I introduce this phrase as if it was a technical term in Gadamer, it is not. Rather, it designates a general emphasis on participation in cultural heritage and the like as a precondition for understanding. Vide

P. Ricoeur's perceptive comments on the relation of participation and distantiation in understanding (1973, pp. 129–41).

13. This point has been emphasized by Habermas (1973, pp. 251–85) in his challenging review of Gadamer translated in Dallmayr, McCarthy (1975). Gadamer does not systematically consider the implications of this feature of hermeneutical reflection for a theory of social action.

14. E. Betti and E. Hirsch are two authors defending these traditional claims of hermeneutics against Gadamer. Vide E. Betti (1955) and E. Hirsch (1976, especially pp. 245–65).

15. I have Habermas' theory of discourse in mind. (Habermas, 1973a, p. 170; 1973b, pp. 211–63, especially p. 259; 1976, pp. 174–273). A theory of discourse, having actual communication situations in mind, concentrates on the relation between the propositional content element of utterances and their performative element. It also distinguishes types of utterances in terms of the distinction between 'constatives' and 'performatives' (Austin). Communication situations can be distinguished in terms of the prevalence of one or the other element. Habermas stresses that the sincerity and truthfulness of speakers can be discursively examined just as much as claims of truth concerning the proposition content of utterances. This is of particular importance in practical discourse.

16. Questions arising out of this conception of a conversation, in which truth claims are at issue, are best examined further. I suggest, by contrasting Habermas' concept of reaching agreement in speaking, operative in every discourse as an anticipation, with the ethnomethodological claim that criteria for the adequacy of what is said in talk are irremediably particular (Garfinkel, Sacks, 1970), that is, dependent for their sense on the very situation of speech in which they are employed. Gadamer's unique contribution to a pragmatically oriented logic of discourse, choosing actual conversation-situations as its representative phenomena, could be to insist neither on universal criteria of validity and truth, or truthfulness, as Habermas does, nor to believe that there are no such criteria, as ethnomethodologists do.

17. Once more I acknowledge Habermas' influence.

18. This is not to say that Gadamer is not aware of their work. He was not, however, at the time of writing *Truth and Method*. For some further comments, vide "The Phenomenological Movement" (Gadamer 1976a, p. 173ff.).

19. Note that Gadamer makes the fascinating claim that Wittgenstein's self-critique takes a direction similar to the one emerging in the evolution of phenomenology. (1976a, p. 174). Gadamer is also critical of Wittgenstein (1976a, p. 177). He argues against Wittgenstein's therapeutic inclinations in saying "that the field of language is not only the place or reduction for philosophical ignorance, but rather itself an actual whole of interpretation . . .

which requires not only to be accepted but to be thought through." This is a matter I take up in the subsequent discussions.

20. I am thinking of ethnomethodology. Vide Eglin, Heap (1975) and Roche (1973) for literature from both traditions relevant to ethnomethodology. The only text I can think of that prepares the ground for an appraisal of hermeneutics, phenomenology and ethnomethodology as having definite themes in common for social and political inquiry is O'Neill (1974). One may also find further interesting starting points in McHugh *et alii* (1974) and Blum (1974). I do not believe any credence should be given to what Meehan and Wood (1975) say about the "Hermeneutic spiral" (p. 365f.)

21. My suggestion is that ethnomethodology is wrong in abstracting from what is said in conversations for the sake of describing formal features of conversational competence. I am specifically thinking of Garfinkel and Sacks' claim that "mastery of natural language" consists in this: "in the particulars of speech a speaker . . . is able to gloss those particulars." The identity of what speakers mean and what they say is never definitely established, in this view. There is room for indefinite and continuous elaboration of what is said. The authors continue to claim that the "recognition that he (a speaker) is speaking and how he is speaking are specifically not matters for competent remarks" (Garfinkel and Sacks, 1970, p. 344). This account of conversations is plainly wrong for these situations in which the truth of what is said is an issue. For then the adequacy, correctness, cogency, etc., of what is said will become a topic for "competent remarks." We do not, in all situations, speak clearly, give correct information, argue cogently or address others sincerely. Gadamer and also Habermas focus on situations in which these more specific competencies are problematic. Garfinkel and Sacks are misled, I think, by their concern with the rejection of claims made by "scientific" or "professional" sociology to know social phenomena, etc., better than members of society ordinarily do. They ignore that some of the most hotly debated issues in everyday life situations revolve around the adequacy, correctness, fairness of certain statements and utterances. In fact, they seem to ignore how much of practical life experience is an experience of competing and incompatible claims to knowledge or fair treatment. We now know that conflicts of this kind do not merely occur in politics, but are also at issue in family-life and in many "daily" situations of life, which involve men and women. Gadamer is closer to this sphere of phenomena in acknowledging that conversations can develop into argumentations. He would share the ethnomethodological view that every such situation may have a rationale of its own, only available to participants, not to "observers."

22. Habermas (1973, translation in Dallmayr, McCarthy, 1977) for this reason places Gadamer's hermeneutics ahead of Wittgenstein, in some respects as a theory of communication in ordinary language. Habermas noticed that

the rules of linguistic communication also include conditions for their interpretation and the translation of what is said from one context into another. This is so, in particular, because with Gadamer "the unity of language, submerged in the pluralism of language games (Wittgenstein) is reestablished dialectically in the context of tradition."

23. This seems to be what conversational analysis does in ethnomethodological sociology (Turner, 1974; Sudnow, 1970). I do not notice any interest in developing criteria for the selection of conversations to be studied, other than an interest in understanding how commonsense knowledge of social structure is organized. This would at least hold for the earlier stage of ethnomethodology, as Heap (1975, p. 407) notes, which searches for invariant features of making sense. The alternative would be, as he points out, to take an interest in contingent practices. This is what conversational analysis seems to do.

24. Pertinent remarks can be found in Gadamer (1967, vol. III, p. 105). Gadamer, I believe, would subscribe to R. Rhees's (1969, pp. 51–58) critical comments on Popper's (1971, pp. 22–25) concept of social engineering. The objection in both cases is not so much to the analogy between machines and institutions, implicit in the metaphorical expression of social engineering. One would object, rather, to the engineer approaching "institutions rationally as means that serve certain ends" (Popper, 1971, p. 24). This instrumental conception of institutions, accounting for them as designed, and resulting from purposive action, omits how institutions are present in social life through the understanding of social norms, which is achieved in communication. Communication cannot be analysed in terms of a concept of instrumental action.

25. See the published portions in Grice (1975).

26. Garfinkel and Sacks (1970) attempt to account for objective sociological formulations and life as conversational phenomena and for sociological inquiries as instances of practical reasoning. The latter concept, however, is unclear, for they do not show in detail how objective sociological formulations, be they meant as literal descriptions or causal-nomological explanations, statements of a theory or observation statements, are of the same kind as formulations done in the course of everyday conversation. They can only claim that both kinds of formulating, actually any kind, are only available to speakers as making sense, due to the availability of natural language and speakers' competence to use it. They analyze properties of natural language coming to the fore in speaking as a situated activity. Garfinkel and Sacks neglect the specific features of utterances made in the theoretical contexts, as they neglect the specific features of utterances made in diverse practical contexts. This seems to be a consequence of their concern with the *formal* features of practical actions as situated events and due to their search for invariant features of practices of making sense. They do not notice that the

very knowledge claims they contest are the ones they themselves must make.

27. In philosophy, the most comprehensive and systematic attempt to connect these traditions has been made by K. O. Apel (1976).

REFERENCES

Apel, K.O. 1976. *Transformation der Philosophie*. 2 vols. Frankfurt.

Betti, E. 1955. *Teoria generale della interpretazione*. 2 vols. Milan.

Blum, A. 1976. *Theorizing*. London.

Dallmayr, F. and T. McCarthy (eds). 1977. *Understanding and Social Inquiry*. Notre Dame, Ind.

Dilthey, W. 1914–1974. *Gesammelte Schriften*. 17 vols. Goettingen.

Eglin, P. 1975. "What Should Sociology Explain." *Philosophy of the Social Sciences* 5, pp. 377–91.

Gadamer, H. G. 1960, 1975. *Wahrheit und Methode*. Tuebingen.

———. 1975. *Truth and Method*. New York.

———. 1967. *Kleine Schriften*. 3 vols. Tuebingen.

———. 1976a. *Philosophical Hermeneutics*, tr./ed. D. E. Linge. Berkeley.

———. 1976b. *Hegel's Dialectic. Five Hermeneutical Studies*, tr. Chr. Smith. New Haven.

———. R. Boehm 1976c. *Seminar: Philosophische Hermeneutik*. Frankfurt.

Garfinkel, H., and H. Sacks. 1970. "On the Formal Structures of Practical Actions," *Theoretical Sociology*, ed. J. McKinney, E. Tiryakian. New York.

Grice, H. P. "Logic and Conversation." The William James Lectures. Unpublished, no date. Sections published in P. Cole and J. L. Morgan (eds.), *Syntax and Semantics*. 1975. vol. 3 "Speech Acts." New York, pp. 41–59.

Heidegger, M. 1962. *Being and Time*. New York.

Habermas, J. 1970. *Zur Logik der Sozialwissenschaften*. Frankfurt.

———. 1971a *Knowledge and Human Interests*. Boston.

———. and N. Luhmann. 1971b. *Theorie der Gesellschaft oder Sozialtechnologie*. Frankfurt.

———. 1971c. "Thoughts on the Foundation of Sociology in the Philosophy of Language," Unpublished Manuscript. Gauss Lectures, Princeton University.

———. 1973a. "A Postscript to Knowledge and Human Interests," *Philosophy of the Social Sciences* 3, pp. 157–89.

———. 1973b. "Wahrheitstheorien." *Wirklichkeit und Reflexion*. Walter Schulz zum 60 Geburtstage. Tuebingen, pp. 211–63.

———. 1976. "Was heisst Universalpragmatik?" In K. O. Apel (ed.), *Sprachpragmatik und Philosophie*, Frankfurt, pp. 174–273.

McHugh, P. et alii. 1974. *On the Beginning of Social Inquiry*. London.

Heap, J. 1975. "Non-Indexical Action," *Philosophy of the Social Sciences* 5, pp. 373–411.

Hirsch, E. 1967, *Validity in Interpretation*. New Haven.

Makkreel, R. A. 1975. *Dilthey: Philosopher of the Human Studies*. Princeton.

Misgeld, D. 1976. "Critical Theory and Hermeneutics: The Debate between Gadamer and Habermas." In O'Neill (ed.), *On Critical Theory*, New York.

Meehan, H. and H. Wood. 1976. "An Image of Man for Ethnomethodology," *Philosophy of the Social Sciences* 5, pp. 365–76

Nietzsche, F. 1874. "Of the Use and Disadvantage of History for Life," in German.

O'Neill, J. 1974. *Making Sense Together*. New York.

Palmer, R. 1969. *Hermeneutics*. Evanston.

Parsons, T. 1951. *The Social System*. New York.

Popper, K. R. 1971. *The Open Society and its Enemies*, vol. 1. Princeton.

Rhees, R. 1969. *Without Answers*. New York.

Rickman, H. P. (ed.). 1962. *Wilhelm Dilthey: Pattern and Meaning in History*. New York.

Ricoeur, P. 1973. "The Hermeneutical Function of Distantiation," *Philosophy Today* 47, pp. 129–41.

———. 1975. "Ethics and Culture," as above, pp. 153–65.

Roche, M. 1973. *Phenomenology, Language, and the Social Sciences*. London.

Sixel, F. W. 1976. "The Problem of Sense: Habermas vs. Luhmann." In J. O'Neill (ed.), *On Critical Theory*, New York.

Strawson, P. F. 1971. *Logico-Linguistic Papers*. London.

Sudnow, D. 1972. *Social Interaction*. New York.

Turner, R. 1970. "Words, Utterances, and Activities." In J. D. Douglas (ed.), *Understanding Everyday Life*, Chicago.

PART III

Tradition and Society

7. FREEDOM AND CONSTRAINT BY NORMS

Robert Brandom

The issue of human freedom classically arises in the context of appraisal of action according to norms, when we seek an account of praise and blame, approval and disapproval. The issue of freedom arises again in the political context of an account of the ways in which an individual is and ought to be constrained by norms imposed by his community. One of the most suggestive responses to the first set of concerns has been developed by the Kantian tradition: the doctrine that freedom consists precisely in being constrained by norms rather than merely by causes, answering to what ought to be as well as to what is. Hegel and his admirers, in their turn, have responded to the second sort of concern with an influential doctrine of freedom as consisting of the self-expression made possible by acquiescence in the norms generated by an evolving community (the social synthesis of objective spirit). The central feature determining the character of any vision of human freedom is the account offered of *positive* freedom (freedom to)—those respects in which our activity should be distinguished from the mere lack of external causal constraint (freedom from) exhibited by such processes as the radioactive decay of an atomic nucleus. In this paper I will examine one way of developing Kant's suggestion that one is free just insofar as he acts according to the dictates of norms or principles,[1] and of his distinction between the Realm of Nature, governed by causes, and the Realm of Freedom, governed by norms and principles. Kant's transcendental machinery—the distinction between Understanding and Reason, the free noumenal self expressed somehow as a causally constrained phenomenal self, and so on—can no longer secure this distinction for us. It is just too mysterious to serve as an *explanation* of freedom. Yet some distinction between the realm of facts and the realm of norms must be established if the notion of freedom as normative rather than causal constraint is to be redeemed. In this paper I will present a version of this distinction which was not envisioned by Kant, and show how a novel response to the dispute between naturalists and non-naturalists concerning the relation of fact to norm can be developed out of that rendering. I will then argue that the account of human freedom which results from this story needs to be supplemented in just the ways in which Hegel claimed Kant's account needed to be supplemented, and will recommend an Hegelian self-expressive successor.

I

In order to clarify the difficult issues associated with accounts of human freedom which center on constraint by norms, we will focus our attention on the special case of norm-governed *linguistic* activity. I am not claiming that there are no significant differences between the way judgments of correctness and incorrectness function for linguistic performances and for actions in general, but I do not think we yet know which differences these are. There are certain respects in which we are surer of what we want to say about the norms that govern language-use than we are about other kinds of norms, so it is reasonable to exploit views about linguistic activity to illuminate the broader issues.

What makes a linguistic performance correct or incorrect, an utterance appropriate or inappropriate? Clearly in some sense the practice of the community which uses utterances of that type generates the standards of correctness by which individual tokenings are to be evaluated. The objective truth or falsehood of claim-making utterances need not concern us here, since appropriate utterances may not be true, and true ones may not be appropriate. I have argued elsewhere[2] that the notions of truth and meaning should be understood as theoretical auxiliaries introduced as part of a certain kind of theory of the practices of using a language which generate norms of appropriateness. For our present purposes we need not invoke these notions, since we need not delve below the level of the practices which constitute the shared use of a language. That it is actual human social practices which determine the correctness as a linguistic performance of an utterance on some particular occasion is clear from the fact that the community whose language is in question could just as well use some other noise on the relevant occasions.

We can express this point in terms of the *conventionality* of the association of particular vocables with standards of usage, so long as we are not seduced by this form of words into thinking of conventions or rules of usage for linguistic expressions as formulated in some ur-language (even mentalese) by the users of the language, an ur-language which they must understand in order to conform to the regularities of usage which constitute the use of the language by that population. We should rather think of those regularities as codified only in the *practices* of competent language-users, including of course the practices of criticizing the utterances of others for perceived failures to conform to the practices governing their linguistic performances and the practices available for adjudicating such disputes as may arise about the appropriateness of some utterance. So long as we think in this way of the norms governing communal usage of linguistic expressions as implicit in the practice of the community, we avoid the pointlessly puzzling regress generated by any rendering of those norms in terms of (linguistically expressed) rules or conventions which must themselves be applied correctly.[3] We can still give whatever causal account we like of the objective capacities in virtue of which individuals are able to engage in the complicated practices we attribute to them, for no regress is generated unless we seek to explain the ability to engage in those linguistic practices in some fashion which appeals to prior linguistic abilities, e.g., the following of a rule.[4]

What sort of a thing is the social practice which embodies a standard of correct and incorrect linguistic usage? Differently put, what makes a given act or utterance an instance of, or performance in accord with, some social practice? Consider a community whose members have a practice of greeting each other with gestures. In virtue of what is some particular arm-motion produced on an occasion an appropriate greeting-gesture according to the practice of the community? Clearly, just in case the community takes it to be one, that is, treats it like one. The respect of similarity shared by correct gestures and distinguishing them from incorrect ones is just a *response* which the community whose practice the gesture is does or would make. To specify a social practice is just to specify what counts as the community responding to some candidate acto or utterance as a correct performance of that practice. The criteria of identity for social practices appeal to the judgment of the community (where "judgment" here is not to be taken as entailing that the response is an explicit verbal evaluation). What the community says or does, goes, as far as the correctness of performances of their own practices are concerned. Classifying the behavior of a community in this way into social practices according to complexly criterioned responses is something that *we* do from the outside, as part of an attempt to understand them. The members of the community need not explicitly split up their activities in the ways we do, though they must do so implicitly, in the sense of responding as we have postulated.

Social practices thus constitute a thing-kind, individuated by communal responses, whose instances are whatever some community takes them to be. *Objective* kinds are those whose instances are what they are regardless of what any particular community takes them to be. *Galaxies more than a hundred light years from the Earth* is such an objective thing-kind. Linguistic practices determining the appropriateness of utterances on various occasions are social practices rather than objective things according to this classification. It may be that for many of these linguistic practices we cannot specify anthropologically just what it is for the community to treat such an utterance as an appropriate performance (we will have more to say about this issue later, under the heading of translation). But whatever epistemic difficulties of *identification* we may have do not alter the criteria of *identity* of such practices, which consist solely of communal responses to utterances. The language-using community has the last word about the linguistic correctness of the performances of its members. As pointed out before, to say this is not to deny that in addition to appraisals of correctness according to the linguistic social practices one must conform to in order to be speaking the language of the community at all there can be appraisals (for instance of the truth or loudness of an utterance) which concern entirely *objective* features of that utterance—which are what they are independent of the responses of the community to those utterances. Our concern, however, is with those norms conformity to which is a criterion of membership in the linguistic community. The truth of utterances is obviously not one such, else languages would be unlearnable since they would presuppose infallibility. It is, on the other hand, probably a condition of having learned a language containing certain minimal formal devices (the conditional, a truth predicate, etc.) that the majority of one's utterances be *deemed* true by the community. *Taking* something as true is a social practice, not a matter of objective fact, however.

One consequence of the criterial dominion communities enjoy over the social practices they engage in is particularly important for our argument in the next section. Consider what one would have to be able to do in order to characterize a social practice objectively. The practice could be expressed by an objective description of past performances which had been accepted as in accord with the practice (were responded to appropriately), together with an account of the dispositions of the community to respond in the specified manner to future activities. These dispositions would be complex along a number of different dimensions. First, notice that it may well matter in what order different candidate performances come up for consideration. Social practices evolve the way case-law does — an issue may be resolved very differently depending upon where in a chain of precedents it comes up for adjudication. Thus the community may accept an act as in accord with a particular practice, and later refuse to accept acts objectively as similar as you like. In addition to the position of a performance in the tradition of precedent performances which comprise the social practice viewed temporally, we would in general have to take into account the location in the structure of the community at which a performance is initially considered. For the community need not be democratically organized with respect to its social practices. There may be experts with various kinds of special authority with respect to judgments of the appropriateness of a performance, as is the case in English with the correct use of words like "molybdenum," or as could well be the case with the determination of the appropriateness of a bride-price in some tribe.[5] The point is that the past decisions of a community as to what accords with a practice of theirs admits of codification in objective rules only with large areas of indetermination as to future possible performances. And even complete knowledge of the complex dispositions of the community will enable the filling-in of these indeterminate areas only insofar as we can also predict exactly when and where in the social structure each possible case will actually arise. This is a formidable undertaking. The trouble is that the community has total authority over their own practices, so that even if in the past they have exhibited a strong objective regularity in their responses, they may depart from that regularity with impunity at any time and for any or no reason.

There is another source of difficulty in capturing social practices in objective terms, namely the possibility of *nested* social practices. We have been talking so far as if the response which a community must make or be disposed to make to a putative performance in order for it to be in accord with a social practice were always some objectively characterizable response. The objective expression of a social practice is then a matter simply of being able to predict when that response will be elicited from the community, a difficult but not mysterious enterprise. But what if the response which for us identifies some social practice is not an objective response, but rather some performance which must be in accord with *another* social practice? There is clearly no problem envisaging such a situation as long as the second, criterial, social practice is itself definitionally generated by some objective response. This being granted, there is no obstacle to even longer chains, just so they terminate eventually in a practice generated by an objectively characterizable response. The objective description of a social practice of a community for which such chains of social responses were the rule rather than the exception (e.g. linguistic practices) might thus require the prediction of everything anyone in the community would ever do. Although it is not obvious at this point, it will be shown in the next section that we can envisage a situation in which *every* social practice of the community has as its generating response a performance which must be in accord with another social practice. This possibility has profound consequences for our account of the relation of the realm of objective things to the realm of social things.[6]

II

Simple as this social practice idiom is, it allows us to describe the relation between norm and fact in a new way. To see this, consider the naturalism/non-naturalism dispute about what sort of distinction we are to envision between norms and facts. According to the naturalist, norms are facts, as objective as any other facts (although, of course, naturalists have various views about what sort of facts are important). Accounts of what ought to be may legitimately be inferred from accounts of what is. According to the non-naturalist, on the other hand, norms and facts are different kinds of things, and this ontological difference reflects or is reflected by the impermissibility of inferences of whatever complexity from "is" to "ought." It is clear that social practices, paradigmatically, *linguistic* ones, generate or express norms insofar as those practices are constituted by traditions of judgments of correctness and incorrectness. At least for the case of these norms which are inherent in social practices,[7] the distinction between norm and fact coincides with the distinction between social practices and any matter of objective fact. The naturalist/non-naturalist dispute here translates into a disagreement about the relation of social practices (with their inherent norms) to objective fact. The naturalist sees no distinction of kind operating, and is committed to viewing social practices as complex objective facts concerning the functioning of various communities. The non-naturalist sees a new category of norm or value emerging in these situations.

When the issue is put in these terms, a *via media* accommodating the motivating insights of both views becomes possible. For we need not choose between the claim that there is an objective difference between the social and the objectively factual and the claim that there is no difference at all between them. We may think instead of the difference as genuine, but *social* rather than objective, according to our criterial classification. On this view, whether a certain body of behavior constitutes a set of social practices (and hence expresses a normative constraint on performance) or merely exhibits complex but objective regularities is not a matter of objective fact. It is not, in other words, independent of how any community treats or responds to that body of behavior. The criterial classification of things into objective and social is itself a social, rather than objective or ontological, categorization of things according to whether we treat them as subject to the authority of a community or not. What, then, is the difference between treating some system as a set of social practices and treating it as consisting of objective processes?

For the possibly special case of *linguistic* practices, a straightforward answer is available. We treat some bit of behavior as the expression of a linguistic social practice rather than an objective process when we *translate* it, rather than offering a causal explanation of it. Let us agree to extend the application of the term "translation" to include any transformation of the capacity to engage in one set of social practices into the capacity to engage in some other set of social practices. Transformation of the ability to engage in those practices which constitute the use of German into those which constitute the use of English will then be a special case of general translation. We are considering two ways of coping with some complex behavior. Objectively, any spatio-temporally locatable performance can be described objectively and explained as part of a causal web consisting of other similarly described events. In practice, this sort of explanation of, say, the reliability of some signal as an indicator of red objects, may involve the causal understanding of quite complex facts about the physiology and training of the signal-producer. Instead of attempting such an objective account, we may instead use our own set of social practices as an unexplained explainer, and be responsible for an account of how the system in question *differs* from what we would do in that situation. Insofar as we adopt this second strategy, we expect the system in question to conform to the same sorts of norms of appropriateness and justification of its performances as govern ours. Translating, rather than causally explaining a performance, consists in assimilating it to our own practices, treating it as a dialect of our own practical idiom.[8]

There are two consequences of this distinction which we should notice. First, causal explanations can proceed atomistically, building up the behavior of a complex system out of independently describable behavioral elements. Translations, however, even in our extended sense, must proceed holistically. One assimilates a complex of behavior to a whole set of our own social practices, providing a commentary to control disanalogies and specify the variety and goodness of fit intended. For our own social practices cannot in general be specified in isolation from one another. A performance is in accord with a particular practice of ours just in case it is or would be responded to in a particular way by our community. But that response typically is itself a performance which must be in accord with a social practice, i.e., one which does or would elicit another response in accord with another practice, and so on. From the point of view of an external objective account of our practices, the invocation of a chain of critical-constitutive practices of this sort which didn't end in an objective criterion of correctness would involve us in a vicious explanatory regress or circle. But for us to engage in a web of social practices no such requirement applies. All that is required is sufficient agreement within the community about what counts as an appropriate performance of each of the practices comprising the web; then holistic objective regularities of performance can take the place of appeal to objective criteria of correctness in any particular case. I am not claiming that this situation always arises—we can specify a social practice generated by an objectively characterized response. The point is that it is not a necessary condition of the possibility of our community engaging in a set of social practices that we or anyone else be able to dissect that set into inferential or critical chains of practices, each ultimately governed by some objective response.

Next, notice that on this account, the measure of social practice is *our* social practice. When we treat a performance in this way we treat the performer as a member of *our* community, subject to *our* norms of appropriateness and justification. By translating, rather than causally explaining some performance, we extend our community (the one which engages in the social practices into which we translate the stranger's behavior) so as to include the stranger, and treat his performances as variants of our own. What we should remark about this is that who is or isn't a member of a particular community is a paradigm case of a matter which is social rather than objective according to our criterial classification. The community has final say over who its own members are. That is just the sort of issue that the community could not coherently be claimed to be wrong about. It might be inconvenient, or arbitrary for them to draw the boundaries around "us" in a certain way, but it is clearly not the sort of issue there is an objective fact to be right or wrong about, independent of what the community takes its own membership to be (of course they can *say* false things about who is in their community—what is decisive according to our criteria is how they behave or respond to the various candidates). So insofar as the distinction between the social and the objective is to be drawn as we have suggested, depending upon whether one copes with the behavior in question by causal explanation and manipulation or by translation, that distinction, while genuine, is social rather than objective, a matter of how the behavior is treated by some community rather than how it is in itself.[9] We will have some more to say about the crucial distinction between translation and explanation in the next section. For now, let us notice the consequences which this way of approaching things has for the larger issues we are concerned with.

If we can make the distinction between translation and causal explanation stick as two distinguishable ways of responding to the same behavior, then we can bypass the naturalism/non-naturalism dispute about the relation of norm to fact. For both parties to that dispute assumed that if there were any distinction between norms and facts it was an *objective* (factual, descriptive) difference. On our account, however, the difference between the normative order expressed in social practices and the factual order expressed in objective events and processes is a social difference in two ways of treating something. The social/objective distinction is social rather than objective.[10] If we now transfer this account of the distinction between the Realm of Nature (fact, description, cause) and the Realm of Freedom (norm, evaluation, practice) back to Kant's original suggestion that freedom consists in constraint by norms rather than simply by causes, the difference between being free and not being free becomes a social rather than an objective difference. The difference between these two "realms" is not an ontological one. The real distinction in the vicinity is between two ways of treating someone's behavior. According to this line of thought, we treat someone as free insofar as we consider him subject to the norms inherent in the social practices conformity to which is the criterion of membership in our community. He is free insofar as he is one of us. Insofar as we cope with him in terms of the causes which objectively constrain him, rather than the norms which constrain him via our practices, we treat him as an object, and unfree. There is no objective fact of the matter concerning his freedom to which we can appeal beyond the judgment of our own community. Of course the community can appeal to what it takes to be objective facts about a candidate for the extended membership granted by translation, but it is how they finally behave toward the candidate that matters. On this view, then, man is not objectively free.[11] Our talk about human freedom is rather a misleading way of talking about the difference between the way in which we treat members of our own community, those who engage in social practices with us, and the attitude we adopt toward those things we manipulate causally. Being constrained by or subject to norms is a matter of belonging to a community, and that is a matter of being *taken* to be a member by the rest of the community.

III

Reason for doubting that this notion of freedom is a finally satisfactory account emerges when we remember that anything at all can be treated as objective, and can also be treated as social. The two stances do not exclude each other. That any set of spatio-temporally locatable events is in principle capable of an objective causal explanation needs little arguing. It is a regulative ideal of natural science. When we translate another's utterance we need not presume that that utterance cannot also be explained as a part of the objective causal order, that it was not predictable (at least statistically) given sufficient information about the physiology, training, and recent environment of the speaker. Of course in situations where we are not now actually capable of such an explanation in terms of causes, there will be a certain amount of strain involved in treating an utterance as merely caused. But there is no difficulty of principle. Less obviously, anything can be treated as subject to the norms inherent in social practices, with a greater or lesser degree of strain. Thus a tree or a rock can become subject to norms insofar as we consider it as engaging in social practices. We can do this either by giving it a social role, for instance that of an oracle, or simply by translating its performances as utterances. Thus we can take the groaning of a branch to be the expression of exhaustion, or take the record-changer to be telling us that the record is over. Of course in such cases we must allow that the item in question is only a member of our community in a derivative and second-class fashion, for it is not capable of engaging in very many of our practices, or even of engaging in those very well. This is the strain involved in translating ordinary occurrences rather than simply explaining them, and no doubt this strain is the reason we usually don't do this. But there are border line cases, as with infants, cats, and temperamental automobiles. The force of the claim that the difference between the social and the objective is a difference in how they are treated by some community (by *us*) rather than an objective matter about which we could be right or wrong is that differences in convenience of one kind or another are the only differences to be accommodated here. If we want to treat the tree like one of us, the wind in its branches translated as utterances suggesting various courses of action, debating and justifying these, then the difficulty of finding a scheme which will make the tree sound sensible is the only obstacle.

It does not seem implausible to treat the difference between the social and the objective, and therefore the difference between the normative and the factual, as itself a social difference in this way. There are clear differences between translation and causal explanation of environing occurrences, and it is equally clear how those differences can generate criterial differences in objects treated one way or the other, once we have seen that such criterial classifications are not objective, ontological ones. But the account of freedom which results from conjoining this explanation of the norm/fact distinction to Kant's doctrine that freedom is constraint by norms is unattractive. Hegel objected to Kant's restriction of Reason and the norms and principles involved in it to the purely *formal* features of conduct. He regarded any account of freedom in terms of constraint by norms to be doomed to empty abstractness insofar as it ignores the *content* of the norms involved, linking freedom to the purely formal fact of constraint by some norm or other. The sort of cultural-historical particularity of the content of norms which Hegel sought in vain in Kant is secured by the token-reflexive reference in the formula — to be a Kantian rational-moral agent is to be one of *us*. This establishes only one side of the dialectic of social and individual development which Hegel urges, however. Communal autonomy is a necessary presupposition of the development of individual freedom. This latter, the freedom of the artist and the genius, is not to be identified with the former, the freedom of the peasant and the worthy Pietist. Hegel envisaged a higher form of positive freedom as self-expression and Bildung, enabled by but not reducible to constraint by communal norms. In the rest of this paper we consider such a notion, elaborated from Hegel's hints, but not intended as an exposition of the account presented by Hegel in his own original and ferocious idiom.

As above, we will take our lead from the consideration of the norms which govern linguistic activity. Our concern before was with the social dimension of these norms, with what constitutes membership in the community which has those norms, and consequently with what it is to be constrained by them. Our present concern is not with the nature of such social constraint, but with its issue. In particular, we want to examine the possibility that for some sets of norms, at any rate, constraint can be balanced by the creation of a new sort of "expressive freedom" of the individual. It is a striking fact that learning to engage in the social practices which are the use of a shared language does not simply enable us to use stock expressions ("Pass the salt," "Good morning," and so on) so as to navigate the common social situations which elicit them (communal feeding, working, and so on). In fact most of the sentences that make up our ordinary conversation are sentences that have never been uttered before in the history of the language, as Noam Chomsky has forcefully pointed out.[12] To acknowledge this fact is not to retreat from the characterization of language as a set of social practices in our sense, since it is still the linguistic community which decides whether some novel sentence is appropriately used or not. But we must not think of the social practices governing such communal judgments of appropriateness for novel utterances the way we think of those governing common sentences like "This is red," as the product of selective reinforcement of many different utterances of that very expression on various occasions.[13] Learning the language is not just learning to use a set of stock sentences which everybody else uses too. One has not learned the language, has not acquired the capacity to engage in the social practices which are the use of the language, until one can produce *novel* sentences which the community will deem appropriate, and understand the appropriate novel utterances of other members of the community (where the criterion for this capacity is the ability to make inferences deemed appropriate by the community). This emergent expressive capacity is the essence of natural languages.

We ought to understand this creative aspect of language use as the paradigm of a new kind of freedom, *expressive* freedom. When one has mastered the social practices comprising the use of a language sufficiently, one becomes able to do something one could not do before, to produce and comprehend novel utterances. One becomes capable not only of framing new descriptions of situations and making an indefinite number of novel claims about the world, but also becomes capable of forming new intentions, and hence of performing an indefinite number of novel *actions*, directed at ends one could not have without the expressive capacity of the language. This is a kind of positive freedom, freedom *to* do something rather than freedom *from* some constraint. For it is not as if the beliefs, desires, and intentions one comes to be able to express when one acquires a suitable language have been there all the time, hidden somehow "inside" the individual and kept from overt expression by some sort of constraint. Without a suitable language there are some beliefs, desires, and intentions that one simply cannot have. Thus we cannot attribute to a dog or a prelinguistic child the desire to prove a certain conjectured theorem, the belief that our international monetary system needs reform, or the intention to surpass Blake as a poet of the imagination. One comes to be able to do such things only by becoming able to engage in a wide variety of social practices, making discriminations and inferences and offering justifications concerning the subject matter in question to the satisfaction of the relevant community. And this is to say that it is only by virtue of being constrained by the norms inherent in social practices that one can acquire the freedom of expression which the capacity to produce and understand novel utterances exhibits.

As a form of positive freedom, this expressive capacity does not consist simply in a looseness of fit in the constraining norms. One is able to express novel contents not simply because an utterance can be linguistically appropriate on many different occasions, nor again because the boundaries between appropriate and inappropriate utterances are vague (as is always the case with social practices, whose "boundaries" — the division between what is and what is not in accord with them — are not objective but social, a matter of how the community does or would respond). No novelty is generated by the fact that the constraint constitutive of social practice has such an open texture that lots of antecedently possible performances are acceptable. Expressive freedom consists in the generation of new possibilities of performance which did not and could not exist outside the framework of norms inherent in the social practices which make up the language. One acquires the freedom to believe, desire, and intend the existence of novel states of affairs only insofar as one speaks some language or other, is constrained by some complex of social norms. Expressive freedom is made possible only by constraint by norms, and is not some way of evading or minimizing that constraint.

It is clear that not all sets of social practices, in the sense we have given to that term, will generate the sort of expressive freedom which we can discern as enabled by natural languages. So an account of positive freedom modelled on the creative use of language — the possibility of novel performances — will not take that freedom to be constituted by the abstract and purely formal fact that one is constrained by norms (that one engages in the social practices of some community, i.e. is accepted as doing so by some community). Not just constraint by norms but constraint by a particular kind of norms makes possible individual expressive freeedom, as Hegel envisaged. Nor should we think of that freedom merely as a fact or a state to be achieved and enjoyed. Expressive freedom, as the capacity to produce an indefinite number of novel appropriate performances in accord with a set of social practices one has mastered, is an ability which must be exercised to be maintained. Following Hegel's hint a little further, we can see the exercise of positive, expressive freedom as part of a process of cultivation [Bildung] of the self and of the community. For the capacity of individuals to produce novel performances in accord with a set of social practices makes possible novel social practices as well. For as the community becomes capable of novel responses (themselves subject to judgments of appropriateness), new social practices are generated. A social practice is defined as a respect of similarity evinced by performances which do or would (under circumstances which must be specified whenever we specify a particular practice) elicit some response from the community. Some sets of social practices, paradigmatically natural languages, make possible novel performances on the part of those who participate in them, and these in turn make possible further social practices. Particular novel performances and the social practices which make them possible and are made possible by them, on the one hand, and individuals and the community they comprise on the other, thus develop together in a fashion Hegel marked with the term "dialectical." Thus a child's relative mastery of a natural language first makes possible the production and comprehension of appropriate novel utterances. This capacity in turn enables the child to submit to stricter social linguistic disciplines, such as govern the criticism or production of literary works or legal briefs. At the level of the community, new disciplines are founded by the novel productions of individuals—the social practices which comprise a scientific or academic discipline are produced in this way, and make possible further novel performances and their appreciation. The self-cultivation of an individual consists in the exercise and expansion of expressive freedom by subjecting oneself to the novel discipline of a set of social practices one could not previously engage in, in order to acquire the capacity to perform in novel ways, express beliefs, desires, and intentions one could not previously even have, whether in arts or sports. The cultivation of the community consists in the development of new sets of social practices, at once the result of individual self-cultivation (producing novel performances which, institutionalized as responses to other performances make possible new social practices) and the condition of it. It is in this sense that we speak of the "culture" of a group as the set of social practices they engage in.[14]

It is clearly not possible to specify in advance the expressive capacities of different sets of social practices, for instance in an attempt to compare two languages along this dimension. For the peculiar dialectical pattern of development of expressive capacities itself continually creates novel expressive dimensions by making possible desires and intentions which could not operate at earlier stages in the cultivation of a particular community or individual. Self-cultivating individuals and communities, developing their expressive capacities according to this dialectic of shared practice and novel performance will accordingly be a *great* deal more difficult to account for in terms of objective causal processes than will social practices which don't make possible indefinite numbers of novel performance-types. Here the quantitative difference in convenience between coping with behavior by treating it as objective and seeking a causal explanation and treating it as social and seeking a translation of it into our own practices assumes such proportions that it is plausible to treat it as a qualitative difference[15] (this does not, of course, entail that we take it as an objective difference rather than as a social difference of how things are treated which is based on the objective difficulty of discovering adequate causal accounts. We are, after all, familiar with objective processes which generate new types of behavior.) Expressive freedom is thus a species of the Kantian genus of freedom as constraint by norms, a specification and supplementation of that general notion.

The final suggestion I want to make by way of recommending this way of talking about human freedom, both individual and social, is to note the sort of legitimation of political and social constraint which it makes possible. Hegel and some of his admirers (notably Marx and T. H. Green) rejected the liberal enlightenment account of justification of constraint of the individual by social and political institutions which had found that justification in the extent to which social organization made possible the greater satisfaction of individual wants, considered as fixed and specifiable in abstraction from the sort of community the individual participates in. The Hegelian tradition was acutely aware of the debt which an individual's desires owe to his community, but did not wish to succumb entirely to the antidemocratic and anti-individualist implications of an account which made the community paramount. The general form of their resolution of this dilemma, which can be reproduced in less metaphysical terms in the idiom of social practices, is this. Constraint of the individual by the social and political norms inherent in communal practices may be legitimate insofar as that constraint makes possible for the individual an expressive freedom which is otherwise impossible for him. Creative self-cultivation is possible only by means of the discipline of the social practices which constrain one, just as the production of a poem requires not only submission to the exigencies of a shared language, but the stricter discipline of the poetic tradition as well. One must speak some language to say anything at all, and the production and comprehension of novel performances requires a background of shared constraint. Political constraint is illegitimate insofar as it is not in the service of the cultivation of the expressive freedom of those who are constrained by it.

To say this is not so much to present a theory as to present the form of a theory, a way of talking about political legitimation and human freedom, an idiom. It does not, for instance, even begin to settle questions about trade-offs between different varieties of negative and positive freedom. For one cannot project a Utopia from these considerations, nor can one abstractly evaluate political institutions according to the kinds and quality of expressive freedom and self-cultivation they enable and encourage. For it is precisely the production of *novel* expressive possibilities which is admired in this account, and that novelty in principle escapes classification and prediction by a priori theorizing. The idiom of expressive freedom is useful, insofar as it is useful, for those caught up in the dialectic of individual and communal cultivation, of shared practice and novel performance, to reflectively control possible changes in practice within a concrete situation. The value of this idiom, as of any other, consists in the possibilities for novel expression which it engenders, by way of comprehending and directing this dialectical process.[16]

NOTES

1. I am not concerned to *expound* Kant (or, later, Hegel), but to develop various consequences of quite general features of his views which can be discussed in abstraction from detailed consideration of particular texts.

2. "Truth and Assertibility," *The Journal of Philosophy* 73 (1976): 137–89.

3. See Ludwig Wittgenstein's *Investigations* I, sec. 198ff.

4. The distinction between these two sorts of explanation will be our topic in the next section.

5. On such linguistic division of labor, and in particular the importance of the possibility of adjudication of some disputes by expert elites to be socially constituted only in the *future*, see Putnam's "Meaning of Meaning" on pages 215–72 of his *Mind, Language and Reality, Philosophical Papers*, vol. II (Cambridge, 1976).

6. Among contemporary philosophers, Wilfrid Sellars has made the most of this basic sort of distinction between the objective and the social. He has argued throughout his works for the importance of such a distinction between a causal or descriptive order and a normative order of justification and reason giving (a dualism indebted to Kant, Schopenhauer, and the early Wittgenstein, rather than Descartes). This point is one of the keys to the classic "Empiricism and the Philosophy of Mind" in Sellars' *Science, Perception, and Reality* (London, 1963). See also chapter 7 of *Science and Metaphysics* (London, 1968). Richard Rorty elaborates this perspective in his *Philosophy and the Mirror of Nature* (Princeton, 1979), to which I am indebted.

7. Although I cannot argue the matter here, I believe that the social practice idiom offers a quite general account of the nature of normative constraint. To show this, however, would entail discussing such issues as the relation of moral norms to other sorts of social norms, a project I don't want to enter here.

8. Jurgen Habermas, In *Knowledge and Human Interests* (Boston, 1971), distinguished the sort of explanation one gives of causal phenomena "logically" — claiming that causal explanation employs a "monologic" of impersonal inference, while interpretation is always "dialogic" in character. While I am not sure what this logical rendering comes to, the account developed here of the difference between the social and objective coincides in many particulars with Habermas' story about the differences between control and conversation.

9. The point here is reminiscent of D. C. Dennett's view about the justification of the adoption of the "intentional stance" (in "Intentional Systems," *Journal of Philosophy* 68 [1971]: 87–106). A difference is that social practices need not exhibit any "intentional" character. I have discussed elsewhere (see note 2) some of what is required of a social practice in order for it appropriately to be taken as making a claim that something is the case. I would thus seek to account for intentionality in terms of social practices. J. F. Rosenberg has argued forcefully against the cogency of the reverse order of explanation in the opening chapters of his *Linguistic Representation* (Dordrecht, 1975).

10. It is a measure of the superiority of this idiom over more traditional ones that the possibility of this sort of view would not come readily to mind so long as the issue is formulated as a norm/fact, or evaluation/description distinction. For what does it mean to say that these distinctions are not factual or descriptive, but normative and evaluative? And yet this is what we are claiming, in the specific sense captured by the social/objective rendering.

11. Though of course on this account that freedom is not merely subjective and imaginary either. It is rather a social matter, and the criterial

classification distinguishes the social from both the subjective (which is whatever some individual takes it to be) and the objective (which is what it is regardless of how anyone takes it to be). I have argued that this criterial classificaton is itself social rather than objective.

12. *Aspects of the Theory of Syntax* (Cambridge, Mass., 1965), chap. 1.

13. W. V. Quine's elephant topiary example in the first chapter of *Word and Object* (Cambridge, 1960), suggests that he has in mind the latter type of sentences exclusively, for it is difficult to see how his story is appropriate to the former.

14. Defining culture in this way, we may distinguish three sorts of substructure: individual repertories, traditions, and institutions. Each individual member of the community has a repertory of social practices comprising all those he is capable of engaging in (producing performances appropriate according to) at a particular time. Such a repertory has a history, insofar as it is different at one time than at another. Those practices have in common a particular human being who engages in them. The practices which make up a *tradition* share a common ancestry. A tradition is a tree structure whose nodes are sets of social practices engaged in by individuals (one individual per node, perhaps not his entire repertory) and whose branches are the transmission or training to engage in the social practices which are transformed. A social institution is then composed at any time of individuals and sub-sets of their current repertories which are their *institutional roles*. The development of the institution is the evolution of those roles in their mutual relation.

15. Although we cannot pursue the matter here, it is plausible to identify the difference between objective causal explanation and translation of social practices (where the criterion for adopting one or the other stance is the appearance of dialectical development by the cultivation of expressive freedom as described above) with the difference which neo-Kantians of the last century perceived between the methods of *Erklärung* and *Verstehen*, which were the distinguishing features of the natural and cultural sciences respectively (and which we might think of as codifying the difference between things which have *natures* and things which have *histories*).

16. I would like to acknowledge the many helpful comments Richard Rorty and Annette Baier kindly provided on an earlier version.

8. THE RATIONAL GOVERNANCE OF PRACTICE

Frederick L. Will

Throughout modern philosophy, and especially after the brief confident upsurge of early rationalism, there have been questions and controversies about the capacities and limits of rational processes in the governance of practice. More recently, in the past two decades, developments in a variety of fields, and particularly in the philosophy of science, have brought to the forefront of attention the social determinants of a variety of processes hitherto presumed to be paradigmatically rational ones. These developments have given to the questions and controversies about rational governance a new turn. To the extent that the processes of observation, reasoning, criticism, judgment, evaluation, and so on, traditionally associated with rational governance, are recognized to be thoroughly determined by, thoroughly rooted in, social practice, it has seemed to many philosophically sensitive writers increasingly difficult to continue to maintain for them their claims to rationality. The question, then, to which this paper is addressed is, Can a view of reason that recognizes and indeed emphasizes its determinants in social practice adequately account for the function that reason is commonly conceived capable of performing in the governance of practice?

I

As is illustrated in the preceding paragraph, the terms "reason," "rationality," and similar ones are, in one accepted philosophical usage, employed to cover a very broad set of forms of procedure, departures from which by relevant activities would correspondingly justify their classification as arational or irrational. In this broad usage reason is not contrasted with, but rather embraces, a vast variety of procedures in the cognitive disciplines, the practical arts, and everyday life. It *includes*, for example, observation, experimentation, the collection and processing of data, and attending to and assessing testimony, as in a court of law.

Another common usage of these same terms is much narrower than this. In it the main contrast signified by "reason" and "rational" is with other cognitive activities, such as observation and the others just mentioned. Here the terms are reserved for activities closely associated with *reasoning*: with inferring, deducing, calculating, and similar activities that fit easily into the rubric of rational *thought*. In the question posed above, whether certain processes of governance can properly be viewed as rational, it is the former, broader sense of this key term that is intended. A consequence of the impulse in the classic modern rationalist philosophers to identify reason with rational thought was that for them the question of the rational governance of practice tended to become translated into the question of the competence in this regard of the reflective processes that fall under this rubric.

The term "governance" is used here in a very broad way to cover all the processes by which, in both individuals and groups, social practices are developed and regulated; strengthened or weakened; changed or preserved against change; and sometimes extinguished. These processes may be gradual and slow, or rapid and abrupt; and there are great variations among them in the degree to which they are conscious, intentional, or deliberate. The more conscious, reflective forms of these processes are of special but not exclusive relevance to the topic of rational governance. That there are rational processes that at times affect the character of practices does not of course imply that at these times the effect has, as it were, its sole ontological source in these processes, that they stand to the effect in the relation of a quite sufficient condition. As in the case of what are discriminated as the causes of physical states or events, what we discriminate as rational determinants of social practice produce their effects, not as solitary creators, but as joint producers in conjunction with a set of background conditions which for the purpose of the attribution of effectiveness and responsibility in this situation normally may be neglected.

The term "practice" likewise is used here very broadly. It applies to modes of procedure of *both* thought and action, and in all fields of thought and action: in morals, politics, and law; in intellectual disciplines such as mathematics, the physical sciences and the social studies; in art, religion, and in philosophy itself. Commonly the singular term "practice" carries the connotation of actual modes of procedure, practices actually followed in some community; and that usage is generally followed here. It is sometimes necessary to refer to accepted modes of procedure plurally. In such cases the plural form will be used with some qualifying term like "accepted," except where such a reading is already sufficiently indicated by the context.

"Practice" and "practices" are not usual ways of referring to modes of thought in the theory of knowledge. In that field important broad patterns of thought are for a variety of reasons more commonly referred to by means of such expressions as "concepts," "ideas," or "conceptual schemes." These terms have the serious disadvantage of suggesting, almost irresistibly to many, that the items whose criticism or governance is under examination are features, components, or states of one or more private minds. If one uses the popular language of "concepts," for example, one needs to take special pains to emphasize and issue reminders that what are being referred to under this title are in a very real and profound sense social.[1] There may be important disanalogies, but there are also strong analogies which support the proposals of such diverse recent writers as Ernest Gellner and Stephen Toulmin to assimilate them to social institutions.[2] Concepts are connected with linguistic signs of a certain sort. But they are not internal mental correlates of these signs. They represent ways of proceeding that entail, that require in order to be what they are, their generation and preservation in the rich matrix of communal and social living. In order to give emphasis to this aspect of our intellectual resources the terms "practice" and "practices" have been preferred here.

II

The thought that the processes of governance of practice could be both rational and deeply rooted in practice has not been much favored in modern philosophy, which has in the main followed a contrary view forcefully advanced by Descartes in the *Discourse on Method* and the *Rules for the Direction of the Mind*. The extreme divorcement maintained between reason and accepted practice in the dominant tradition of modern philosophy was a consequence of a presumption that since reason, as a resource in the governance of practice, must be granted to have the capacity to transcend and oppose practice, it must be conceived, as an authority and agent of governance, to be independent of practice. The passage from condition to consequence in this conviction excluded the possibility, little contemplated in this philosophical tradition, that rational governance of practice represented a capacity in accepted practice to transcend, oppose, and in other ways modify itself. Adhering to this conviction, a long line of modern philosophers through the years persevered in the search for resources in the governance of practice that are identifiable as rational and independent of all established institutions and accepted practices.[3] The plausible general loci of such resources were clearly *experience* and *reason*, employing the latter term now in its more narrow common usage to signify rational *thought*. But these familiar resources, as they are normally employed, are thoroughly permeated by social practices. It was therefore proposed that by careful intellectual analysis we might eliminate from them their conceived unessential and invalidating social elements, arriving at, as a purified form of experience, pure sensation, and a purified form of thought engaged solely with the relations of what were conceived to be certain very intimate, personal intellectual resources, namely, our own "ideas."

This general conception of rational governance, whether fleshed out in the general rationalist way exemplified by Descartes or in the empiricist way pioneered by Bacon and later refined by Hume, was riven by a fundamental contradiction. The more that philosophical analysis succeeded in eliminating the social components from these apparently competent resources, the less competent were the resultant forms for the purpose for which they were sought. By the time of Locke confidence in what in the way of knowledge could be achieved by "the perception of the connexion and agreement, or disagreement and repugnancy, of any of our ideas" was beginning seriously to fade. Fifty years later the incapacity of both the would-be pure surrogates of experience and thought were exposed by Hume. Neither of these, Hume convincingly demonstr ed, could provide the sought-for governance separately; nor could they do it in conjunction. As governors of practice, experience and thought, in their impure and socially infected forms, were competent but fundamentally illegitimate; in their pure and asocial forms, they were legitimate but utterly incompetent. Striking examples of this incompetence cited by Hume were, in knowledge, the incapacity of rational thought, joined with experience, to validate *any* conclusions from that experience (induction), and in ethical inquiry, the incapacity of these to discern any differences in value, even so gigantic a one as that between the scratching of a finger and "the destruction of the whole world." Rational governance of practice Hume therefore judged to be a myth, concluding that something altogether different, which he called "custom," not only is but must be the great guide of life. A true child of the Enlightenment, operating within a thoroughly Cartesian divorcement of reason and practice, he was constitutionally incapable of recognizing, what sometimes seems to be obtruding into his reflections, that rational governance of practice and life is to be found, not external to these, but resident in them, in custom-guided life itself.

The historical trial of the claims of independent sense and thought was recently reenacted in a shortened form in the rise and subsidence of logical positivism, and indeed in the life of one philosopher, namely, Wittgenstein. After having formulated in the *Tractatus* a constitution for logical positivism, in his later philosophy he advanced most profound arguments against the claims of those two classical resources, sensory and rational intuition, to constitute sources of governance altogether external to and independent of practice. His criticism of putative independent sense is illustrated in his discussion of a private language and of "seeing as" in the *Philosophical Investigations*. His criticism of independent a priori thought, rational intuition, is illustrated in his discussions of logical necessity in the same book and in the *Remarks on the Foundations of Mathematics*.

The views of Wittgenstein on reason that are implicit in his writings on mathematics, perception, and knowledge generally are recent examples of an opposed tradition that goes back now about a hundred and fifty years. The pioneering expositor in this tradition, occupying the position in it that Descartes occupied in the more dominant tradition, was Hegel. Other, more recent expositors have been the two giant figures in American pragmatism, Peirce and Dewey. One most important point upon which this newer tradition opposed the older one was the relation between reason, as a governor of practice, and practice itself. Where the older view, following the divorcement of reason from practice to a logical conclusion, conceived of reason as a resource accessible to individuals independently of their relations with other individuals, independently of their membership in communities, the newer view has maintained that reason, and rational governance with it, can only be understood when they are conceived to be themselves fundamentally social.

III

Among the considerations that must count favorably for a social view of rational governance are the striking reversals encountered by advocates of the older individualist view in their efforts to locate a rational touchstone for thought and action in some resource quite independent of social life and practice. Some of these reversals were briefly noted in the preceding section. More positive considerations for regarding rational governance as immanent in social life and practice lie in the capacity of such a view to perform more satisfactorily with respect to rational governance in the two chief ways that any theory of governance must perform with respect to its subject matter. Such a theory must, first, account satisfactorily for what, independently of these rival theories, are recognized to be clear cases of rational governance. And, secondly, on the basis of success in performing the first function, it must apply illuminatingly to the unclear and controversial cases in such a way as to give guidance concerning how individuals and groups should act in those situations in which rational governance is called for and in which alternative paths of thought or action open to them affect the way in which governance shall proceed.

Rational governance is not some strange exotic plant that we need to visit intellectual conservatories to see. We are acquainted with it from our earliest years. And its ancestry in our individual personal lives includes aspects of our lives and experience that are features of our original nature. If we conceive of practices on the model of the habits, the recurring patterns of response that we as individuals display in our behavior, there is no doubt that to some extent our behavioral patterns are determined by our physical and psychological inheritance, and not exclusively by our physical and social environment. Once developed from whatever original physical and original determinants they have, a primary feature of human habits, and likewise practices, is their flexibility, their capacity, as dispositions to act, to adapt to and be modified by a great variety of conditions in the contexts in which they are translated for dispositions into actual performances. Included under the wide term "conditions of performance" are both personal aspects of those engaged in the performances and aspects of the impersonal environment in which they are performing. In this terminology the personal environment of any particular performance will include, as a most important component, many and varied other dispositions to act with which any given disposition is related and which may inhibit, intensify, or otherwise modify its realization.

In respect to their relations with such conditions of performance, the habits of individuals and the social practices with which they greatly intersect are very much alike. When habits are learned, when practices are mastered, more is acquired by the individuals engaged in the process than a simple connection in action between some specific occasion and some equally specific response. The driver follows a practice when, upon seeing the green arrow on the traffic signal, he moves the car in the direction of the arrow; or when, hearing a rapidly approaching siren, he moves the car out of the main traffic lanes. But this description by no means includes all he has learned to do, if he is a competent driver, in these and similar circumstances. The forms of action exemplified here extend far beyond the sequences of these immediate occasions and responses. They include a capacity to adjust one's way of proceeding to an array of wider conditions of performance. These will include in these cases other aspects of the present driving and traffic situation, and also other habits or practices with which the driver is equipped and which likewise help to determine what is proper procedure in situations like these.

We miss an aspect of practices that is vital for philosophical understanding if we restrict ourselves to those features that may be thought of as molecules composed of atomic bits of behavior, themselves thought of as fixed responses to limited sensory cues. Three-quarters of a century ago, John Dewey, a prominent psychologist of the day as well as philosopher, emphasized this point in an important paper on reflex theory, arguing that we thoroughly misunderstand learned human behavior when we think of it as a congeries or collection of bits of responses to bits of stimulation.[4] One who learns a practice as if he were a beginning soldier being imprinted with elements of close-order drill learns to behave in a way so odd and eccentric that Bergson could make it an important element in his theory of laughter. One essential thing missing from such learning is an understanding of how the more obvious, immediate responses that exemplify the practices are determined in character by features of the conditions of performance, including therewith other dispositions to act, other forms of procedure, in short, other practices. This means that in following practices one is performing in a way that is governed in a great degree and in a highly complex way. Action is suited to circumstances, with of course varying degrees of success; and an essential aspect of this suiting of action to circumstances is the coordinating with each other of dispositions to action represented by divergent practices. Practices do, so to speak, confront circumstances, but not as individuals. Rather, in the metaphor employed by W. V. Quine in speaking of the coordination of statements with sense experience, they do so as corporate bodies.

Some rational governance, according to the view taken here, is an integral part of our accepted practices, of practice itself. One cannot be trained in these practices without being in some degree infused with rational governance as it is entailed in the following of these practices, in the consequent coordination and adjustment of them with each other and with various other components of the conditions of performance. Neither of these two chief components of the coordinating conditions of practices may be neglected. That practices adjust *in concert* with other practices to the circumstances in which the performance of the practices takes place should not obscure from us that they do adjust; and that they do adjust should not obscure from us that they adjust to circumstances while adjusting to each other. Both these aspects of coordination are indispensable and interdependent components of that form of rational governance that is learned with practices, because it is incorporated in the practices learned. It is governance of this kind, among other things, that a soldier or sailor learns when he learns how to occupy a post to stand watch. It includes a kind of flexibility of response that the once celebrated boy on the burning deck in a signal degree did not display when he stood fixed amid the rolling flames and booming shots simply because there was no one to inform him that his duty to remain had under these circumstances been overridden. It is this, in a very fine and complex way, that the skilled surgeon is expected to learn, partly through instruction and partly through experience about what is possible, desirable, optional, and necessary, in his craft. And it is this, in a simpler, more homely way, that one learns when one learns to cook, do carpentry, make cabinets, paint houses, drive a motor car, pilot an airplane, play a game like tennis, or participate in a sport like fishing.

IV

Thus far, emphasis has been upon the point that rational governance is learned by individuals in learning practices, because governance is integral to the practices themselves. This kind of governance might be called "governance *in* practice." It is governance in application to actual instances of action, governance primarily engaged in the control of such instances, utilizing relations of coordination between practices and the conditions of their performance that are already instituted and implicit in accepted practices. This may be contrasted with another aspect of the governing process, the one that is the primary object of concern in this paper. It might be called "governance *of* practice," being those processes by which the relations of coordination utilized in the governance of action are instituted, annulled, or altered. Though these processes are contrasted here, what needs to be stressed is their common character and close relations. They may be viewed as complementary phases of one fundamental process. To varying extents, depending upon circumstances, they commonly go together, since ordinarily one effect of the employment of practices in the governance of action is some alteration, which in some cases may be minute, in the practices themselves, and since ordinarily, as is exemplified in the case of such instances of governance as are represented in legal decisions defining laws, the occasion for governance *of* practice is ordinarily some difficulty encountered by governance *in* practice. Grasping the close relations between these two phases of the governantial process is a most important step toward answering the chief question to which this paper is addressed.[5] Taking advantage of this distinction, one may say that when an individual learns practices, he learns governance in both these respects. Part of what is instilled in the learner is what is accepted in the community in the way of an achieved coordination or governance of these practices. The culture provides for its continuance by, among other things, reproducing this aspect of itself, more or less adequately, and with some attendant variation, in the learning individual. But the individual who learns does so, not just as passive matter being given form by a cultural mold, but as, in this respect, a reproduction in miniature of the teaching community. Reproduced in him is not merely the product achieved, but also in some degree the process. In acting as a member of the community in accordance with these practices he replicates naturally in some degree the process by which the community has achieved and repeatedly continues to re-achieve composition among these practices.

Some proficiency in the skill or art of rational governance is thus in an obvious way inherent in accepted practices, and, in addition to whatever of this skill or art is transmitted to new members of the community by physical or psychological inheritance, is transmitted with these practices in the processes of culturation. In a less obvious way, inherent in the practices is some proficiency in the skill or art of altering this governance from the state already achieved. This likewise is an endowment of the individual, and likewise partly from nature and partly from nurture. This proficiency varies widely as a community endowment from one community to another. There appears to be wide divergence in this respect in the education of the young between mainland China and, say, Israel, and, by and large, between the Catholic and the Protestant churches in the United States. The proficiency also varies widely, in the same community, from individual to individual. The practices with which he is launched upon the world, like the laws which at any given time have to be interpreted in government by the judiciary and administered by the executive, are components of systems of governance that are designed to achieve coordination of practices in two main respects: with each other and with further conditions of performance, including those of neither a psychological nor a social nature. Governance may fail in its coordination of practices with each or, more typically, jointly with both of these components of the conditions of performance.

Each individual, in the governance of his own conduct, is thus in some degree in the position of a judge in the legal system when the latter is called upon to make decisions effecting determinations in case law or in constitutional provision that are similarly called for by some serious lack of coordination of what is manifest, recognized law either with other similarly manifest laws or with non-legal aspects of the conditions to which these laws apply. To some extent the settled governance that came to the individual largely from his community, but which, as he matures, becomes in further degrees of his own making, needs to be further determined, refined, redefined, rectified, even reconstituted.

V

The very fact that the rational governance of social practice effected by the social processes just described can and does change has appeared to many to lead to a most serious skeptical consequence. This has been the subject of much discussion during the past two decades.

The elements of the apparent problem are simple. If rational governance, as a product, is identified with the result achieved by these processes, and if that result is subject to change—sometimes striking and rapid change—has not the identification of governance with these changeable and changing products excluded from rational governance the processes by which changes in these products occur? This has seemed to many to lead to a view of rational governance that applies only to and within systems of governed practices, that does not therefore apply to the processes by which one system is replaced by another, and which therefore has the result that these changes of governance—"revolutions" when the changes are large and abrupt—must be conceived to be effected by other than rational means. Rational governance of social practice, on this reading of the matter, is restricted to governance within such systems of practices as have been referred to in recent philosophy of science as paradigms, conceptual frameworks, systems of categories, or conceptual schemes.

It should now begin to be apparent that this difficulty, urged repeatedly against a social view of rational governance, does not necessarily accompany such a view. In particular, it is not a difficulty for the version of the view advanced here, but arises rather from a view of practices and their governance that the preceding pages have been careful to reject. This is a view which logically separates governance from practices, or what amounts to much the same thing, separates governance *in* practices from governance *of* practices and then identifies rational governance with the former, with the consequence that the processes by which the latter are effected are rendered intractable to rational governance. The roots of such a view lie in a tendency in much thought about social practices to think of them in the way that was criticized in detail in Section III, that is, exclusively as templates for limited segments of action. When practices are thought of in this abstract way, detached from life, there is no dynamism in them, no fundamental internal ground of change. And the same holds for any changes of governance that can be regarded as normal features of the functioning of practices in individual and social life. Fundamental change in governance is then thought to entail processes of a kind radically different from those of rational governance. On the other hand, when practices are looked upon more concretely, and the radical separation between them and their rational governance eliminated, fundamental changes in governance need no longer be regarded as beyond the capacities of rational governance itself. Such changes may be produced, though assuredly they are not always produced, by processes that differ greatly not in kind, but in dimension, from those adjustments of practices to the conditions of procedure that are in some degree constant features of living practice and that have been identified here as defining characteristics of the kind of governance that is rational.

Indeed the very changes that for some views of rational governance are surds or anomalies, are for the view sketched here prime, paradigm examples of rationality itself. That there are such changes is an immediate corollary of this view in its application to both individuals and social groups. Changes of governance are sometimes stimulated by perceived or somehow dimly felt inadequacies in governance as it has been achieved and is in place at any given time. The impulse to change in this manner need not be attributed to some mystic urge toward fulfilment present throughout individual and social life. Some change in governance is a natural consequence of governance, of life lived in accordance with practices coordinated in achieved governance. For not only do the conditions under which life is lived and practices engaged in change, generating inadequacies in previously achieved arrangements; so that present inadequacies may be attributed simply to failure of old governance to meet intervening new conditions. It is also the case that the success of previous arrangements may alter life in such a way as to lead to the modification or rejection of some of the very arrangements of practices and governance that have made this state of life possible; so that in these instances the inadequacy of old arrangements to meet new conditions, their failure, is a consequence of their preceding success. As it is characteristic of life lived through certain practices to undergo change that in some degree, sometimes small and sometimes great, renders the conditions of life, including the achieved governance of practices, inadequate, it is the soberest of truths that change is endemic to governance. Though some changes in governance, both large and small, are imposed upon governance from without, some are in some degree the natural products of governance itself. And however widely these latter changes may vary in dimensions, they are natural extensions of the homely day-to-day processes by which individuals and groups adapt general modes of action, within accepted parameters, to each other and to specific conditions of application.

What those parameters are, how strictly or how loosely particular action is determined by accepted practices, varies widely among practices and, even for the same practices, from one set of circumstances to another. Similarly, with respect to governance of the practices themselves, there is wide variation in the amount of indeterminacy that various systems of governance permit. Indeterminacy of governance in itself represents no failure in governance, since governance is not needed at every point at which practices impinge upon one another. It is needed at those points at which indeterminacy leads to conflict in action or incipient action, to either intrapersonal or interpersonal conflict, or, as commonly, a complex combination of both. Significant changes in large-scale governance of social practice are for the most part made by community action. And this, again for the most part, is not by referenda, or legislation, or judicial decision, but by direct changes taking place in modes of action as a natural consequence of living according to these forms. These changes take place, both in individuals and in communities, by far mostly in alterations in modes of action made by agents who have no clear understanding or appreciation of the process in which they are engaged. They are aware principally that they are responding to difficulties in accepted routines, accepted ways of acting and thinking. But in so doing, from time to time, more or less unknowingly, they make minor changes in the design of the governance which cumulatively they eventually realize, sometimes with a sharp shock of surprise, have produced a grand change in the *Gestalt*, in the grand design of the whole. The individual awakes one morning, as it were, to discover, what perhaps others understood long before, that he is no longer an agnostic but a believer, just as Pascal ("*Cela vous fera croire*") predicted, or no longer a believer but an infidel, as Pascal with equal logic, in different circumstances, might have expected. The community similarly awakes to find that it no longer believes that its kings rule by divine right, or, to take a striking historical example, now believes that the mother of Jesus Christ, though not fully divine like her son, was indeed a demigoddess. What these examples exhibit in changes in practices of belief can easily be exhibited as replicated in changes in practices of overt action. The individual more or less unwittingly has become a drunkard, or a teetotaler; the nation has become imperial rather than republican, the community hedonistic rather than moralistic in its attitude toward sexual practices.

The more conscious, deliberate forms of rational governance exemplified in philosophic judgment in science, morals, history, law, or whatever, whether these judgments are made by individuals or by groups, are all of a piece with the less conscious and less deliberate forms from which they take their rise. The story of the development leads back in individuals and the race through a regression of generally simpler forms to kindred primitive resources for response that are now part of our native endowment as members of this biological species and that perhaps have their material basis in us, not in the pineal gland, but in the central nervous system. What the more conscious, deliberate forms of governance are capable of contributing to the governance process in a special measure is understanding of the process (Hegel would have described it as reason becoming aware of itself) and, with that understanding, also in special measure, some sense of the present movement of governance, some vision of the character that this governance, if permitted to move according to its own inner logic, will have in its immediately next stages. To adapt to this situation the metaphor employed by Plato in the *Crito*, philosophical thought, in whatever field it is generated and nurtured by "the Laws," has some capacity, the Laws having been assimilated in it, and itself assimilated to the Laws, to perform a service for the Laws. As a portion of the photosensitive tissue of the Laws, developed into a kind of intellectual eye, it is capable of looking with special depth and breadth into some aspects of life lived according to and through the practices and institutions of the Laws. On the basis of a capacity for discernment somewhat broader and deeper than that commonly generated in the conduct of the affairs of ordinary life, philosophical thought—be it in doctor, lawyer, merchant, prince, teacher, preacher, or whatever—can offer to the Laws informed judgment and advice (often disguised as categorical imperatives) concerning the nurture of the practices and institutions with which it is concerned. Embraced under the term "nurture" here are both the strengthening and the weakening, the cherishing and the depreciating, the invigorating and the debilitating, in whole or in part, of individual items in the complex of practices and institutions. The availability of this specially informed judgment and advice may in some cases be decisive in determining in a substantial way the course that the practices and institutions will take; but ordinarily the effect is much more modest. Even where not decisive it may, if well-founded, be helpful—in an intermediary way analogous to that of Socrates with the knowing slave boy—in facilitating a course of development already substantially determined by other grounds. By rendering the determination of certain developments more patent, it may also render their realization easier, less generally disruptive, less costly in harmful side-effects than they would otherwise be. Thus philosophic judgment based upon the Laws, speaks for the Laws. It attempts to say, in however tentative and fallible a way, what the Laws, yet inarticulate upon the point, would say, if they could speak upon it now: what, if the anticipated developments should be realized, the Laws will say when in the idiom of concrete historical reality they eventually do speak.

So speaks the court, when, performing this philosophical function in its own domain, it makes a *juridical* judgment upon a contested point of law, as distinguished from a judgment of fact. So speaks the judge when he supports such a judgment with a corresponding juridical opinion. So he speaks when the interpretation of the law, as he engages in it, is the kind that it is his vocation to make, when the term "interpretation" is not a misnomer for a form of covert, oligarchical legislation. Much of current discussion of activism versus strict interpretation of the law, particularly of constitutional law, would be helpfully illumined by a recognition of the implication of this point upon the seemingly obvious but greatly deceptive familiar distinction between the operations of making new law and discovering what the law already is. Here, as at many other places, a neat, well-worn distinction may serve to distort, rather than clarify the reality in which it is drawn. A decision speaking for the law, interpreting the law as it is, does not necessarily pronounce old law, since the law changes; and a pronouncement of *old* law, does not necessarily pronounce recognized law, since what needs to be explored in old law, and what is recognized or understood therein, is likewise subject to change. If we do suppose that interpretation of the law, as thus construed, is an example of a process that can be fully rational, and its results legitimate or valid, we can then begin to understand how a process that is fundamentally social in its basis and dynamics, can itself be a fully rational, legitimating one: and, furthermore, rational and legitimating, not in spite of but *because* of its being thus fundamentally social. Those whose vision has not been obscured by the blinding clarity of the distinction between "is" and "ought" will be in a position to recognize how, in this particular way in this context, "is" itself established "ought." Others further off the present beaten path in their philosophical tuition may recognize here a kernel of truths in those seemingly perverse pronouncements of Hegel, already misinterpreted in his own day, assimilating the rational to the real (the actual: *das Wirkliche*).

VI

Two remaining points about the general process of rational governance call for attention here. First, having come to the point of recognizing the relation of mutual dependence and corrigibility that hold among those segments of social practice that we mark off and identify as individual practices, it is important that one not overestimate the degree of changeability at any one time in the whole system of practices that these relations entail. The philosophical skepticism that has haunted modern philosophy since its beginnings in the seventeenth century no doubt has something to do with the fact that up to the present time the changeability and hence instability of practices has tended to be exaggerated. It is as if without some firm center of unchangeable practices, the totality must resolve into flux; as if the only alternative to Plato or Kant on these matters is Heraclitus; as if once pried loose from the fixity of the forms or the categories, there are no elements whatever of ballast making for stability in the system.

Some remedy for the intellectual vertigo that such thoughts as these are capable of generating lies in the emphasis, implicit in the term, upon the social character of practices. This is by no means sufficient, however. Typically it leads to a displacement of the relativism from a relation between individuals to one between communities, often speech communities, and we are invited, then, to consider the contingency of our practices in relation to those of Eskimos, exotic aborigines, the inmates of the closed society of George Orwell's *1984*, strangers from outer space, or even porpoises. There is no one specific remedy that can be invoked at this point. But it is some help to emphasize a further character of practices which is much more readily apparent than when one employs the idiom of concepts, namely, that practices are rooted in and depend for their continuance, not only upon the common native components of human nature, but also upon a non-human, extra-personal and extra-social environment in which life is carried on in accordance with the practices. With these materials and upon this stage the dramas of life are played, and the nature of the materials and the character of the stage are most important determinants—representing both opportunities and hindrances—of the kind of plays that may be performed. Over the millennia of biological evolution nature, in the process of forming us, has implanted in us physical and psychic structures that now constitute native internal determinants, which may nevertheless tolerate a wide range of parameters in the practices we engage in. Through our activities in these practices in manifold ways we learn more and more about the determinants of practice, both the external and the internal ones. Much of this learning is embedded in common sense. Since the sixteenth century there has been an increasingly rapid explosion of learning about certain facets of the material world. But not all that we learn about ourselves or our environment comes to us in the form of explicit statements, judgments, hypotheses or theories *about* the world. Nature, in and beyond ourselves, makes its presence and character known not only in our scientific and other broadly scientific practices, but in other practices as well, such as, for example, in politics, law, and morals. It was the limitations imposed upon us and opportunities offered to us by external and internal nature, and the revelations of nature itself effected by these limitations, that were grasped and stressed by the adherents of natural law in the long tradition of that name in the above fields of study. While their positivist opponents were surely in the right in stressing that the learning in these fields begins with the specific, limited modes of response with which we are indoctrinated, the adherents of natural law were equally right and have performed a great service in stressing something that now especially needs to be stressed, namely, that in external and internal nature there are, as well as opportunities for the development of practices, limitations upon the kinds of practices which may be developed, and that these limitations we ignore at the risk of the health and well-being of the system of practices and the quality of the life that is lived through them.

All these limitations upon the variability of practices and governance, not least of which is that independent character of the objects of investigation with which in scientific and other cognitive practices we are directly concerned, represent sources of stability greatly counterbalancing any tendency there may be in governance and practices toward general, unmanageable instability. If, having given up the thought of fixed sources of governance residing in some Platonic reserve altogether external to practices, we are prone to think ourselves cast adrift rudderless upon the sea of practice, we need to remind ourselves that we never do, because we never can, face so desperate a predicament. And this, not only for physical, psychological, or social reasons, but also for firm logical ones. The primary reason why the incapacitating consequences of extreme conceptual relativism are not to be feared is that the predicament contemplated as threatening in that doctrine and from which these consequences are supposed to follow is one the very thought of which is logically incoherent in an extreme degree. To suppose an individual or a community to be in a situation in which all practices have, as it were, become unstuck, is in the first place to suppose a being that only remotely, if at all, resembles an individual, and likewise something, perhaps a collection of totally asocial animals, that is not a community. But, waiving that point, and supposing there to be such an individual or community, for either of them there would be no residue of practices which at the time are unquestioned and which form the critical mass of accepted practices necessary in order for a problem about governance to arise. There is, in short, no way in which we, either as individuals or as communities, can so saturate ourselves in skepticism about practices that we can divorce ourselves, even in thought, from all of them. And, were this possible, there would in consequence be insufficient logical material with which to construct a problem concerning the rationality of governance and governantial change. That there is always a residual mass of more or less well-governed accepted practices available, when questions about rational changes of governance arise, and that, further, this residual mass is our fundamental resource for devising answers to these questions, does not, as has already been indicated, mean that this residue is always adequate for the purpose. It means, rather there is a resource that is no more always and in principle sufficient for the purpose than it is always and in principle insufficient. The sober truth, much less philosophically exciting than either of those extreme alternatives, is that sometimes this resource is sufficient and sometimes it is not.

VII

The second and final general point that needs to be emphasized about rational governance follows hard upon the first. The first point concerned the stability of governance and practices, and the limits that this stability imposes upon the extent to which at any given time these practices, and governance with it, are subject to change and challenge. The second point also concerns limits, this time limits upon rational governance itself.

However the notion of rational governance of practice is explicated, there is little doubt that limits must be recognized in the capacity of the processes of this governance to achieve their ends. There have been, are, and will continue to be numerous situations in which, for one reason or another, these processes falter in a variety of ways. They may falter in the maintenance or invention of needed features of governance, or in the divestiture of established or arising forms of governance of seriously deleterious features. And there is no guarantee that every time established governance falters, there is an adequate restorative, that for every disease of governance there is a remedy. First, granting that such restoratives or remedies are possible, there is no guarantee that available rational processes, in either their communal or individual forms, will be sufficiently sensitive to detect their needs; or that responding to the need they will be sufficiently clever and wise to devise them, that the measures they do devise may not be ones that, if taken, would exacerbate the very difficulties they were intended to reduce, or would generate difficulties as serious as, or more serious than, those that they were devised to meet. And if these incapacities must be recognized in rational processes generally, they may be expected in those more reflective, more conscious, more previsionally endowed forms of the processes that have been identified as those of rational reflection. In contrast with the attitude of unqualified confidence which is common among the philosophical toward something discerned by them in the more conscious, more deliberate forms of governance and identified with reason, the attitude toward rational processes that issues from the view set forth here is, without denigration, more sober and, it is hoped, more realistic. One consequence of the view is that there are occasions in which the residual mass of unquestioned practice is sufficient to demonstrate to philosophical reflection the need for criticism and change in practices and governance, but is yet insufficient to provide reflection with adequate guides either for that criticism or for the discovery of means by which amelioration may be achieved.

Nothing that has been said so far about the processes of rational governance provides any guarantee that what these processes yield at one time in the form of changes of governance may not at other times and from other points of view be rightly judged to have been deficient in rationality. There are some who readily concede the possibility of reversal in steps taken by individuals in the governance of habits in their own lives, but would demur in some degree concerning governance viewed on the broad stage of world history, where individuals, as agents of governance, are to a considerable extent replaced by social groups or institutions. Yet the hard facts of social life and proximate history count heavily against placing unqualified trust in any social agent of governance, however grand and impressive, whether it be a universal church, a dominant nation-state, or a rising economic class. A device commonly employed at this point to avoid the conclusion that rational governance, reason itself in its communal large-scale forms, may falter, is the advancement of some ground intended to guarantee that in the long run the proximate discrepant facts will be cancelled, that in the long sweep of history episodes of weakness or fault will be minor, minor ripples or eddies in some irresistible progressive tide. Grounds—of various degrees of respectability: logical, mathematical, historical, or theological—are sought for demonstrating that somehow in the main, regardless of supersessions or because of them, the course is upward through improved versions of itself, toward rationality in some absolute form, which it may either eventually in some cases reach (Hegel), or progressively approximate (Peirce).[6]

That there has been progress in approximation to truth in some domains of inquiry seems, as it seemed to Peirce, undeniable. That the process must continue, as Peirce thought it must in the community of investigators, is much more questionable. The divergence of the present view from that of Hegel is at this point wide. A judgment of the course of practices and governance in the world, reflecting and depending upon what we have been able to learn through these practices and their governance, will have to be much less bold and unqualifiedly optimistic than his. What we are acquainted with as reason in our lives and can further define in our deepest, most careful thought, what we can discern as reason in the world and in some degree attain in ourselves, has neither of the attributes of an omniscient and omnipotent God, striding triumphantly through the world or speaking infallibly to us. It is not the function of reason, as we thus know it, to ensure that the human journey of this world will terminate in some Promised Land, as did the fabled pillars of cloud and of fire in the

Wilderness. Nor is its function to give infallible instructions, written in stone, of how we should conduct ourselves on this journey, like the fabled injunctions delivered to Moses on Sinai. The function of reason is much more homely, modest, mundane and, to change the myth, less Promethean than this. Drawing upon the most pertinent features of practices and governance we are able to say that, with these as with other things, new revised versions are not necessarily better; new manifestations of reason itself, are not necessarily improved ones; though they sometimes are. And who, or what, is to say? Who, but us? And upon what basis than these practices and what rational governance we have at any time achieved in them: not these in general, but those that are most pertinent, this too being a matter susceptible of judgment only by practices and their governance, though of course not the same ones that are the objects of question when a question of pertinence itself arises.

Peirce was speaking of this aspect of rational governance when in his 1905 essay on pragmatism he emphasized that although it is plain that what we do not at any time doubt is not thereby established as true, nevertheless what we do not *at all* doubt, we must and do regard as truth—or as he actually put it, with some exaggeration and perhaps exasperation with "Mr. Make Believe" and his would-be doubts— we "must and do regard as infallible, absolute truth."[7] What holds for truth here seems to hold generally. On the other hand, those determinations which our practices enable us to make at any one time, and for which, judged by the pertinent arrangement of governance, there is no positive basis for doubt, no ground for singling out this rather than any other accepted item for doubt except that it *is* an accepted matter—those determinations we may, as we must, accept, as true, and without any twinges of Cartesian guilt. In this respect, as Justice Oliver Wendell Holmes wrote over fifty years ago, "imitation of the past, until we have a clear reason for change, no more needs justification than appetite."[8] One perhaps expresses only what is implicit in this striking remark when one closes with the reminder that, just as there are circumstances in which it is manifestly in accordance with rational governance to conform to accepted practices in our individual and collective actions, there are others in which it is manifestly in accordance with the same governance to act differently and in such a manner that, in a deeper sense than Hamlet intended by this phrase, we do honor the custom more in the breach than in the observance.

NOTES

1. The objective but non-social components of ideas or concepts were elaborated upon by this writer in "Thoughts and Things," *Proceedings and Addresses of the American Philosophical Association* 42 (1968–69): 51–69. These, and also the social components, were treated in chapters 7 and 9 of his *Induction and Justification* (Ithaca, N.Y., 1974).

2. Toulmin, S., *Human Understanding*, vol. I (1974), 158–66; Gellner, E., "Concepts and Society" (1962), reprinted in B. R. Wilson, ed., *Rationality* (1970), pp. 18–49.

3. The story of the appeal of this quest and the reasons why it was and is doomed to fail cannot be detailed here. A detailed examination as the product of inductive inferences erected upon sensory intuitions, is given in Part II of *Induction and Justification*.

4. "The Reflex Arc Concept in Psychology," *Psychological Review* 3 (1896). See also *Human Nature and Conduct*, Pt. I, Sect. I. Dewey served as president of the American Psychological Association for the year 1899–1900. His presidential address was entitled, "Psychology and Social Practice."

5. This emphasis upon continuity is fundamentally opposed to the emphasis upon discontinuity at a corresponding point in the well-known account of scientific revolutions advanced by T. S. Kuhn (*The Structure of Scientific Revolutions* [Chicago, 1962]). The view of governance advanced here provides a more general epistemological ground for a criticism that was frequently made of Kuhn's account of historical grounds, namely, that in it the distinction drawn between "normal" and "revolutionary" science is unrealistically sharp.

6. For Peirce's views see *Collected Papers*, "Three Logical Sentiments" (1878), 2: 652–55; "The Social Theory of Logic" (1868), 5: 341–57; "How to Make Our Ideas Clear" (1878), 5: 388–410; "Definitions of Truth" (1901), 5: 565–73. Perhaps the best brief, though typically obscure, statement on this matter by Hegel himself is in his own Introduction to the *Phenomenology of Spirit*. Much more of Hegel's thought in the *Phenomenology* or elsewhere needs to be assimilated before one can appreciate what he took to be grounds for that famous proclamation early in the *Lectures on the Philosophy of History*: "The only thought which philosophy brings to the treatment of history is the simple concept of *Reason*: that reason is the law of the world and that therefore, in world history, things have come about rationally." *Reason in History*, trans. by R. S. Hartman, 1953, p. 11.

7. *Collected Papers*, "What Pragmatism Is," 5: 416.

8. "Holdsworth's English Law," *Collected Legal Papers* (1920), pp. 285, 290. Quotation from Herbert Wechsler, *Principles, Politics and Fundamental Law* (Cambridge, Mass., 1961), p. 23.

9. POSTMODERNIST BOURGEOIS LIBERALISM

Richard Rorty

Complaints about the social irresponsibility of the intellectuals typically concern the intellectual's tendency to marginalize herself, to move out from one community by interior identification of herself with some other community—for example, another country or historical period, an invisible college, or some alienated subgroup within the larger community. Such marginalization is, however, common to intellectuals and to miners. In the early days of the United Mine Workers its members rightly put no faith in the surrounding legal and political institutions and were loyal only to each other. In this respect they resembled the literary and artistic avant-garde between the wars.

It is not clear that those who thus marginalize themselves can be criticized for social irresponsibility. One cannot be irresponsible toward a community of which one does not think of oneself as a member. Otherwise runaway slaves and tunnelers under the Berlin Wall would be irresponsible. If such criticism were to make sense there would have to be a supercommunity one *had* to identify with—humanity as such. Then one could appeal to the needs of that community when breaking with one's family or tribe or nation, and such groups could appeal to the same thing when criticizing the irresponsibility of those who break away. Some people believe that there is such a community. These are the people who think there are such things as intrinsic human dignity, intrinsic human rights, and an ahistorical distinction between the demands of morality and those of prudence. Call these people "Kantians." They are opposed by people who say that "humanity" is a biological rather than a moral notion, that there is no human dignity that is not derivative from the dignity of some specific community, and no appeal beyond the relative merits of various actual or proposed communities to impartial criteria which will help us weigh those merits. Call these people "Hegelians." Much of contemporary social philosophy in the English-speaking world is a three-cornered debate between Kantians (like John Rawls and Ronald Dworkin) who

214

want to keep an ahistorical morality-prudence distinction as a buttress for the institutions and practices of the surviving democracies, those (like the post-Marxist philosophical left in Europe, Roberto Unger, and Alasdair MacIntyre) who want to abandon these institutions both because they presuppose a discredited philosophy and for other, more concrete, reasons, and those (like Michael Oakeshott and John Dewey) who want to preserve the institutions while abandoning their traditional Kantian backup. These last two positions take over Hegel's criticism of Kant's conception of moral agency, while either naturalizing or junking the rest of Hegel.

If the Hegelians are right, then there are no ahistorical criteria for deciding when it is or is not a responsible act to desert a community, any more than for deciding when to change lovers or professions. The Hegelians see nothing to be responsible to except persons and actual or possible historical communities; so they view the Kantians' use of 'social responsibility' as misleading. For that use suggests not the genuine contrast between, for example, Antigone's loyalties to Thebes and to her brother, or Alcibiades' loyalties to Athens and to Persia, but an illusory contrast between loyalty to a person or a historical community and to something "higher" than either. It suggests that there is a point of view that abstracts from any historical community and adjudicates the rights of communities vis-à-vis those of individuals.

Kantians tend to accuse of social irresponsibility those who doubt that there is such a point of view. So when Michael Walzer says that "A given society is just if its substantive life is lived in . . . a way faithful to the shared understandings of the members," Dworkin calls this view "relativism." "Justice," Dworkin retorts, "cannot be left to convention and anecdote." Such Kantian complaints can be defended using the Hegelian's own tactics, by noting that the very American society which Walzer wishes to commend and to reform is one whose self-image is bound up with the Kantian vocabulary of "inalienable rights" and "the dignity of man." Hegelian defenders of liberal institutions are in the position of defending, on the basis of solidarity alone, a society which has traditionally asked to be based on something more than mere solidarity. Kantian criticism of the tradition that runs from Hegel through Marx and Nietzsche, a tradition which insists on thinking of morality as the interest of a historically conditioned community rather than "the common interest of humanity," often insists that such a philosophical outlook is—if one values liberal practices and institutions — irresponsible. Such criticism rests on a prediction that such practices and institutions will not survive the removal of the traditional Kantian buttresses, buttresses which include an account of "rationality" and "morality" as transcultural and ahistorical.

I shall call the Hegelian attempt to defend the institutions and practices of the rich North Atlantic democracies without using such buttresses "postmodernist bourgeois liberalism." I call it "bourgeois" to emphasize that most of the people I am talking about would have no quarrel with the Marxist claim that a lot of those institutions and practices are possible and justifiable only in certain historical, and especially economic, conditions. I want to contrast bourgeois liberalism, the attempt to fulfill the hopes of the North Atlantic bourgeoisie, with philosophical liberalism, a collection of Kantian principles thought to justify us in having those hopes. Hegelians think that these principles are useful for *summarizing* these hopes, but not for justifying them (a view Rawls himself verges upon in his Dewey Lectures). I use 'postmodernist' in a sense given to this term by Jean-François Lyotard, who says that the postmodern attitude is that of "distrust of metanarratives," narratives which describe or predict the activities of such entities as the noumenal self or the Absolute Spirit or the Proletariat. These metanarratives are stories which purport to justify loyalty to, or breaks with, certain contemporary communities, but which are neither historical narratives about what these or other communities have done in the past nor scenarios about what they might do in the future.

"Postmodernist bourgeois liberalism" sounds oxymoronic. This is partly because, for local and perhaps transitory reasons, the majority of those who think of themselves as beyond metaphysics and metanarratives also think of themselves as having opted out of the bourgeoisie. But partly it is because it is hard to disentangle bourgeois liberal institutions from the vocabulary that these institutions inherited from the Enlightenment — e.g., the eighteenth-century vocabulary of natural rights, which judges, and constitutional lawyers such as Dworkin, must use *ex officiis*. This vocabulary is built around a distinction between morality and prudence. In what follows I want to show how this vocabulary, and in particular this distinction, might be reinterpreted to suit the needs of us postmodernist bourgeois liberals. I hope thereby to suggest how such liberals might convince our society that loyalty to itself is morality enough, and that such loyalty no longer needs an ahistorical backup. I think they should try to clear themselves of charges of irresponsibility by convincing our society that it need be responsible only to its own traditions, and not to the moral law as well.

The crucial move in this reinterpretation is to think of the moral self, the embodiment of rationality, not as one of Rawls's original choosers, somebody who can distinguish her *self* from her talents and interests and views about the good, but as a network of beliefs, desires, and emotions with nothing behind it—no substrate behind the attributes. For purposes of moral and political deliberation and conversation, a person just *is* that network, as for purposes of ballistics she is a point-mass, or for purposes of chemistry a linkage of molecules. She is a network that is constantly reweaving itself in the usual Quinean manner—that is to say, not by reference to general criteria (e.g., "rules of meaning" or "moral principles") but in the hit-or-miss way in which cells readjust themselves to meet the pressures of the environment. On a Quinean view, rational behavior is just adaptive behavior of a sort which roughly parallels the behavior, in similar circumstances, of the other members of some relevant community. Irrationality, in both physics and ethics, is a matter of behavior that leads one to abandon, or be stripped of, membership in some such community. For some purposes this adaptive behavior is aptly described as "learning" or "computing" or "redistribution of electrical charges in neural tissue," and for others as "deliberation" or "choice." None of these vocabularies is privileged over against another.

What plays the role of "human dignity" on this view of the self? The answer is well expressed by Michael Sandel, who says that we cannot regard ourselves as Kantian subjects "capable of constituting meaning on our own," as Rawlsian choosers,

> . . . without great cost to those loyalties and convictions whose moral force consists partly in the fact that living by them is inseparable from understanding ourselves as the particular people we are—as members of this family or community or nation or people, as bearers of this history, as sons and daughters of that revolution, as citizens of this republic.[1]

I would argue that the moral force of such loyalties and convictions consists *wholly* in this fact, and that nothing else has *any* moral force. There is no "ground" for such loyalties and convictions save the fact that the beliefs and desires and emotions which buttress them overlap those of lots of other members of the group with which we identify for purposes of moral or political deliberations, and the further fact that these are *distinctive* features of that group, features which it uses to construct its self-image through contrasts with other groups. This means that the naturalized Hegelian analogue of "intrinsic human dignity" is the comparative dignity of a group with which a person identifies herself. Nations or churches or movements are, on this view, shining historical examples not because they reflect rays emanating from a higher source, but because of contrast-effects—comparisons with other, worse communities. Persons have dignity not as an interior luminescence, but because they share in such contrast-effects. It is a corollary of this view that the moral justification of the institutions and practices of one's group—e.g., of the contemporary bourgeoisie—is mostly a matter of historical narratives (including scenarios about what is likely to happen in certain future contingencies), rather than of philosophical metanarratives. The principal backup for historiography is not philosophy but the arts, which serve to develop and modify a group's self-image by, for example, apotheosizing its heroes, diabolizing its enemies, mounting dialogues among its members, and refocusing its attention.

A further corollary is that the morality/prudence distinction now appears as a distinction between appeals to two parts of the network that is the self—parts separated by blurry and constantly shifting boundaries. One part consists of those beliefs and desires and emotions which overlap with those of most other members of some community with which, for purposes of deliberation, she identifies herself, and which contrast with those of most members of other communities with which hers contrasts itself. A person appeals to morality rather than prudence when she appeals to this overlapping, shared part of herself, those beliefs and desires and emotions which permit her to say "WE do not do this sort of thing." Morality is, as Wilfrid Sellars has said, a matter of "we-intentions." Most moral dilemmas are thus reflections of the fact that most of us identify with a number of different communities and are equally reluctant to marginalize ourselves in relation to any of them. This diversity of identifications increases with education, just as the number of communities with which a person may identify increases with civilization.

Intra-societal tensions, of the sort which Dworkin rightly says mark our pluralistic society, are rarely resolved by appeals to general principles of the sort Dworkin thinks necessary. More frequently they are resolved by appeals to what he calls "convention and anecdote." The political discourse of the democracies, at its best, is the exchange of what Wittgenstein called "reminders for a particular purpose" — anecdotes about the past effects of various practices and predictions of what will happen if, or unless, some of these are altered. The moral deliberations of the postmodernist bourgeois liberal consists largely in this same sort of discourse, avoiding the formulation of general principles except where the situation may require this particular tactic — as when one writes a constitution, or rules for young children to memorize. It is useful to remember that this view of moral and political deliberation was a commonplace among American intellectuals in the days when Dewey — a postmodernist before his time — was the reigning American philosopher, days when "legal realism" was thought of as desirable pragmatism rather than unprincipled subjectivism.

It is also useful to reflect on why this tolerance for anecdote was replaced by a reattachment to principles. Part of the explanation, I think, is that most American intellectuals in Dewey's day still thought their country was a shining historical example. They identified with it easily. The largest single reason for their loss of identification was the Vietnam War. The War caused some intellectuals to marginalize themselves entirely. Others attempted to rehabilitate Kantian notions in order to say, with Chomsky, that the War not merely betrayed America's hopes and interests and self-image, but was *immoral*, one which we had had no *right* to engage in in the first place.

Dewey would have thought such attempts at further self-castigation pointless. They may have served a useful cathartic purpose, but their long-run effect has been to separate the intellectuals from the moral consensus of the nation rather than to alter that consensus. Further, Dewey's naturalized Hegelianism has more overlap wih the belief-systems of the communities we rich North American bourgeois need to talk with than does a naturalized Kantianism. So a reversion to the Deweyan outlook might leave us in a better position to carry on whatever conversation between nations may still be possible, as well as leaving American intellectuals in a better position to converse with their fellow citizens.

I shall end by taking up two objections to what I have been saying. The first objection is that on my view a child found wandering in the woods, the remnant of a slaughtered nation whose temples have been razed and whose books have been burned, has no share in human dignity. This is indeed a consequence, but it does not follow that she may be treated like an animal. For it is part of the tradition of *our* community that the human stranger from whom all dignity has been stripped is to be taken in, to be reclothed with dignity. This Jewish and Christian element in our tradition is gratefully invoked by free-loading atheists like myself, who would like to let differences like that between the Kantian and the Hegelian remain "merely philosophical." The existence of human rights, in the sense in which it is at issue in this meta-ethical debate, has as much or as little relevance to our treatment of such a child as the question of the existence of God. I think both have equally little relevance.

The second objection is that what I have been calling "postmodernism" is better named "relativism," and that relativism is self-refuting. Relativism certainly is self-refuting, but there is a difference between saying that every community is as good as every other and saying that we have to work out from the networks we are, from the communities with which we presently identify. Postmodernism is no more relativistic than Hilary Putnam's suggestion that we stop trying for a "God's-eye view" and realize that "We can only hope to produce a more rational conception of rationality or a better conception of morality if we operate from within our tradition."[2] The view that every tradition is as rational or as moral as every other could be held only by a god, someone who had no need to use (but only to mention) the terms 'rational' or 'moral,' because she had no need to inquire or deliberate. Such a being would have escaped from history and conversation into contemplation and metanarrative. To accuse postmodernism of relativism is to try to put a metanarrative in the postmodernist's mouth. One will do this if one identifies "holding a philosophical position" with having a metanarrative available. If we insist on such a definition of "philosophy," then postmodernism is post-philosophical. But it would be better to change the definition.[3]

NOTES

1. *Liberalism and the Limits of Justice* (New York: Cambridge, 1982), p. 179. Sandel's remarkable book argues masterfully that Rawls cannot naturalize Kant and still retain the meta-ethical authority of Kantian "practical reason."

2. *Reason, Truth and History* (New York: Cambridge, 1981), p. 216.

3. I discuss such redefinition in the Introduction to *Consequences of Pragmatism* (Minneapolis: Univ. of Minnesota Press, 1982), and the issue of relativism in "Habermas and Lyotard on Postmodernity," in *Praxis International* vol. 4, no. 1 (April 1984), pp. 32–44, and in "Solidarité ou Objectivité?" forthcoming in *Critique*.

10. MORAL ARGUMENTS AND
SOCIAL CONTEXTS
A Response to Rorty

Alasdair MacIntyre

In place of the hierarchical relationship of intellectuals to plain persons we might entertain the hope of developing a form of social conversation in which professors are as likely to learn from farmers or coalminers as *vice versa*. But on what resources could such conversation draw? Rorty's answer is that, given the failure of all attempts to construct the kind of rationally-justifiable-as-such morality presupposed by Held's thesis,[1] it has nothing to draw upon but our common stock of conventions and anecdotes. But once again dissensus is the obstacle. There are too many rival conventions, too many conflicting anecdotes; and the repetition of assertions and denials does not constitute conversation. What postmodern bourgeois liberalism exhibits is not moral argument freed from unwarranted philosophical pretensions, but the decay of moral reasoning.

That decay is unsurprising in a society whose world view, oscillating between *Moralität* and *Sittlichkeit*, obscures the connection between the possibility of moral reasoning and the existence of a certain type of tradition-bearing community. Any particular piece of practical reasoning has rational force only for those who both have desires and dispositions ordered to some good and recognize that good as furthered by doing what that piece of practical reasoning bids. Only within a community with shared beliefs about goods and shared dispositions educated in accordance with those beliefs, both rooted in shared practices, can practical reason-giving be an ordered, teachable activity with standards of success and failure. Such a community is rational only if the moral theory articulated in its institutionalized reason-giving is the best theory to emerge so far in its history. The best theory so far is that which transcends the limitations of the previous best theory by providing the best explanation of that previous theory's failures and

222

incoherences (as judged by the standards of that previous theory) and showing how to escape them.

The succession of such institutionalized theories in the life of a community constitute a rational tradition whose successive specifications of human good point forward to a never finally specifiable human *telos*. To be a rational individual is to participate in social life informed by a rational tradition. It is when modern societies reject this kind of rootedness in rational tradition that moral theorists either with the Enlightenment and Held attempt to construct a morality from the resources of reason-as-such or with Rorty seek to come to terms with the fragmented *status quo*.

NOTE

1. Virginia Held was the other symposiast when Richard Rorty's immediately preceding paper was delivered at an American Philosophical Association symposium on December 28, 1983.

PART IV

Hermeneutics and Pragmatism: Confrontation, Convergence, and Critique

11. HOLISM AND HERMENEUTICS

Hubert L. Dreyfus

I

Of the many issues surrounding the new interest in hermeneutics, current debate has converged upon two:

1. Is there any difference between the natural and the human sciences?
2. If there were such a difference, what personal and political difference would it make?

In this paper I will argue first that there is an essential difference between theoretical and practical holism and thus there is an essential difference between the natural and human sciences. I will then argue that, if one holds that there is no crucial difference between things and people one must embrace some form of nihilism — a way of life in which all values have the same value, everything is equal, or, to put it another way, there are no meaningful differences. Richard Rorty's view that how we treat people depends solely upon what sort of lives we happen to prefer, is one form such nihilism can take. However, if there *is* a crucial difference between self-interpreting human beings and other sorts of entities, one can counter the nihilistic possibility of what Rorty calls "conversations" between those who have opposed "preferences" with the possibility of genuine conflicts of interpretation as to the serious issues worth conversing about.

Such conflicts cannot be settled by traditional philosophical or empirical argument since traditional debates operate within a taken-for-granted understanding of what considerations can be taken seriously. In conflicts of interpretation, moreover, the question is not which view of what is important corresponds to the way things are in themselves, but rather, which is the better account of our condition, i.e., which allows a deeper appreciation of the cultural commitments we cannot help sharing because they make us what we are.

II

Let us first consider theoretical holism. This view that science involves interpretation and that interpretation is a kind of translation is generating a great deal of interest and spreading much confusion in current philosophical circles. It holds that the reason the social sciences cannot live up to the scientific objectivity of the natural sciences is that there is no such objectivity even in natural science. The very conception of objective knowledge, it is said, is a philosophical mistake left over from Descartes' rationalist interpretation of the implications of Galilean science. This critique of the accepted view of scientific method emphasizes the fact that science, like any other human cognitive activity, involves interpretation. Even natural scientists must determine what are to count as the relevant facts and what their theoretical significance is, so that there is no possibility of finding neutral uninterpreted data for deciding between competing hypotheses.

Pierre Duhem already noted in the last century that in science individual sentences are not tested against experience one by one, but only as a whole via a theory. In our time philosophers of science have worked out the implications of this view arguing that in science data are what Hanson called "theory laden." In verifying a theory we move in a circle from hypothesis to data, and data to hypothesis, without ever encountering any bare facts which could call our whole theory into question. Thus we arrive at the "anarchist" philosophy of science of Paul Feyerabend which concludes that there is no fundamental difference between the truth of the natural and the social sciences or, indeed, between these and witchcraft since there can be no objective verification, only the confrontation of incommensurable holistic interpretations. The only difference between the natural and the social sciences, on this view, is that in natural science this battle of interpretations is repressed whereas the social sciences, for some unknown reason, have never succeeded in covering up the conflict.

If one accepts this general approach, the philosopher's job becomes one of meta-interpretation. He tries to understand these incommensurate interpretations of reality by making them commensurable. Rorty calls this "discourse about as-yet incommensurable discourse" hermeneutics, and claims that this understanding of hermeneutics "links up with the use of the term by such writers as Gadamer."[1] Dagfinn Føllesdal has pointed out that it also connects with Quine who has argued that any attempt to understand another discourse must be like crack-ing a code, and with Donald Davidson who has developed further Quine's notion of "radical translation" by pointing out that in trying to make sense of another language or culture we must try to maximize agreement concerning what seems to us obviously true and false.[2] Once this project of radical translation has succeeded, the hermeneutic in-terpreter can understand some alien episode in his own culture, such as Ptolemaic science (Thomas Kuhn, for example, now says that his studies of Aristotelian science are hermeneutic)[3] or some other culture with a seemingly alien view of reality (as, for example, the cultural interpretations of Clifford Geertz).[4]

The important point for Rorty is that hermeneutics is always necessary whenever there is a failure of communication between com-peting discourses. Thus hermeneutics becomes necessary whenever there is a breakdown in understanding, whether this be between cultures or between conflicting paradigms of explanation in the natural or the social sciences. Conversely, it follows too, that in any of these cases we can dispense with hermeneutics when the two competing discourses have been translated into each other or when one of them has driven out the other. In the case of the natural or social sciences, commen-surability signals that a "scientific revolution" is over and the practi tioners have returned to a normal shared framework.

This notion of interpretation as translation between theories leads Rorty to the conclusion that there is no important difference between the natural and the social sciences.

It might be the case that all future human societies will be (as a result, perhaps, of ubiquitous technocratic totalitarianism) hum-drum variations on our own. But contemporary science (which already seems so hopeless for explaining acupuncture, the migra-tion of butterflies, and so on) may soon come to seem as badly off as Aristotle's hylomorphism. [The important distinction] is not the line between the human and the non-human but be-tween that portion of the field of inquiry where we feel rather uncertain that we have the right vocabulary at hand and that por-tion where we feel rather certain that we do. This *does*, at the moment, roughly coincide with the distinction between the fields of the Geistes and the Naturwissenschaften. But this coincidence may be *mere* coincidence.[5]

Exponents of hermeneutics as radical translation between incommensurable discourses, reach these radical conclusions precisely because they treat all understanding as theoretical. From their point of view a theory is made up of the systematic interrelation of distinguishable elements. In the case of a scientific theory these elements are related by explicit propositions stating laws; in the case of common sense, which they construe as a theory, these elements are related by conscious and unconscious posits and beliefs. Whether explicitly expressed in sentences or implicitly held as behavioral dispositions these beliefs can be regarded as hypotheses which could in principle be stated. As Quine puts it:

> [H]ypotheses in various fields of inquiry may tend to receive their confirmation from different kinds of investigation, but this should in no way conflict with our seeing them all as hypotheses. We talk of framing hypotheses. Actually we inherit the main ones, growing up as we do in a going culture. The continuity of belief is due to the retention, at each particular time of most beliefs.[6]

Thus, on this view, even practical common sense is a crude scientific theory.

> . . . science is itself a continuation of common sense. The scientist is indistinguishable from the common man in his sense of evidence, except that the scientist is more careful.[7]

On this model, understanding a person from an alien culture or understanding a radically different sort of science involves making a total theory about a total theory, that is, making a translation into your language of the theory implied in the other person's behavior or language. This view thus treats all understanding as an *epistemological* problem, as a question of theoretical knowledge, so, on this view, there is no important difference between the knowledge sought in the social and the natural sciences.

III

On the opposed view worked out by Heidegger, *theoretical* holism with its account of interpretation as *translation* must be distinguished from what one might call *practical* holism, which thinks of interpretation as *explication*.

Practical understanding is holistic in an entirely different way from theoretical understanding. Although practical understanding — everyday coping with things and people — involves explicit beliefs and hypotheses, these can only be meaningful in specific contexts and against a background of shared practices. And just as we can learn to swim without consciously or unconsciously acquiring a theory of swimming, we acquire these social background practices by being brought up in them, not by forming beliefs and learning rules. A specific example of such a social skill is the conversational competence involved in standing the correct distance from another member of the culture depending on whether the other person is male or female, old or young, and whether the conversation involves business, courtship, friendship, etc. More generally, and more importantly, such skills embody a whole cultural interpretation of what it means to be a human being, what a material object is, and, in general, what counts as real. This is why Heidegger in *Being and Time* calls this cultural self-interpretation embodied in our practices "primordial truth." Heidegger, Merleau-Ponty, and Wittgenstein suggest that this inherited background of practices cannot be spelled out in a theory because (1) the background is so pervasive that we cannot make it an object of analysis, and (2) the practices involve skills.[8]

The first argument presupposes the second, since if it were merely the pervasiveness of one's own background which made it inaccessible to theory, it could be made an object of theoretical analysis by another culture, or, perhaps, another stage of one's own culture. For Quine and Davidson all one needs in order to understand another culture or epoch is a *theory* that maximizes agreement as to which beliefs are true and which are false. The fact that these beliefs only make sense in a practical situation against a taken-for-granted cultural background seems to them to present no special problem, since on their view the background can itself be made the explicit object of some form of theoretical detached analysis revealing further beliefs. Husserl attempted to answer Heidegger's practical holism in just this way. In *Crisis* he claims that the transcendental phenomenologist objectifies the horizon or background by "reactivating" our "sedimented" beliefs and "validities."[9] This is also the answer to practical holism implicit in any version of "cognitive science," whether artificial intelligence or information processing psychology, which proposes to treat the background of practices as a "belief system."[10] For these various versions of theoretical holism the pervasiveness of the background makes the project of explication at worst what Husserl called an "infinite task."

The practical holist's answer to such a theoretical account of the background is twofold: (1) *What makes up the background is not beliefs*, either explicit or implicit, but habits and customs, embodied in the sort of subtle skills which we exhibit in our everyday interaction with things and people. Foucault calls these social strategies micropractices. Wittgenstein notes that ". . . [I]t is our *acting*, which lies at the bottom of the language game."[11] While one may, indeed, on reflection treat aspects of the background as specific beliefs, as for example beliefs about how far to stand from people, these ways of acting were not learned as beliefs and it is not as beliefs that they function causally in our behavior. We just do what we have been trained to do. Moreover, as practices, they have a flexibility which is lost when they are converted into propositional knowledge. (2) If, given the distortion involved in treating skills as propositional knowledge, the theoretical holist attempts to analyze the background not as a belief system but as a set of procedures, he runs into two new problems. (a) If skills are to be analyzed in terms of the sort of rules people actually sometimes follow, then the cognitivist will either have to admit a skill for applying these rules, or face an infinite regress. Or, if he says that one doesn't need a rule or a skill for applying a rule, one simply does what the rule requires, then he has to answer Wittgenstein's question: why not just accept that one simply does what the situation requires, without recourse to rules at all? (b) If, in the light of these difficulties, the theoretical holist attempts to substitute for the ordinary sort of rule a formal, nonmental rule, as used in computer models, he faces another dead end. A formal rule must be represented as a sequence of operations. But there seem to be no basic movements or ideas to serve as the elements over which such rules would have to operate. Even though bodily skills, for example, are sometimes learned by following rules which dictate a sequence of simple movements, when the performer becomes proficient the simple movements are left behind and a single unified, flexible, purposive pattern of behavior is all that remains. It makes no sense to attempt to capture a skill by using a representation of the original elements used by beginners, since these elements are not integrated into the final skill. And no other simple elements have been proposed. No one has the slightest idea how to construct formal rules for the skills involved in swimming or speaking a language, let alone the skills embodying our understanding of what being means. It seems that the background of practices does not consist in a belief system, a system of rules, or in formalized procedures; indeed, it seems the background does not consist in representations at all.

Heidegger is the first, as far as I know, to have noted this noncognitive precondition of all understanding, and to have seen its central importance. As he puts it in the language of *Being and Time*:

> [T]he "in-order-to," the "for-the-sake-of," and the "with-which" of an involvement . . . resist any sort of mathematical functionalization; nor are they merely something thought, first posited in an "act of thinking." They are rather relationships in which concernful circumspection as such already dwells.[12]

To emphasize the pervasiveness of this shared background which is the foundation of everyday intelligibility and of scientific theory, Heidegger calls it primordial understanding. Whether we describe and interpret our practices as in hermeneutics, or whether we take the background for granted as in normal science and study the "objective" facts, we necessarily presuppose this background. This means that we are always already in what Heidegger calls the hermeneutic circle of understanding.

In explaining this circle Heidegger distinguishes three ways that explicit understanding involves what he calls *pre-understanding*.[13] This threefold distinction includes, but goes beyond, the insight of theoretical holism that all data are already theory laden. We can define Heidegger's three terms, for which there are no satisfactory single-term English equivalents, as follows:

1. *Vorhabe* (fore-having). The totality of cultural practices (not noticed by theoretical holism) which "have us"[14] or make us who we are, and thus determine what we find intelligible. In any science this is what Kuhn calls the "disciplinary matrix"—the skills a student acquires in becoming a scientist, which enable him to determine what are the scientifically relevant facts.
2. *Vorsicht* (fore-sight). The vocabulary or conceptual scheme we bring to any problem. At any given stage in our culture this is captured in a specific theoretical understanding of what counts as real spelled out by the philosophers. In science, *Vorsicht* is whatever is taken to be the relevant dimensions of the problem.

3. *Vorgriff.* A specific hypothesis which, within the overall theory, can be confirmed or disconfirmed by the data.

We can now use Heidegger's distinctions to highlight the difference between theoretical and practical holism's view of the interpretive circle. The Quineian *theoretical* circle results from what Heidegger calls *Vorsicht*, i.e., from the fact that all verification takes place within a theory, and that there is no way out of the circle of holistic hypotheses and evidence. The Heideggerian *hermeneutic* circle, on the other hand, says that this whole theoretical activity of framing and confirming hypotheses takes place not only on the background of explicit or implicit assumptions but also on a background of practices (the *Vorhabe*) which need not—and indeed cannot—be included as specific presuppositions of the theory, yet already define what could count as a confirmation. Thus all our knowledge, even our attempt to know the background, is always already shaped by what might be called our implicit ontology, an "ontology" which is in our practices as ways of behaving towards things and people, not in our minds as background assumptions which we happen to be taking for granted. Of course, this hermeneutic circle does not impose a restriction we should regret or try to overcome: without such *Vorhabe* we would have no facts and no theories at all.

Much of the confusion concerning hermeneutics in the current literature stems from the fact that Gadamer, who claims to be working out the implications of Heidegger's notion of hermeneutics, never seems to have taken a stand on Heidegger's claim that there is a level of everyday practice (the *Vorhabe*) beneath our theoretical presuppositions and assumptions (the *Vorsicht*). Gadamer often employs the right rhetoric, as when he says:

> . . . we always stand within tradition, and this is no objectifying process, i.e., we do not conceive of what tradition says as something other, something alien. It is always part of us . . . a recognition of ourselves which our later historical judgment would hardly see as a kind of knowledge. . . [15]

But at times he seems to side with cognitivists like Quine. In describing the hermeneutic pre-understanding, instead of speaking of *Vorhabe*, he speaks of *Vorurteil* (prejudice or pre-judgment), which seems for him to be an implicit belief or assumption:

The isolation of a *prejudice* clearly requires the suspension of its *validity* for us. For so long as our mind is influenced by a prejudice, we do not *know* and consider it as a *judgment*.[16]

Gadamer's claim to be expounding Heideggerian hermeneutics, when, in fact, he fails to distinguish practice and theory, leads Føllesdal, like Rorty, to assimilate *ontological* hermeneutics to Quine and Davidson's *epistemological* position:

> Gadamer and other hermeneuticists hold that all understanding and interpretation presupposes extensive agreement concerning what is true and what is false. Similar observations have been made by Wittgenstein and many other philosophers. I have quoted several passages where Quine argues for his more limited version of the condition, namely that one should preserve agreement with regard to what one considers obvious.[17]

Incidentally this account also distorts Wittgenstein, who is much closer to Heidegger on this point (and most others), than he is to Quine. For Wittgenstein, agreement in judgments means agreement in what people *do* and *say*, not what they *believe*. As he puts it: "It is what human beings say that is true and false; and they agree in the *language* they use. That is not agreement in opinions but in form of life."[18]

According to the ontological hermeneutics of both Heidegger and Wittgenstein when we understand another culture we come to share its *know-how and discriminations* rather than arriving at agreement concerning which *assumptions and beliefs* are true. This coordination comes about not by making a translation, or cracking a code, but by prolonged everyday interaction; the result is not a commensuration of theories but what Heidegger calls "finding a footing" and Wittgenstein refers to as "finding one's way about."

IV

One reason that the difference between Quineian and Heideggerian holism has not been noted is that both views lead to a nondeterminacy as to what is being interpreted. Føllesdal has seen that hermeneutic phenomenology entails a nondeterminacy thesis but, misled by Gadamer, he has identified this nondeterminacy with Quine's famous notion of the indeterminacy of translation. Quine's rejection of meanings, or what he calls "the idea idea," is the conclusion of an argument that in translation from one belief system to another there are no meanings for us to be right or wrong about. Likewise, the view that shared background practices embody an interpretation of what it is to be human and in general an interpretation of what it is to be, leads to the conclusion that these practices do not have an implicit meaning to which any attempted translation must correspond. Rather, to the question: What is the meaning embodied in this practice? one can only offer an interpretation of an interpretation.

To make this different sort of nondeterminacy clear it helps to start with a discussion of aesthetics. In literary criticism, for example, if we give up the idea that an artist's intentions determine what a work means we have to give up the idea that there is a text with a fixed meaning we can be right or wrong about. What the text means is relative to an interpretation, and interpretations change with changing background assumptions and practices.

But why must we give up appeal to the artist's intentions? One argument has been that our evidence for these intentions is simply more behavior which also must be interpreted. This is true, but it only shows that in literature as in science a theory is always underdetermined by the evidence. These difficulties are shared with natural science where they lead to what Quine has called the *underdetermination* of physics, precisely in order to distinguish it from the *indeterminacy* of translation. Similarly this argument shows only the underdetermination of literary interpretations, not their nondeterminacy.

In search of stronger arguments one could take a Freudian view that the author himself is no authority on what his intentions really are. But this again leaves us with unconsious intentions, and the implication that if we could only get at these intentions they would enable us to decide what the work really meant.

Heidegger's argument for the distinctive nondeterminacy of interpretation of works of art is different from either of these. He would point out that an artist or a thinker, just like anyone else, cannot be clear about the background practices of his life and his age, not just because there are so many of them that such explication is an infinite task, but because the background is not a set of assumptions or beliefs about which one could even in principle be clear. The artist is thus in no better position than his contemporaries to make explicit the per-

vasive individual and social self-interpretation his work embodies. This
is what Heidegger calls the essential unthought in the work.

> The greater the work of a thinker . . . the richer is the unthought
> in the work, i.e., that which through that work and through it
> alone, comes up as never-yet-thought.[19]

As this passage implies, this unthought is not at some unsoundable
depth but right upon the surface. It can best be noticed in the case
of thinkers whose intuitive grasp extends beyond that of their contemporaries (e.g., Melville in *Moby Dick*). These artists lack the language and concepts to focus what their style and choice of details is
nonetheless constantly showing, and their interpretation of their own
is as limited as the comments of contemporary reviewers. A later age,
in which the implications of events (in Melville's case the connection
between the destruction of the whaling industry and technological objectification) have worked themselves out, can assemble and focus the
author's details in a more comprehensive interpretation. We cannot
speak of *the* meaning of a work, not because we can never get at this
meaning since our only evidence of the author's intentions is his behavior, but rather because there is no final determinate meaning to
get at.

So, in spite of their apparent agreement, there is a crucial difference between Heidegger and Quine. For Quinean radical translation there is *nothing*, i.e., no meaning, to be wrong about, so any
holistic translation which accounts for all the data is as good as any
other; for Heideggerian hermeneutic explication there is *no thing* (fact
or theory) to be right or wrong about either — as Foucault puts it, in
making a similar point about Nietzsche's notion of interpretation,
" . . . if interpretation is never finished that is simply because there
is nothing to interpret" — but the job of hermeneutics is still to interpret the interpretation embodied in our current practices in as comprehensive and responsible a way as possible.[20] We can, on this view,
still have better or worse interpretations in literature and in the human
sciences, but not because interpretations can be right or wrong about
a meaning in itself. According to this account, better interpretations
are merely those which are more liberating. For early Heidegger in *Being
and Time* (as for Gadamer and Habermas) this means that a better
interpretation is one that makes the interpreter more flexible and open
to dialogue with other interpretations.

We shall see that Heidegger changed his view on this important point. In the later works he holds that a better interpretation is one which focuses and makes sense of more of what is at issue in a current cultural self-interpretation. But this presupposes that *something really is at issue* — although, of course, there can be no final answer as to what that something is. I will return to this important change in Heidegger's understanding of hermeneutics in the conclusion of this paper.

V

Our distinction between theoretical and practical holism will now enable us to make a distinction between the natural and the human sciences. We have seen that current interest in the role of interpretation in all disciplines has led thinkers such as Rorty to deny that any philosophically interesting distinction can be made between types of disciplines with regard to their subject matter. Since all knowing presupposes a background of assumptions, so the story goes, no theory can correspond to things as they are in themselves, no science can be objective, and all sciences are simply either normal or abnormal. According to Rorty, when the practitioners of a discipline share a taken-for-granted background of assumptions, discourse is commensurable and the discipline is normal; when the background itself is in question, discourse is incommensurable and the discipline is in crisis and needs hermeneutic help. As Rorty puts it:

> . . . there is no requirement that people should be more difficult to understand than things; it is merely that hermeneutics is only needed in the case of incommensurable discourses, and that people discourse whereas things do not. What makes the difference is not discourse vs. silence, but incommensurable discourse vs. commensurable discourse.[21]

We are now in a position to see what leads Rorty to this surprising conclusion. By thinking of understanding human discourse as a theoretical problem of making sense of behavioral facts by conjecturing other facts about beliefs and assumptions, he assimilates the understanding of the meaning of cultures, societies, and individual behavior to the understanding of meaningless physical motions. In Heideggerian terms he understands the role of hypothesis (*Vorgriff*) and conceptual scheme (*Vorsicht*) in all understanding, but he leaves out the essential role of the background of practices (*Vorhabe*) in understanding human beings.

To be clear about this special role of the background practices in the study of man we must first remember that the natural sciences too presuppose a background of techniques, shared discriminations, and a shared sense of relevance — all those skills picked up through training which Kuhn calls the "disciplinary matrix" of a science. An example would be those skills which enable modern scientists to "work-over" objects so as to fit them into a formal frame-work.[22] These more and more sophisticated skills and techniques serve the special purpose of enabling modern scientists to isolate properties from their context of human relevance, and then to take the meaningless properties thus isolated and relate them by strict laws. Like any skills, the practices which make natural science possible involve a kind of know-how (*Vorhabe*) which cannot be captured by strict rules. Polanyi stresses that these skills cannot be learned from textbooks but must be acquired by apprenticeship, and Kuhn adds that they are also acquired by working through exemplary problems. Moreover, these scientific skills themselves presuppose our everyday practices and discriminations so the skills themselves cannot be decontextualized like the context free physical properties they reveal. For both these reasons (the need for examples and for background practices) the practices of scientists cannot be brought under the sort of explicit laws whose formulation these practices make possible. Rather, scientific practice is, according to Kuhn, "a mode of knowing that is less systematic or less analyzable than knowledge embedded in rules, laws, or criteria of identification."[23] But the important point for the natural sciences is that natural science is successful precisely to the extent that *these background practices which make science possible can be taken for granted and ignored by the science.* Thus the holistic point that *Vorhabe* is necessary even in the natural sciences does not preclude the possibility of formulating scientific theories in which the interpretative practices of the observer play no internal role.

The human sciences constantly try to copy the natural sciences' successful exclusion from their theories of any reference to the background. They hope that by seeking a shared agreement on what is relevant and by developing shared skills of observation, etc., the background of practices of the social scientist can be taken for granted and ignored the way the background is ignored in natural science. Behaviorism in psychology and the current vogue of information-processing models in the social sciences are cases where researchers take for granted background analogies such as the computer model and are trained in shared techniques such as programming, in the hope that they can relate by rules the meaningless attributes and factors this information-processing perspective reveals. Given such formalizing techniques, normal social science might, indeed, establish itself, only, however, by leaving out the social skills which make the isolation of features or attributes possible. But such skills and the context of everyday practices they presuppose are *internal* to the human sciences, just as the laboratory skills of scientists are internal to the history and sociology of science, for *if the human sciences claim to study human activities, then the human sciences, unlike the natural sciences, must take account of those human activities which make possible their own disciplines.* If, for the sake of agreement and "objectivity," the human sciences, simply ignore their nonformalizable background practices, these practices will show up in each particular human science in the form of competing schools which call attention to what has been left out. For example, in sociology ethnomethodology insists on pointing out and hermeneutically investigating the background practices of "scientific" sociology, and in linguistics formal transformational grammars have focused new interest on the nonformal aspects of semantics and pragmatics.

Thus, while in the natural sciences it is always possible and generally desirable that an unchallenged normal science which defines and resolves problems concerning the structure of the physical universe establish itself, in the social sciences such an unchallenged normal science would only indicate that an orthodoxy had gained control. It would mean that the basic job of exploring the background of practices and their meaning had been forgotten, and that the unique feature of human behavior, the human self-interpretation embodied in our everyday know-how (*Vorhabe*), was not being investigated but simply ignored.

Another way to put this point is that, generally speaking, the natural sciences are at their best as normal science. For them, revolution means mainly that there is a conflict of interpretations—a lack of stability and agreement—until a new orthodoxy is established. The social sciences, on the other hand, are at their best in the perpetual revolution and conflict of interpretations which inevitably arise when they are trying to account for *all* human behavior, even the pervasive background of cultural interpretation which makes action meaningful. For them, normal science would show that the disciplines involved had become conformist, complacent, and ultimately sterile.

VI

Here the social and political issues come to the fore, and Rorty is clearly aware of the apparent danger:

> The fear of science, of "scientism," of "naturalism," of self-objectification, of too much knowledge turning one into a thing rather than a person, is the fear that all discourse will become normal discourse. That is, it is the fear that there will be objectively true or false answers to every question one asks, so that human worth will consist in knowing truths and human virtue be merely justified true belief.[24]

But, in spite of his belief that the social sciences are just as theoretical and objectifying as the natural sciences and just as capable of becoming normal, Rorty thinks that there is no real danger. He claims that even in a world in which objective science explained and controlled everything, people could still look at the totality of objective facts from an edifying point of view and "ask such questions as: 'What is the point?' 'What are we to do with ourselves now that we know the laws of our own behavior?' "[25] Rorty is clear that such edifying discourses can make no claim to being true about the world, or even to being better or worse accounts of cultural meaning, since nothing falls outside objective theory but individual feelings.

> Whether [the world] seemed to point a moral to an individual would depend on that individual. It would be true or false that it so seemed, or did not seem, to him. But it would not be objectively true or false that it "really did," or did not, have a sense or a moral.[26]

Yet Rorty is confident that:

> Given leisure and libraries, the conversation which Plato began will not end in self-objectification—not because aspects of the world, or of human beings escape being objects of scientific in-

quiry, but simply because free and leisured conversation generates abnormal discourse as the sparks fly upward.[27]

But such discourse could not be anything like serious abnormal discourse as we now understand it. As long as someone feels that something has been left out of the objective account he may be inclined to propose and defend an interpretation of what that non-theoretical residue is and what it means for human action. But if, as in Rorty's projection, all objective truth were settled, and there is no other area of serious investigation of shared phenomena, abnormal discourse could only be the expression of an individual's subjective attitude towards the facts. And once this metatruth was understood, there would be no place for disagreement about any debatable issues, and hence no need for hermeneutic efforts at commensuration. Indeed, there would be no sense to translating one discourse into another by trying to make them maximally agree on what was true and what false as proposed by Gadamer and Quine, since all discoursers would already agree on all the objective facts. All that abnormal discourse would amount to would be the expression of private fantasies, and resulting pro and con attitudes towards the facts. And all that would be left in the place of Rorty's kind of hermeneutics would be the Derridian notion of the play of discourse about discourse. This would seem to be all Rorty could mean by conversation.

Not that acknowledging with early Heidegger that the background practices can never be incorporated into a theory, would be sufficient to explain why there will always be conflicts of interpretation. If, as early Heidegger claims, anxiety reveals the background practices to be meaningless, there would be reason to question the applicability to human beings of objective science, but no reason to propose and defend alternative interpretations of human practices, or to offer proposals for meaningful action. Practical holism's insight that our micropractices cannot be objectified as beliefs, assumptions, norms, rules, stereotypes, or anything else saves us from theoretical nihilism, but, since *Being and Time* can offer no way to distinguish the trivial from the important contents of the nonobjectifiable aspect of the micropractices, it lands us in practical nihilism. Holding onto anxiety can make us flexibly free of all objectification, but Heidegger can give no account of why any flexible interpretation should be taken more seriously than any other, or taken seriously at all.

VII

In conclusion, before turning to the political implications of the difference between the natural and social sciences as understood by *later* Heidegger, let us review and generalize our analysis. We have argued that in the human sciences the background is internal to the science while in the natural sciences it is external. This follows from the fact that theory succeeds by decontextualizing while the human sciences have to deal with the human context. But the importance of this difference depends on a further ontological question, whether the background can itself be treated as a belief system or a set of rules, i.e., whether there can be a theory of practice. That there can be such a theory is the unargued assumption of the view that theoretical holism is the only kind of holism.

The consequences of the acceptance of *theoretical holism* for political action is a choice between two kinds of nihilism: secular and religious. Each of these, in turn, can take two forms. Rorty's nihilism can take either the form of a liberal, pragmatic, naturalism which simply opts for the specific beliefs one happens to share with others about the value, lovableness, etc., of human beings. But, of course, any such values, since they are themselves merely the result of subjective preferences and pragmatic choices, could equally well be rejected. So one lets those who disagree opt for their own preferences. Or Rorty, like Derrida, can push this theoretical nihilism one step further. Although talk of meaning is mere discourse about nothing, such talk can itself become the source of enjoyment as the object of our interpretive playfulness. Derrida expresses this last stage of theoretical nihilism when he advocates with Nietzsche "the joyous affirmation of the free play of the world . . . without truth, without origin, offered to an active interpretation."[28]

The religious response to this secular nihilism, which we have not had time to discuss here, tries to save seriousness in either of two ways: (1) By pointing out that, although all our beliefs about value and meaning are *in principle* objectifiable and, hence, just more facts about the world, there are *in fact* always some beliefs so close to us that we cannot treat them as objects. This seems to be Gadamer's move. He claims that each epoch of history has pervasive shared beliefs about human beings and the meaning of Being in general which those living in that epoch cannot objectify. Or, (2) by Ricoeur's approach, which is the opposite of Gadamer's. Instead of finding the source of religious meaning in the ineffable depths of culture, Ricoeur finds that religious symbols point to an ineffable source about and beyond all experience. Then, in the name of this "numinous" realm, he justifies the special nature of human beings.

But this religious move in either version is still nihilistic. With Gadamer, it bases its claims that pervasive "prejudices" are unchallengeable simply on their inaccessibility to the people who hold them, which runs the risk of making a virtue of obscure, pervasive obsessions and compulsions, while with Ricoeur, the numinous is so unrelated to this world that it gives us absolutely no guidance when it comes to political action. Both views relativize *all* particular commitments. But if what makes human beings special is absolutely ineffable it makes absolutely no difference, and where action is concerned we are back to endless conversation between competing preferences.

Once we see, however, that the human practices or *Vorhabe* which gives us our understanding of reality and of ourselves do not consist of representations and so cannot be treated as a theory, then this *practical holism* gives us two new possible positions: one "secular" and nihilistic, and one "religious" and safe from nihilism. These positions were held successively by Heidegger. In *Being and Time* Heidegger thought that those practices which cannot be captured as beliefs and procedures and which thus distinguish us from computer-like objects, are nonetheless, at least in this stage of our culture, relentlessly subjectifying and objectifying. (Later Heidegger comes to see this tendency as technology; Foucault sees it as the encroachment of disciplinary society.) We can, however, early Heidegger holds, experience the fact that we are neither subjects nor objects in attacks of metaphysical anxiety. But since this experience of Nothing with a capital "N" only gets us to recognize what we are not, rather than getting us in touch with anything specific that we *are*, it gives us no motive or focus for action. In order to act at all we must return to the World of *Das Man*, and act in terms of the typified situations, roles, and goals which the disciplinary society presses upon us.

Only the "religious" alternative, sketched by later Heidegger, especially in "The Origin of the Work of Art," offers a way out of nihilism. Later Heidegger assumes the practical holism of *Being and Time,* thus avoiding both the secular and religious varieties of theoretical nihilism. He then holds open the possibility that there still exists in our micro-practices an undercurrent of a pretechnological understanding of the meaning of Being, presumably once focused in the Greek Temple. Now scattered in our inherited background practices this understanding involves nonobjectifying and nonsubjectifying ways of relating to nature, material objects, and human beings. Heidegger asks us to strengthen these practices, to "foster the saving power . . . in little things,"[29] and points out that artists are especially sensitive to this saving power and devoted to preserving endangered species of inherited practices. To take examples close to home, Faulkner personifies the wilderness, Pirsig speaks with respect of the quality even of technological things such as motorcycles, and Melville opposes Ishmael as mortal and preserver to Ahab as the willful mobilizer of all beings towards his arbitrary ends.

Nontechnological micro-practices, if they still exist at all, are not hard to discern, not because they are so pervasive as to be ineffable, or so numinous as to be unreachable—they were once palpably present in cultural exemplars such as the Greek Temple—but because they are dispersed by the objectifying practices which have had such success since the Enlightenment. Nor can the existence of such "saving" practices be proved by philosophical arguments. Still, only their existence and continued efficacy would account for our otherwise mysterious preference for anything rather than the disciplinary technological society.

The practical "religious" form of resistance to nihilism in late Heideggerian hermeneutics requires a two-stage strategy. First, one must deconstruct theoretical holism, and give what Heidegger in *Being and Time* calls a "concrete demonstration" that human beings and the objects they encounter are formed by cultural practices which cannot be objectified. Second, one must give an interpretation of our current cultural situation by finding a cultural paradigm (for Heidegger, the hydroelectric power station on the Rhine; for Foucault, the prison), which focuses our dominant practices, while at the same time assembling all the evidence in our micro-practices—and this of course includes our linguistic practices—that an alternative understanding of human beings once existed and still continues, although drowned out by our everyday busy concerns. Finally, having done this job, one can only hope that the micro-practices excluded by technology will find a new focus in a new paradigm.

Since this last step lies beyond our will, Heidegger has said that only a God can save us. The *first* two stages of this hermeneutic strategy, however, require our efforts. Although, as Rorty eloquently argues, philosophical debate is no longer relevant, the alternatives are not animated conversation, or silent waiting for being to speak, but rather *first*, what Foucault calls genealogy, i.e., amassing and interpreting the historical details of how we got to where we are, and *second*, the as-yet-unnamed hermeneutic activity devoted to interpreting and preserving the inherited understanding of what it means to be, dispersed in our everyday activities—an understanding which makes possible normal as well as abnormal disciplines and gives meaning and seriousness to our lives.[30]

NOTES

1. Richard Rorty, *Philosophy and the Mirror of Nature* (Princeton: Princeton University Press, 1979), pp. 343–44.

2. Dagfinn Føllesdal, "Experience and Meaning" in *Mind and Language*, ed. Samuel Guttenplan (Oxford: at the Clarendon Press, 1975), p. 38.

3. Thomas Kuhn, *The Essential Tension* (Chicago: University of Chicago Press, 1977), p. xiii.

4. Clifford Geertz, *The Interpretation of Cultures* (New York: Basic Books, 1973).

5. Rorty, p. 352.

6. W. V. O. Quine and J. S. Ullian, *The Web of Belief* (New York: Random House, 1978), p. 81.

7. W. V. O. Quine, *The Ways of Paradox and Other Essays* (Cambridge, Mass.: Harvard University Press, 1976), p. 233.

8. Cultural practices obviously involve a lot more than bodily skills. For example they include the parks, furniture, etc., which Dilthey called "objectifications of life," symbols, and the general cultural moods which Heidegger calls *"befindlichkeiten"* and Wittgenstein calls "cultural styles." I will focus my discussion on skills because they are a concern common to Heidegger, Wittgenstein, and Merleau-Ponty, and because the two kinds of holism can be sorted out by distinguishing their differing treatment of skills.

9. Edmund Husserl, *The Crisis of European Sciences and Transcendental Phenomenology* (Evanston, Ill.: Northwestern University Press, 1970), sec. 40.

10. Roger Schank and Kenneth Colby, *Computer Models of Thought and Language* (San Francisco: W. H. Freeman, 1973).

11. Ludwig Wittgenstein, *On Certainty* (New York: Harper & Row, 1969), p. 28, no. 204.

12. Martin Heidegger, *Being and Time* (New York: Harper & Row, 1962), p. 122.

13. Ibid., sec. 32.

14. This is admittedly a forced reading of *Being and Time,* but one which, I think, is true to what Heidegger is trying to get at. In a later marginal note added to his copy of *Sein und Zeit* Heidegger remarks a propos of a passage where he speaks of Dasein *having* a world, that it would have been better to speak of a world being given to Dasein. "Dieser 'gebe' entspricht die 'Habe'. Da-sein 'hat' niemals Wel." *Sein und Zeit* (Niemeyer, 1977), p. 441.

15. Hans-Georg Gadamer, *Truth and Method* (New York: Seabury Press, 1975), p. 250.

16. Ibid., p. 266. (My italics.)

17. Føllesdal, p. 39.

18. Ludwig Wittgenstein, *Philosophical Investigations* (Oxford: Blackwell, 1953), p. 88, no. 241.

19. Martin Heidegger, *Der Satz vom Grund* (Pfullingen: Neske, 1957), pp. 123–24.

20. Michel Foucault, "Nietzsche, Freud, Marx," *Cahiers de Royaumont*, Philosophie Numero 6: *Nietzsche* (Paris: Les Editions de Minuit, 1967), p. 189.

21. Rorty, p. 347.

22. According to Heidegger the objects with which science deals are produced by a special activity of refined observation which he calls "*Bearbeitung*." "Every new phenomenon emerging within an area of science is refined to such a point that it fits into the normative objective coherence of the theory." "Science and Reflection" in *The Question Concerning Technology* (New York: Harper & Row, 1977), pp. 167, 169.

23. Kuhn, p. 192.

24. Rorty, pp. 388 89.

25. Ibid., p. 383.

26. Ibid., p. 388.

27. Ibid., p. 389.

28. Jacques Derrida, "Structure, Sign, and Play in the Discourse of the Human Sciences," *The Structuralist Controversy* (Baltimore: Johns Hopkins University Press, 1968), p. 264.

29. Martin Heidegger, "The Question Concerning Technology" in *The Question Concerning Technology* (New York: Harper & Row, 1977), p. 33.

30. Earlier versions of this paper were presented at Johns Hopkins University and the 1979 annual meeting of the American Association for the Advancement of Science. I am indebted to Paul Rabinow and Jane Rubin for their help in developing the account of nihilism which forms the conclusion of the present version.

12. THE THOUGHT OF BEING AND THE CONVERSATION OF MANKIND: THE CASE OF HEIDEGGER AND RORTY

John D. Caputo

I

Although hailed as a sign of a thaw in the cold war between Anglo-American and continental philosophy, Richard Rorty's beguiling appropriation of the thought of Heidegger in his recent writings[1] has produced no small measure of confusion. How seriously, one wonders, has Rorty moved towards Heidegger? Or contrariwise, just how close does Heidegger come to saying the sorts of things Rorty does? Is Rorty just trying to shock the Anglo-American community by invoking the name of Heidegger? Is he being intentionally outrageous in order to draw attention to what he takes to be the more sober part of his argument? Is there only a grain of truth to this assimilation of Heidegger, while the real positions of the two thinkers are vastly different?

I will argue in the present paper that, despite Rorty's daring and imaginative appropriation of Heidegger's critique of metaphysics, he has excised what seems to me to belong to the very substance of Heidegger's thought — what Heidegger calls *"die Sache des Denkens,"* the matter for thought. I will hold that the "hermeneutics" which Rorty advocates is a shadow of the real thing: Rorty is delighted with the critique of "method" in Gadamer and Heidegger, but he is stalled at the notion of a "truth" which eludes method.[2] I want to raise the question of Rorty's appropriation of Heidegger not only as a contribution towards settling the exegetical question as to where Heidegger ends and Rorty begins, but also as an occasion to debate the substantive philosophical questions that are posed by this surprising wedding.

And although I come at this question with avowedly Heideggerian sympathies, I do not wish to be mistaken as a reactionary who wants nothing to do with bridging the disparate traditions represented by Heidegger and Rorty. I have more than a little sympathy for Rorty's project, for the attempt to find a non-absolutist position which is at the same time beyond relativism, to develop a bravely finite philosophy which recognizes our historical and human limitations, to find a new way beyond the old metaphysics, beyond philosophy as a strict science and foundation of the particular sciences. And I am, I hope, worlds removed from arguing that Rorty has not "understood" Heidegger, which is in my view the first and last refuge of the Heideggerian epigones who think that to understand Heidegger is to talk as Heidegger talks, to write as Heidegger writes and to read Heidegger on one's knees—*die knieende Philosophie*. I have no doubt that Rorty sees what Heidegger is up to with his critique of metaphysics, but he has no taste for it. Although he cites Heidegger a good deal and with a good deal of approval, he does not agree with Heidegger on what is, to my mind, most essential about Heidegger. And since my own sympathies are with Heidegger I want to point out the side of Heidegger which Rorty dismisses and to say a word in its defense. For I think that Rorty has taken up only the "deconstructive" side of Heidegger, the critique of metaphysics (*Destruktion der Geschichte der Ontologie, Überwindung der Metaphysik*), but that he remains quite hostile to Heidegger's project of retrieval (*Wiederholung, Andenken*). In the end we get from Rorty neither Heideggerian "thought" nor Gadamerian "hermeneutics," but—if there is anything "continental" here—Derrida's play of signs. If philosophy has abandoned the mirror of nature, it appears in Rorty to have ended up with a mirror play of words in which words lead to more words but never to the matter itself. And is that not after all what has driven philosophers of this century into two hostile camps? If that is so, it blows a chill wind over the thaw.

I will work this argument out in five stages: (1) I will begin with a brief sketch of the main lines of Rorty's position, and then undertake a critical confrontation with it on the question of (2) Being, (3) language, and (4) hermeneutics, and then add (5) a concluding note of my own.

II

The argument which Rorty has been making in recent years draws its inspiration from three sources (*PMN*, 8, 12–13). From Heidegger he takes the overarching aim of an historical critique of metaphysics from Plato to the present, insofar as metaphysics is based on the mistaken conception of truth as *orthotes*, correctness.[3] From Wittgenstein he draws the notion of a plurality of irreducible language games, and from Dewey the pragmatic conception of truth as a social process hammered out by the hard work of public discussion.

Like Heidegger Rorty is opposed to the "meta-physical" opposition between a pure soul or mind on the one hand and the body on the other. Like Heidegger he locates the origin of this dualism in the Platonic conception of knowledge.[4] Rorty demonstrates the progressive trivialization of this problem so that in the end absolutely nothing depends upon showing that what nowadays goes under the name of mind and body are in fact distinct. What was once, in classical philosophy, an argument about the dignity of man, has degenerated into a claim that incorrigibility is the sole mark of the mental, so that purely private pains and raw feels — states which we surely share with brute animals — are alone mental (*PMN*, 17 ff.). Indeed even if one could demonstrate the existence of such states, nothing would follow (whence Rorty's ingenious mental experiment of a race which reports neural but not mental states but nonetheless shares with us the whole range of culture) (*PMN*, 70 ff.). The history of this metaphysical problem has spun itself out; the contemporary mind-body problem is at "the end of philosophy."[5]

Like Heidegger, Rorty is opposed to a representationalist theory of knowledge in which the mind is taken to be the mirror of nature, which is what Heidegger would call the power of *Vorstellung*, of "representing" the objective world to a conscious subject.[6] Like Heidegger Rorty is not interested in a new and improved theory of knowledge but in dismantling the entire epistemological project. For Heidegger epistemology is a kind of *hubris* according to which human subjectivity presumes to hold court over Being itself. For Rorty philosophy is a discipline in search of a subject matter. Having turned over the task of generating new knowledge to the experimental sciences, philosophy redefined itself as the science of necessary truths rather than matters of fact, and hence as the science which seeks the necessary conditions beneath the particular sciences. Philosophy switched metaphors: instead of calling itself the summit or queen of the sciences, it now proclaims itself the ground or foundation of the sciences. This Neo-Kantian project of foundationalism was also at the heart of Husserl's phenomenology, and Heidegger himself, despite his later disavowals, explicitly embraced this program in section 3 of *Being and Time*.[7] It was only in his later works that Heidegger gave up the foundationalist program. Rorty thinks that there is a comparable reversal in Anglo-American thought (from early, logical analysis to later ordinary language analysis). But when Quine, Wittgenstein, and Sellars attacked the distinction between the analytic and synthetic, the necessary and the contingent, the purely given and what is added on by the mind, they cut the nerve of philosophy as epistemology and foundation (*PMN*, 165 ff.). Truth as it emerges from their writings is not the representation of reality but a holistic coherence of beliefs, settled by an on-going social debate. Philosophers on this view are not experts on knowledge but para-professionals with a taste for debate (*PMN*, 393).

What then remains for philosophers at the "end of philosophy"? What is there to do besides teaching the opinions of the "great dead philosophers" (*PMN*, 393)? For Heidegger the end of philosophy poses the "task of thinking" (*die Aufgabe des Denkens*), of a meditative openness to a matter which has been progressively concealed yet concealedly present in the history of metaphysics. The task of thinking is hermeneutic: to heed the message which Being ambiguously sends, to listen to the silent call of Being. But for Rorty that is a reactionary, indeed "pathetic" attachment on Heidegger's part to the old philosophy.[8] Rorty too sees in the end of philosophy the birth of hermeneutics. But this has, to say the least, rather a different sense for him. If the old philosophy as epistemology wanted to create a master, canonical discourse, the new hermeneutics seeks only to recognize the plurality of discourses and is content to keep a civil conversation going (*PMN*, 315–16). There is strict method in neither the natural sciences (Kuhn) nor the human sciences (Gadamer), but simply diverse spheres of discourse, some of which assert themselves for a while as normal. There is no hard and fast distinction between the human sciences and the natural sciences, nor between man and nature. Sartre was only half right: not only does man have no essence, nature has none either (*PMN*, 361–62, n. 7). The natural and the human sciences do not differ as explanation from understanding; rather a hermeneutically governed conversation is going on in all the disciplines, none of which can be canonized as representing true Being. The real mistake is to think that there is a "deep nature"—whether it be matter or spirit or Being—and hence an absolute sphere of discourse (*PMN*, 373). We cannot say that anything has an essence, *pour soi* or *en soi*. We can only have recourse to the plurality of language games, each of which has its own rules, its own advantages, its own contribution. There is no final truth, no final flooding of the mind with an overwhelming truth. We cannot escape our freedom, Rorty says with Sartre, that is, from the radical contingency and replaceability of language games. That is to try to shake off one's finitude, to try to become God (*PMN*, 376–77).

III

There is, as I have said above, much to recommend the argument which Rorty is making here. Like Heidegger and Gadamer, Rorty pursues a philosophy of finitude, which recognizes the inability of man to rise to an absolute standpoint and to issue ahistorical declarations about what Being "is" as if there were no man, and about what man is as if the philosopher himself were not caught up in his own humanity. There is here something of an "Hegelianism for the people," reflecting its Deweyan origins, in Rorty's proposal about the conversation of mankind, a social and cultural conversation without the Absolute, a *Bildung* without the divine spirit, which is also in keeping with Gadamer's own appropriation of Hegel.[9] And although the notion of truth as a social process is not without problems of its own,[10] it points towards a way in which one can establish a forum in which to debate the pressing needs of the day, a task for which I take Heidegger's "*Denken*" to be singularly ill-equipped, as does Heidegger.[11] But at best I think that Rorty is advising us to swear off metaphysics, to abstain from it as one would abstain from a bad habit, but not to think it through, and to think through it, to its more primordial source, which is the sense of Heidegger's "overcoming" of metaphysics. This attachment to metaphysics Rorty takes to be Heidegger's ultimate illusion and infirmity, his own "fatal attachment to the tradition."[12]

And so I want to discuss two issues—the question of Being and the question of language—in order to show the subtle way in which Rorty, while making use of Heidegger, turns Heidegger against himself. Rorty often enough speaks in Heidegger's name when in fact he is worlds apart from Heidegger. I want to show how that is so and to say a word on Heidegger's behalf. We will take up the question of Being in this section, that of language in the next, and after that the question of hermeneutics.

Rorty wants us to swear off making ontological claims and frankly to concede that we have to do only with a plurality of ontologically neutral language games, games which are bound by an internal criterion of self-coherence but to which we should steadfastly refuse to attach any ontological weight. The alternative is to make the mistake of metaphysics, which is to think that our propositions mirror the world. We are thus presented with a dichotomy: either a metaphysical correspondence theory or a kind of neo-nominalism;[13] either we are speaking about reality or we are just talking; either our talk has ontological bearing or it is just talk (*PMN*, 371).

But Heidegger's critique of metaphysics moves in precisely the opposite direction and hence it eludes Rorty's dichotomy. Heidegger's antidote to the correspondence theory is not ontological but rather propositional abstinence, that is to say, to give up propositional discourse as a form of "objectifying" thought. Metaphysics suffers from the illusion — first instigated by Plato's notion of a pure *nous* looking on at a distance at a pure *eidos* — that there is a world-less subject on the one side and a subject-free object-in-itself on the other (cf. *Being and Time*, section 13). And metaphysics holds that the bridge over this abyss is propositional rectitude. Heidegger rejects objectifying thought not because every attempt to build a bridge is a failure — although he agrees that it is — but because man *already belongs* to Being (the world) in a more primordial way, long *before* propositional discourse arrives on the scene. We are already part of its sweep, we are already part of that from which we would stand apart. Instead of this metaphysical representationalism Heidegger proposes to us a "topological" model of thought (*Da sein*) as the "there" (*da*) of Being's own self-disclosure. Thought is not a "subject" standing over and against "reality" (*realitas*, *Vorhandensein*), or an "object" (*Gegen-stand*), but it is wholly given over to Being as the place where Being emerges into manifestness.[14] Propositional discourse tries to objectify that to which we already belong. There is then a more primordial belonging of Dasein to Being, a "commitment" which Dasein does not *make*, propositionally, but which is *already there*, which belongs to its essential make-up. Heidegger does indeed disavow making "ontological claims" — but only inasmuch as we are always and already (*immer schon*) claimed by Being and hence the posture of making propositional claims upon Being is the *hauteur* of metaphysics. Thinking does not make claims upon Being but is claimed by it (*ins Anspruch nehmen*). We do not enunciate "propositions" which have ontological "commitments" to reality because we are always and from the start "pre-committed" to Being and world. Hence the critique of metaphysical correspondence has the effect of imbedding thought more deeply into Being than is dreamt of in metaphysics, of acknowledging the "identity" (*Zusammen-gehören*) of Being and thinking. And so it is worlds removed from Rorty's ontological abstinence and altogether evades the dichotomy—between mirroring and language-games—which he constructs.

If Rorty accepts Heidegger's critique of the correspondence theory, he rejects the point of this critique, viz., the movement from *orthotes* to *aletheia*. He cuts Heidegger's argument off in its deconstructive phase and never allows it its recollective moment. Since we cannot "represent reality" we must be content with propositions which are only propositions, excise correspondence in favor of a self-enclosed system of propositions. That is no overcoming of metaphysics for Heidegger, but its simple negation which in fact contents itself with the charred ruins of metaphysics. Propositional discourse denuded of correspondence still moves within the framework of metaphysics as its inverse coin. Because it remains within the sphere of propositional discourse, Rorty's shift from a correspondence to a coherence theory of propositional truth is of no consequence to Heidegger. It remains within the sphere of influence of *logos* as *ratio*, as warranted assertions and is unmindful of *logos* as the gathering of thought to Being. Adjudicating claims by a social process in which propositions are understood to refer only to other propositions, and verifying them by their correspondence to reality, do not differ in kind for Heidegger. Each is a species of metaphysics.[15]

Rorty has taken Heidegger's critique of metaphysics and managed to turn it against him. This is aptly illustrated by their common critique of "ocular" metaphors. Knowledge for Rorty is a matter of propositions and the evidence for a proposition is other propositions which are forthcoming in its support. But metaphysics, which turns on the ontological commitment of propositions to reality, wants to be "constrained" by an object of knowledge (*PMN*, 375–76). This is because ever since the time of Plato and Aristotle, metaphysics has thought of propositions on an analogy with perception and hence it wants to be flooded with the presence of an object which compels our assent, just as if we were commanded by Zeus himself (PMN, 157–58). As Rorty rightly points out, Heidegger rejects such "ocular" metaphysics and exposes the roots of it in the Platonic theory of the *idea* (*PMN*, 159, n. 40). But Heidegger has nothing to do with Rorty's remedy against ocularism, which is to sever the bonds between Being and thought in favor of purely intra-linguistic relations. Indeed Heidegger's point is exactly the opposite: ocularism is at fault precisely because of the distance it erects between the disinterested spectator and the spectacle of the world, a distance which cannot be crossed by some theory of "transcendence" which thinks itself able to walk the waters between subject and object. Rorty agrees with Heidegger on the futility of all such remedies and on the need not to solve but to dissolve the problem. But if Rorty's deconstruction of the visual metaphor results in a blind-folded language game, Heidegger turns to acoustical and aural metaphors. He attacks the very notion of a disinterested on-looker, of thought gazing at a distant object, of looking on at a distance. Ocular metaphors presuppose distance and detachment, and Heidegger is constantly replaying them in aural terms which stress the *belonging* of Dasein to Being. Hence Heidegger frequently invokes the kinship between *Hören*, *Hörchen* and *Gehören*: hearing, hearkening to and belonging.[16] Ocular metaphors give way to aural ones in order to regain our sense of the primordial belonging of thought to Being, of man to world.

Heidegger has not therefore given up the idea of constraint so much as he has "retrieved" it in a more radical way. He does not think that the bond between Being and thought can be broken and hence he thinks that all such theories of a self-evident object which compels our assent are solutions to a problem which does not exist. We do not need constraining grounds to assert Being because we are *already in* Being's hold. We are held (*gehalten*) in a relationship (*Ver-hältnis*) to Being by Being itself, he says.[17] And in *A Letter on Humanism* he says that because man is held in the hold of Being, Being alone issues the true *nomos* for man, assigning him his essence and true abode.[18] Man thus is never in a situation where he would require constraining evidence, inasmuch as he is always and already (*immer schon*) bonded to Being, held by Being, sustained by Being.

To sum up this section: the critique of metaphysics in Heidegger and Rorty are at distant removes from one another. Rorty is interested in evading metaphysics by way of purely linguistic theory, by a language purified of all ontological commitments, a language which is just language. Heidegger is not interested in evading metaphysics but in thinking it through to its origins, origins which are indeed unknown to metaphysics itself. The whole point of Heidegger's critique of metaphysics is to regain the ground on which we already stand. If Rorty wants us to take up a language with no strings attached, with no ontological bearing, Heidegger wants us to understand that we are always borne by Being. If the notion of the *Sache*, the matter, of thought is the whole point for Heidegger, it is precisely what Rorty wants to dismiss. If for Rorty a philosophy without mirrors is a philosophy of words, for Heidegger it is a belonging to Being and world.

IV

Like Wittgenstein and Rorty, Heidegger turns everything over to language. He denies that anything comes to presence outside of language.[19] The event by which things emerge fleetingly into presence and drop back into absence is the event of language itself. Language (*Sprache*) and the event of manifestness(*Ereignis*) name one and the same matter (*Sache*). One can even go so far as to say that for Heidegger Being is language. But none of this is to say that Heidegger turns everything over to words, or to a language in which words and propositions have only internal relations with other words, which is Rorty's view.[20] If in the preceding section we argued that for Heidegger thought belongs essentially to Being, we will continue this argument in this secton by adding that we belong to language and that our belonging to language is essentially a way of being bound to Being and world. These are one and the same for Heidegger, not because Being reduces to language, but because the event of Being occurs in and through language, because the world in which we already have our pre-ontological bearings is always and already linguistic. Language is the house of Being for Heidegger not in the sense that we are confined to words — he does not have in mind Rorty's linguistic house-arrest — but in the sense that language houses, shelters, and protects Being. More straightforwardly, language is the way the world is experienced, disclosed, encountered.

Once again the same pattern unfolds in the dialogue between Heidegger and Rorty. Rorty follows Heidegger's critique of the notion that language is here, on the subjective side, and the world there, on the objective side, and that the task of philosophy is to build a bridge between them. That is a dead end. But Rorty's solution is to break the bond of language to Being altogether, whereas Heidegger's remedy is to recover the more primordial belonging of Being to language and of language to Being. Language for Heidegger is not a subjective representation of an object but rather Being's own taking over of man in order to come to words. When man speaks he is not verbalizing inner representations which correspond to outer objects, but letting things come to language in his talk. Hence Heidegger says it is not man who speaks, but Being; man's speaking is in truth a response to a more primal address.[21] And if Rorty would take Heidegger's notion of the language of Being as a vestigial nostalgia for metaphysics, Heidegger would locate Rorty's language games squarely within metaphysics. Rorty and Heidegger, more deeply considered, are not the allies that Rorty leads us to believe; rather each belongs to the other's history of metaphysics. I want to make that clear and then to defend Heidegger's point of view.

In a metaphysical conception of language, according to Heidegger, language is viewed as man-made, as the free creation of the conscious subject, and secondly as a tool or instrument for human purposes—two theses which Rorty enthusiastically embraces. Against these metaphysical conceptions Heidegger holds that it is not man who speaks but language itself, and that before it is an instrument of any sort language is more primordially the disclosure of the world. Let us look briefly at each of these points.

For Rorty language is a game people play, a language game devised by men, a tribute to the resourcefulness and inventiveness of the beings which we are (*PMN*, 378). There is nothing more to language than what we put into it; it has no ontological bearing. The one lesson which Rorty wants us to draw from the edifying philosophers is to keep alternate descriptions alive, to prevent the freezing-over of culture, the translation of the plurality of discourses into one canonical discourse. But in all of this Rorty comes closer to early Sartrean "existentialism" than to Heidegger. If anything, Rorty defends the rights of human resourcefulness to generate new and alternate discourses—but he cuts off the relationship of language to Being. But Heidegger has warned us over and over again not to assimilate his thought to the categories of existential anthropology. And that is why I say that even at his irreverent best Rorty still remains within a metaphysical conception of language. The multiplicity of language games is a tribute to the ability of man to redescribe himself indefinitely, to come up with alternate linguistic formulations, and the search for a single, commensurable discourse is an escape from freedom, bad faith (*PMN*, 384). But that means that language is entirely a human doing, a product of human freedom and subjectivity, uprooted from its bond to Being, to world and to history.

Rorty's view is at the furthest remove from Heidegger's declaration that it is language which speaks, not man (*die Sprache spricht*). Language originates not in the inventiveness of subjectivity but in the openness of Dasein, not in the subject's ingenuity but in letting-be. A man does not create his language but he is born into it, is taken possession of by it. When he speaks his words are heavy with the tradition to which his language belongs. When he speaks his words are heavy with the things themselves to which his language is a response. Genuine, authentic speaking is more fundamentally a listening, and it comes to pass in a silence which Heidegger likens to the stillness outside the *Hütte* on the morning after a night of howling wind and snow. The authentic speaker—the poet is the best example for Heidegger—is taken over by the things themselves, yields to them, lets them come to words in him. Now this paradigm—a very "abnormal" one—is at the furthest remove from the noisy chatter of language games which Rorty defends. Rorty wants what he himself calls "kibitzing" (*PMN*, 393), not the language of Being. There is no higher or deeper hearkening or responding in this language, no sense whatsoever of hearing the things themselves—not because we *represent* them correctly, but because we *belong* to them long before propositional discourse has a chance to get a word in.

By the same token Rorty takes language in pragmatic terms as a man-made creation serving human purposes, and that interpretation of language belongs squarely to what Heidegger calls *Technik*. Language games are devised, revised, and even discarded to meet changing human purposes, to help people cope. Poetry, science, and interpersonal communication are the uses to which language is put; there are as many possible language games as there are human needs to serve. In opposition to this metaphysical-technological conception of language Heidegger thinks language as *logos*, as the original letting-be-seen, the primordial showing,[22] which allows things to be what they are. Language is not a system of words devised for human purposes but the event which gives birth to things, the event in which phenomena are first constituted and take shape for us. Language is not a creature of man's inventiveness but a gift bestowed upon him in which things come to presence.

Indeed at times Rorty's language games seem to me hardly distinguishable from what Heidegger calls "inauthentic discourse" (*Gerede: Being and Time*, section 35). Authentic discourse arises from the silence in which we are addressed by the things themselves; but in inauthentic discourse we are cut off from the *Sache* and trapped in a sphere of words. In inauthentic discourse we take up already formulated assertions and pass them along. But the language games are like that: denuded of ontological bearing they are just talk, just words which lead to other words. In inauthentic discourse we cultivate words for their own sake, keeping our eyes steadily on what others are saying and never on the *Sache* itself. Thus edifying philosophers love conversation, not argument, Rorty says (*PMN*, 372), and want to keep the conversation going. Rorty never mentions the silence from which all language springs. However fundamental this silence may be for Heidegger, it conflicts with Rorty's fundamental paradigm of more and more talk.

This point is effectively brought out when one considers the way in which Rorty has levelled off the plurality of discourses. We can distinguish normal from abnormal discourse, he says, but we can never single out a privileged discourse which has some kind of inside road to the things themselves (*PMN*, 315–22). Now this position, which Rorty invokes in the name of Heidegger and Gadamer, contradicts both thinkers, in my opinion, both of whom clearly think in terms of the originary and the derivative, the primordial and the fallen. In *Being and Time* authentic discourse differs from inauthentic not simply as two different language games, but as the primordial and the fallen or the "uprooted."[23] And in the later works Heidegger clearly singles out the poet and the thinker as speaking a more primordial discourse than that of the objectifying sciences. The poet is preeminent among all artists and among all speakers because he dwells closest to the origin of language, to the pulse of "*Sprache*" itself.[24] Objectivistic language is derivative, made possible only by breaking the primary bond of thinking to Being and artificially "constructing" a subject-object relationship. Such languages are not without rights of their own, to be sure,[25] but there can be no mistaking the fact that they are derivative modes of discourse, achieved by way of modifying our *primary* relation to the world. There is nothing like a sheer plurality of games in Heidegger; there is rather a hierarchy of primordial and founded, and that is why Heidegger is criticized as an elitist.

I believe that there is a good deal more of Derrida in this "Heidegger" than Heidegger himself. Anti-establishment thinkers like Heidegger, Rorty says, "Hammer away at the holistic point that words take their meaning from other words" and that "vocabularies acquire their privileges from the men who use them." Then in a telling footnote Rorty adds, "This Heideggerian point about language"—which in my view contradicts Heidegger's express teachings and represents a metaphysical conception of language—"is spelled out at length and dialectically by Derrida in *La Voix et le Phénomène*" (*PMN*, 368–69). That I take to be something of a give-away. Rorty is not interested in the real matter to be thought in so far as Heidegger is concerned, in *aletheia*, *physis*, and *logos*. He is instead much closer to Derrida, who has adopted the deconstructive phase of Heidegger's thought, declaring the end of philosophy, but who rejects the "task of thought," the "recollective" phase of Heidegger's thought. Rorty is interested in the destruction of the history of ontology in its negative sense; its positive sense is Heidegger's final illusion. The conversation of mankind is not thought, but talk, just "saying something" (*PMN*, 371). I do not hear Heidegger in all this, nor do I think that Rorty hears Heidegger in a really serious sense. He hears only destruction, deconstruction, but not the truly disconcerting: retrieval, recollection. And that it seems to me is a hermeneutic failure, a will to translate everything into one's own terms, to find a commensurable discourse after all (*PMN*, 381). According to Rorty, "hermeneutics" means listening to what is other, to the strange. Yet one wonders if he has not appropriated Heidegger only insofar as Heidegger is familiar and dismissed what is truly strange in Heidegger.

V

That brings us to our final questions: what Rorty thinks hermeneutics is, and how he practices it—which are not unrelated issues.

I have argued that one must be on the alert when Rorty cites the name of Heidegger, for Rorty has in mind only the end of philosophy, not the task of thought. I am not arguing that Rorty does not *know* what Heidegger is saying, that destruction is only a part of the larger movement of retrieval, but that he *rejects* this as an illusion. Now I want to add that not only is Rorty's "Heidegger" suspect, so also is his "hermeneutics" (*PMN*, 315–22). One cannot but applaud Rorty's thrusts at the arrogance of one-dimensional thought, at the monotonous and superficial uniformity of discourse in the age of *Technik*. But Rorty's critique of Western ontology is not positively motivated. He denies metaphysics in order to make room for a plurality of languages. He wants to curb the pretensions of reason, whether in the form of naturalism or idealism, not like Kant, because of what he believes, but because of what he does not believe, viz., that it is ever possible to have more than a more or less successful language game. He does not want to overcome the history of ontology because of something more essential, but because he wants nothing to do with anything more or less essential, with *Wesen*, with Being. All that he asks from his destruction is to preserve the lines of communication among the resulting plurality of discourses. And hermeneutics is the name for the open-endedness of this ongoing conversation. But my difficulty with this hermeneutics, and here I stand with Heidegger, is that it belongs in a fundamental way to the metaphysics it wants to lay aside. For even if one makes the shift from *episteme* to *phronesis*, from truth as a strict science to a social process, from argument to conversation, one still gets no further than propositional discourse, and that means what Heidegger calls "subjectivity." The point is that we belong so fundamentally to the world and to the things themselves that our talk can only proceed from out of the experience of them (*aus der Erfahrung*).[26]

And that is why I think that Rorty takes not only the name of Heidegger but also of Gadamerian hermeneutics in vain (*PMN*, 353–65). Hermeneutics for Rorty is the open-endedness of this discourse, a resolve not to close off innovative redescriptions of ourselves which are fresh and interesting. It is a meta-rule for language games aimed at checking their tendency to absolutize themselves. But hermeneutics for Heidegger is our openness to the messages of the gods, listening to the silent address of Being.[27] And in Gadamer, in whom this dark Heideggerian saying takes on more manageable proportions, hermeneutics bears the full weight of our historical situatedness in the world (in Being), of the whole ontological commitment which Rorty denies but which, in the form of our belonging to the world and Being—our "pre-committedness" to the world—constitutes the essence of Gadamer's and Heidegger's thought.

In Gadamer, hermeneutics arises precisely because of the weight of the tradition and of the impossibility of disengaging ourselves from it.[28] We belong to the world, to the historical tradition, to Being, and hermeneutics is the way thought comes to grips with its own Being-in-the-world. Hermeneutics arises from the limitations of objective thinking, of setting ourselves apart from the world, from that imbeddedness in the world which can never be objectified. The true hermeneutic circle is that we stand already in Being, already belong to Being, and the hermeneutic task is to reestablish contact with that to which we already belong. But for Rorty that is just another version of the illusion of privileged access,[29] and hence Rorty, in my view, denies the genuine hermeneutic circle. For Heidegger and Gadamer we stand already in an understanding of that which is to be understood, and in denying the hermeneutic circle, Rorty has also undermined what Heidegger calls the "hermeneutic situation." For the language we speak has been handed down to us by the tradition. We do not inventively devise language games, but we are historically rooted speakers whose speaking is anchored in the world, speaking a language which bears ontological and historical weight. Rorty's language games are weightless creatures and his hermeneutics a mechanics of weightlessness. There can be no hermeneutic situation, no bond of thought to Being, to the world, to history.[30] The hermeneutic situation means that we are always caught up in the historical sweep, thrown, factical, historical. Our language is handed over to us by the tradition. We are delivered over to a tradition and hermeneutics is the way to find what that tradition says to us here and now. Hermeneutics thus means listening to the voice of the tradition and to the voice of the things themselves as they speak to us in the tradition. It is hearing hitherto neglected possibilities, hitherto unspoken words which have been all along sounding.

If these language games have no ontological weight, if they do not bespeak our primary bond to the world and to Being, if they are not the way our relationship to the world — that is to say, Being's hold on us — comes to words, then the very historical facticity out of which hermeneutics arises is invalidated. What remains is the free play of discourse which hermeneutics rules over, not only by denying any game absolute authority, but by denying that any discourse has primordiality as well. Hence in the place of hermeneutic understanding, of the attempt of an historically rooted understanding to hear what the work of art or what the historical tradition says to us about ourselves and our world, we have the open-endedness of language games.

The alpha and the omega of Rorty's hermeneutics is to be done with the tradition and he considers Heidegger's life-long attempt to hear what is said there as his final illusion:

> Heidegger's attachment to the notion of "philosophy"—the pathetic notion that even after metaphysics goes something called "Thought" might remain—is simply the sign of Heidegger's own fatal attachment to the tradition: the last infirmity of the greatest of the German professors.[31]

Here the cards are on the table. Hearing what is still unspoken in the tradition, the very essence of hermeneutics for Heidegger and Gadamer, is an illusion. The attempt to hear what the tradition says is precisely to remain a victim of the tradition:

> By offering us "openness of Being" to replace "philosophical argument," Heidegger helps preserve all that was worst in the tradition he hoped to overcome.[32]

Heidegger remains stuck in metaphysics for Rorty insofar as he remains attached to the fundamental illusion that instigated metaphysics in the first place: that there is a depth dimension, a *Sache*, a matter for thought. Rorty's whole project thus amounts to an attempt to short-circuit what Heidegger takes to be the one thing which is most genuinely worthy of thought.

Now that, as I see it, is the gulf which separates Heidegger and Rorty—a gulf which separates them on Being, on language, on hermeneutics. One has to be impressed with Rorty's range, with his ability to move back and forth between both traditions, with his intercontinental ambidexterity. But I have tried in these pages to expose the serious differences between Heidegger and Rorty and to show that each is for the other the latest victim in the history of metaphysics. Now on Rorty's own terms hermeneutics is a matter of keeping the conversation going, of listening to what is truly, genuinely other. But one wonders to what extent Rorty confronts the genuinely incommensurable in Heidegger's thought. He listens to the critique of the correspondence theory of truth, of metaphysics as representationalism, of the traditional metaphysical distinctions, but he hears only language games and social practice. Is this not to translate everything into one's own terms, to establish a normative, commensurable discourse, after all? Does not everything which Heidegger says get translated back into some kind of statement about language games? Is there not a trace of "reductionism" in holding that thinkers like Heidegger and Kierkegaard are providing us with "alternate descriptions" of ourselves? Did Kierkegaard take himself to be giving an "alternate description" of becoming a Christian? Is this anything more than a reductionistic translation?

It is Rorty who poses for himself the project of a dialogue with Heidegger, of listening to his incommensurable discourse. Yet he rejects the truly incommensurable and "abnormal" thought in Heidegger: that the Being of language is the language of Being, that the critique of truth as *orthotes* is aimed at recovering truth as *aletheia*, that language itself speaks, not man. He rejects Heidegger's call to go beyond a humanistic conception of thought and language, to think in terms of Being and not man, in terms of Being and not beings. The Heidegger with whom Rorty dialogues is not an autonomous voice from another tradition but a Heidegger who has been integrated into a critique of metaphysics which is not at all uncommon among English-speaking philosophers. There is no fusion of horizons here but rather an assimilation into one's own already established horizon. Rorty denies the strangest of the strange in Heidegger, the abiding incommensurability of the thought which thinks that which is not a thing.[33] From the beginning Heidegger warned us that the wages of raising the question of Being is anxiety. Hermeneutics on that account is readiness for anxiety. But for that hermeneutics Rorty does not seem to me as ready as Wittgenstein himself, who said: "I can readily think what Heidegger means by Being and anxiety."[34] One wonders if there is not a depth structure, not only in Heidegger, but also in Wittgenstein, which is drowned out by the conversation of mankind.

VI

In my view, the point that the continental philosophers have been making, first under the name of "existentialism," then of "phenomenology," and nowadays of "hermeneutics" — all of which, to use Rorty's term, is "edifying" philosophy — is to make of philosophy a concerted effort to put man back in touch with himself. Their attack upon metaphysics has been aimed at reawakening a sense of the human drama, at recovering the lived quality of our experience and the historicality of the dialogue into which we have all been entered. On this account, everything turns on what Heidegger, following Kierkegaard, called the "repetition" or "retrieval" (*Wiederholung*) of a primordial but latent pre-understanding in which we all always and already stand. If that pre-understanding is denied, if it is called the fallacy of privileged access, as in Rorty, or a vestige of the metaphysics of presence, as in Derrida,[35] then the essential nerve of the critique of metaphysics which philosophers from Kierkegaard to Gadamer have been making has been cut. For the "edifying" philosophers have been saying that metaphysics has systematically suppressed this authentic pre-understanding in favor of speculative constructions which are more to the liking of its own theoretical tastes. Their work of "retrieval" is meant to bring to a halt the flight of metaphysics from the finitude and limitations of man. Ever since its inauguration in Platonism metaphysics has sought the antidote to finitude and the cure for mortality. Soul, substance, *Geist*, transcendental subjectivity — all of these are so many constructions meant to insulate man from his finitude, to preserve for him some kind of inner absolute core, some sort of contact with absolute knowledge.

Now it is precisely Rorty's attempt to break with such metaphysical idols, his pursuit of a non-absolutistic philosophy of finitude, which most strongly recommends the work in which he is presently engaged and which, it seems to me, is his most genuine point of contact with the great continental tradition of the last two centuries. But the attempt to overcome the diverse forms of Platonism through which metaphysics has passed must not become a denial of a truth behind or beneath metaphysics, a denial of what Heidegger has called the sphere of the "primordial" or "originary" (*ursprünglich*), an origin which is, I hasten to add, more originary than any metaphysical *arche* or *principium*. The overcoming of metaphysics has always meant the "regression," the way back (*Rückgang*), into this more originary sphere. It is true enough, as Derrida says, that the overcoming of metaphysics must not be content with the higher man, in whom there is still a trace of pity for metaphysics, but must bring forth the *Übermensch* himself, who truly overcomes metaphysics. But let us not forget that the *Übermensch* is not signified by the lion, whose destruction is only preparatory, but by the child, who is creative and a new beginning.[36]

And it is for this new beginning, for this recovery of a sense of the beings which we ourselves are, that the work of the edifying philosophers has been undertaken.

That is indeed the point which is constantly being made when Heidegger speaks of the "oblivion of Being" (*Seinsvergessenheit*). Now I frankly concede that the word "Being" has always had a mystifying effect upon Heidegger's readers, particularly his Anglo-American readers, and I rather think he did better when he avoided using this word and spoke instead of *physis*, *aletheia*, event (*Ereignis*), or world. In fact his most illuminating accounts of what "Being" means, and hence of what he wants to retrieve, are to be found in those later essays which speak of the earth and the heavens, gods and mortals.[37] Here as nowhere else it becomes plain that Being for him means the world in which mortals—in which man as *homo, humus* (*Being and Time*, section 42)—dwell. World is the place of birth and death, growth and decline, joy and pain, of the movement of the seasons, of the mysterious rhythm of human time. It is the silence of that primordial rhythm which has been shattered by metaphysics—by the ontology whose natural outcome is technology—and which Heidegger in particular wants to restore.

What I hear in the edifying philosophers—with whom, I hope, Rorty has opened up a permanent dialogue—is a call, or better a recall, back to the human setting of our lives, back to a sense of finitude and mortality, to the joy and the tragedy of the human condition, to an understanding of ourselves in which we can *recognize* ourselves. In my view, everything in hermeneutics depends upon this recognition, upon our ability to *find ourselves* in the account. Hermeneutics, as Heidegger said, puts something into words for the first time which we have all along understood but for which we have hitherto lacked the words.[38] The point of the overcoming of metaphysics is precisely that metaphysics has been oblivious of this understanding, that it has suppressed it, or distorted it beyond recognition, that it has substituted for it intellectualistic reconstructions in which we are experientially unrecognizable. Johannes Climacus liked to quip that when one is talking with a Hegelian the first thing to do is to wring from him a concession that he is after all only a human being, and not absolute science, or the speculative standpoint, or some other fantastic creature.[39] And Johannes' point is well made. For metaphysics has always been on the look-out for a way around finitude; it is always looking for the cure.

The great continental thinkers of the last two centuries have been anti-metaphysical, not out of a negative urge to raze, but because they saw in metaphysics a flight from that which it should have been its first order of business to affirm. Their anti-metaphysical polemics have had the positive sense of recalling us to a sense of ourselves and of the structure of our world, a sense which we have all along understood but have been unwilling or unable to say. It is this sense of recalling, retrieving, recovering, which belongs to the heart of Heidegger's project and which is altogether missing in Rorty.

What I find in Rorty, and in Derrida too, is that the deconstructive moment, the moment of critique, has been detached from its original matrix, discharged from the service of hermeneutic retrieval, and put on the loose to lead a life of its own. And a deconstruction of that sort can only come to grief. I am troubled by the new alliances, by Rorty's Anglo-Heideggerian alliance and by Derrida's Franco-Heideggerian alliance. I do not hear in either the voice which calls us back to ourselves, which bids us to say what we already know. And that, as I understand them, is the essential point which Heidegger and the other "edifying" philosophers have been making and which separates them from these new alliances in the most decisive way.

NOTES

1. I have in mind *Philosophy and the Mirror of Nature* (Princeton: Princeton University Press, 1979), hereafter *PMN*; "A Reply to Dreyfus and Taylor," *The Review of Metaphysics* 34 (September 1980): 39–46, 47–56; "Overcoming the Tradition: A Reply to Heidegger and Dewey," in *Heidegger and Modern Philosophy*, ed. Michael Murray (New Haven: Yale University Press, 1978) pp. 239–58, reprinted from *The Review of Metaphysics* 30 (December 1976): 280–305. We will cite the Murray edition. See also "Pragmatism, Relativism, and Irrationalism," *Proceedings and Addresses of the American Philosophical Association* 53 (1980): 719–38; and "Nineteenth-Century Idealism and Twentieth-Century Textualism," *The Monist* 64, 2 (April 1981): 155–74.

2. This is the ironic title of Gadamer's major work, *Wahrheit und Methode* (Tübingen: Mohr, 1975). See also David Hoy's comment on this title in *The Critical Circle* (Berkeley: University of California Press, 1978), pp. 92–93.

3. Martin Heidegger, *Zur Sache des Denkens* (Tübingen: Niemeyer, 1969), p. 78; Eng. trans. *On Time and Being*, trans. J. Stambaugh (New York: Harper & Row, 1972), p. 70. See also Heidegger's essay "Vom Wesen der Wahrheit" for his best account of the movement from *adequatio* to *aletheia*. This essay is in *Gesamtausgabe*, B. 9, *Wegmarken* (Frankfurt: Klostermann, 1976), pp. 177–202, and in a good English translation by John Sallis in *Martin Heidegger: Basic Writings*, ed. David Krell (New York: Harper & Row, 1977), pp. 117–41.

4. Heidegger's critique of Plato is to be found in *Wegmarken* ("Platons Lehre von der Wahrheit"), pp. 203–38; the currently available English translation is not reliable.

5. Cf. *PMN*, 163, n. 42; this is a favorite expression of Heidegger's which he uses in an important essay entitled "Das Ende der Philosophie und die Aufgabe des Denkens," in *Zur Sache des Denkes*, pp. 61 ff. (*On Time and Being*, pp. 55 ff.).

6. This is an omnipresent theme in Heidegger's work. See *Being and Time*, translated by John MacQuarie and Edward Robinson (New York: Harper & Row, 1962), sections 13, 28, and 43a (this edition also provides the pagination in the margins to the German edition: *Sein und Zeit*, [Tübingen: Niemeyer, 1963]). See also *Der Satz vom Grund* (Pfullingen: Neske, 1965), pp. 13–61 and my commentary on these pages in *The Mystical Element in Heidegger's Thought* (Athens: Ohio University Press, 1978), pp. 51–60.

7. Heidegger, *Being and Time*, sections 3–4; in the "Seminar" which was held on "Time and Being" Heidegger denied that anything was to be erected on this "fundamental" ontology; cf. *Zur Sache des Denkens*, p. 34 (*On Time and Being*, pp. 31–32).

8. Rorty, "Overcoming the Tradition," p. 256.

9. See *Wahrheit und Methode*, p. 451 where Gadamer speaks of avoiding a "metaphysics of infinity in the Hegelian manner." English translation: *Truth and Method* (New York: Seabury Press, 1975), p. 433; this translation should be used with caution.

10. See Richard Bernstein, "Philosophy in the Conversation of Mankind," *The Review of Metaphysics* 33 (June 1980): 745–75.

11. Heidegger frustrates his interviewers by constantly claiming that "thought" (*Denken*) can give no concrete advice in the present political situation, not even indirect advice. Cf. " 'Nur noch ein Gott Kann Uns Retten,' Der Spiegel-Gesprach mit Martin Heidegger am 23 September, 1966," *Der Spiegel* (Hamburg), no. 26, 31 May 1976, pp. 193 ff.; English trans.: "Only a God Can Save Us: *Der Spiegel's* Interview with Martin Heidegger," trans. M. Alter and J. D. Caputo, *Philosophy Today* 20 (Winter 1976): 267–84.

12. Rorty, "Overcoming the Tradition," p. 256. In the same vein Der-

rida wants to go beyond Heidegger's critique of metaphysics which attempts deconstruction "without changing ground, by repeating what is implicit in the founding concepts and original problematics, by using against the edifice the instruments or stones available in the house"—as opposed to his own deconstruction which means: "To decide to change ground, in a discontinous and eruptive manner, by stepping abruptly outside and by affirming absolute rupture and difference." See Jacques Derrida, "The Ends of Man," trans. E. Morot-Sir et al., *Philosophy and Phenomenological Research* 30 (1969): 56.

13. I use the word nominalism in the sense that we are restricted to the words we use, the language we speak, whereas for Heidegger it is in language that our world is disclosed. I do not mean nominalism in the classical sense in which it is words, not concepts, which correspond to things—obviously a metaphysical sense for Rorty—nor the sense criticized by Wittgenstein in which all words are thought of as nouns. See Wittgenstein's *Philosophical Investigations*, trans. G. E. M. Anscombe (New York: Macmillan, 1953), pp. 2–3.

14. The "identity" of Being and Dasein, in the sense of their "belonging together" (*Zusammen-gehören*) is argued throughout Heidegger's later writings, but see especially "Der Satz der Identität" in *Identity and Difference*, trans. by J. Stambaugh (New York: Harper & Row, 1969).

15. I might add parenthetically that I am not here defending a pre- or non-linguistic experience, which is a myth that Sellars rightly criticizes (*PMN*, 182ff.). The pre-predicative sphere is not pre-linguistic; it is the language of the poet, or of a man buried in a matter of urgent business, whereas the proposition is the language of a detached observer. See *Being and Time*, section 33.

16. See *Being and Time*, section 34 and *Der Satz vom Grund*, p. 91.

17. "Ein Verhältnis zu etwas wäre somit dann das wahre Verhältnis wenn es von dem, wozu es sich verhält, in seinem eigenen Wesen gehalten wird." Heidegger *Gelassenheit* (Pfullingen: Neske, 1959), p. 50; English trans.: *Discourse on Thinking*, trans. J. Anderson and E. Freund (New York: Harper & Row, 1966), p. 72.

18. Heidegger, *A Letter on Humanism*, trans. F. Capuzzi, in *Basic Writings*, pp. 238–39; *Ein Humanismusbrief* in *Wegmarken*, pp. 360–61.

19. "Language, by naming beings for the first time, first brings beings to word and to appearance. Only this naming nominates beings *to* their Being from out of their Being." Heidegger, "The Origin of the Work of Art," trans. A. Hofstadter, in *Poetry, Language, Thought* (New York: Harper & Row, 1971), p. 73; "Der Ursprung des Kunstwerkes," *Gesamtausgabe*, B. 5, *Holzwege* (Frankfurt: Klosterman, 1977), p. 61. Heidegger's overall view of language is presented in *Unterwegs zur Sprache*, (Pfullingen: Neske, 1959); I would particularly recommend "Der Weg zur Sprache," pp. 239ff.; English

trans.: *On the Way to Language*, trans. Peter Hertz (Harper & Row, 1959), pp. 111 ff. See also "Die Sprache," *Unterwegs zur Sprache*, pp. 11–33; English trans.: "Language," *Poetry, Language, Thought*, pp. 189–210.

20. This is also the structuralist view which is trenchantly criticized by Paul Ricoeur in "Structure, Word, Event," in *The Philosophy of Paul Ricoeur*, ed. C. Reagan and D. Stewart (Boston: Beacon Press, 1978), pp. 109 ff.

21. Heidegger, *Unterwegs zur Sprache*, pp. 254–262; *On the Way to Language*, pp. 124, 131.

22. Heidegger, *Unterwegs zur Sprache*, pp. 252–53; *On the Way to Language*, pp. 122–23.

23. *Being and Time*, section 35, p. 214. The same attack on the distinction between primordial and derivative is also found in Derrida: "Yet is not the contrast between primordial and derivative properly metaphysical? Is not a demand for an *arche* in general—whatever precautions are taken with this concept—the essential operation of metaphysics? Is there not at least some Platonism in the notion of *Verfallen?*" See J. Derrida, "*Ousia* and *gramme*: A Note to a Footnote in *Being and Time*," trans. E. Casey, *Phenomenology in Perspective*, ed. J. Smith (The Hague: M. Nijhoff, 1970), p. 89.

24. Heidegger, "Der Ursprung des Kunstwerkes," pp. 60–62; "The Origin of the Work of Art," pp. 73–74.

25. See Heidegger's "Wissenschaft und Besinnung," in *Vorträge und Aufsätze* (Pfullingen: Neske, 1954), pp. 45–70; Eng. trans. "Science and Reflection," in *The Question Concerning Technology*, trans. W. Lovitt (New York: Harper & Row, 1977), pp. 155 ff.

26. Heidegger, "Aus der Erfahrung des Denkens," the title of a short but penetrating piece in *Aus der Erfahrung des Denkens* (Pfullingen: Neske, 1965). English trans.: "The Thinker as Poet," in *Poetry, Language, Thought*, pp. 1–14.

27. Heidegger, *Unterwegs zur Sprache*, pp. 121–22; *On the Way to Language*, pp. 29–30; Heidegger refers to Plato's *Ion*, 534e.

28. This is argued throughout Gadamer's *Wahrheit und Methode*, but see especially pp. 324–60; *Truth and Method*, pp. 305–41.

29. "I don't think that one should try to find numinous depths in the prereflective consciousness any more than that one should try to find absoluteness in the in-itselfness of atoms. The two attempts seem to me to be merely the Romantic and the Classic forms of the same Cartesian obsession with 'immediate contact with the object'." "A Reply to Dreyfus and Taylor," *The Review of Metaphysics* 34 (September 1980): 42.

30. It is clear that Rorty *wants* to think historically (*PMN*, 9–10, 367), but my question is how language games which are devised with a Sartrean freedom, and which bear no ontological weight, can stand in a history of effects. If our language has no bearing on the world, then how can history

have any bearing on it?

31. Rorty, "Overcoming the Tradition," p. 256.

32. Ibid., p. 258.

33. In a lecture given in February 1981 in Haverford, Pennsylvania, Rorty seemed to me to want to improve upon his earlier rendering of Heidegger in "Overcoming the Tradition." He said among other things that "Being" is what the world would be like if poetry were the normal discourse. That makes considerable progress over calling it a pathetic illusion. Once again, though, I presume that poetry is just one more discourse, with no special privileges. And again I have the distinct sense that Rorty is saying that the thought of Being means "talking poetically," and not an experience of Being. As if Hölderlin had written "poetically does man talk," and not "poetically does man dwell."

34. Ludwig Wittgenstein, "On Heidegger on Being and Dread," with commentary by Michael Murray, in Murray, *Heidegger and Modern Philosophy*, p. 80. I have rendered *Angst* as "anxiety," not "dread." For more on the depth structure in Wittgenstein, see Allan Janik and Stephen Toulmin, *Wittgenstein's Vienna* (New York: Simon & Schuster, 1973), pp. 194–95 *et passim*.

35. Derrida, "The Ends of Man," pp. 46–48.

36. Derrida, "The Ends of Man," p. 57; the reference is to Friedrich Nietzsche, *Thus Spoke Zarathustra*, trans. R. J. Hollingdale (Baltimore: Penguin Books, 1969), "Of the Three Metamorphoses," pp. 54–56 and "Of the Higher Man," pp. 296–306.

37. See Heidegger, *Poetry, Language, Thought*, pp. 143–86.

38. Heidegger, *Being and Time*, section 63, p. 362.

39. S. Kierkegaard, *Kierkegaard's Concluding Unscientific Postscript*, trans. D. Swenson and W. Lowrie (Princeton: Princeton University Press, 1941), p. 99.

13. FROM HERMENEUTICS TO PRAXIS

Richard J. Bernstein

One of the most important and central claims in Hans-Georg Gadamer's philosophical hermeneutics is that all understanding involves not only interpretation, but also application. Against an older tradition that divided up hermeneutics into *subtilitas intelligendi* (understanding), *subtilitas explicandi* (interpretation), and *subtilitas applicandi* (application), a primary thesis of *Truth and Method* is that these are not three independent activities to be relegated to different sub-disciplines, but rather they are internally related. They are all moments of the single process of understanding. I want to explore this integration of the moment of application into hermeneutic understanding which Gadamer calls the "rediscovery of the fundamental hermeneutic problem."[1] For it not only takes us to the heart of what is distinctive about philosophical hermeneutics but it reveals some of the deep problems and tensions implicit in hermeneutics. First, I want to note some of the central features of what Gadamer means by philosophical hermeneutics. Then I can specify the problem that he is confronting when dealing with application. This will enable us to see what Gadamer seeks to appropriate from Aristotle, and especially from Aristotle's analysis of *phronesis* in book VI of the *Nicomachean Ethics*, in elucidating the sense in which all understanding involves application. Gadamer certainly realizes that "Aristotle is not concerned with the hermeneutical problem and certainly not with its historical dimension, but with the right estimation of the role that reason has to play in moral action" (*TM*, p. 278; *WM*, p. 295), and yet Gadamer claims that "if we relate Aristotle's description of the ethical phenomenon and especially the virtue of moral knowledge to our own investigation, we find Aristotle's analysis is in fact a kind of model of the problems of hermeneutics" (*TM*, p 299; *WM*, p. 307.)[2] But Gadamer's own understanding, interpretation, and appropriation of Aristotle has much richer consequences. It is itself a model of what he means by hermeneutical understanding. It is an exemplar of effective-historical consciousness

(*Wirkungsgeschichtliches Bewusstsein*), the fusion of horizons (*Horizontverschmelzung*), the positive role of temporal distance, how understanding is part of the process of the coming into being of meaning, the way in which tradition "speaks to us" and makes a "claim to truth" upon us, and what it means to say that "the interpreter dealing with a traditional text seeks to apply it to himself." Furthermore, when we see how Gadamer appropriates Aristotle's text, we gain a deeper understanding of why the *Geisteswissenschaften* are moral-practical disciplines in the sense in which the *Ethics* and the *Politics* are practical disciplines, and why Gadamer thinks that "hermeneutic philosophy is the heir of the older tradition of practical philosophy" whose chief task is to "justify this way of reason and defend practical and political reason against the domination of technology based on science."[3] Gadamer's own understanding of philosophical hermeneutics can itself be interpreted as a series of footnotes and reflections on his decisive intellectual encounter with Aristotle, an encounter to which he frequently refers and which was initiated by his participation in Heidegger's seminar on the *Nicomachean Ethics*.[4]

In order to orient our discussion, it is important to recall some of the primary characteristics of philosophical hermeneutics. As Gadamer frequently reiterates, "the hermeneutic phenomenon is basically not a problem of method at all. It is not concerned with a method of understanding, by means of which texts are subjected to scientific investigation like all other objects of experience. It is not concerned primarily with amassing ratified knowledge which satisfies the methodological ideal of science—yet it is concerned, here too, with knowledge and with truth" (*TM*, xi; *WM*, xxvii). The task is to elucidate the distinctive type of *knowledge and truth* that is realized whenever we authentically understand.[5] From Gadamer's perspective, it has been the obsession with *Method*, and with thinking that the primary task of hermeneutics is to specify a distinctive method of the *Geisteswissenschaften* that can rival the scientific method of the *Naturwissenshaften* which plagued and distorted nineteenth-century hermeneutics. This led to a view of understanding as primarily a psychological subjective activity, as involving some sort of empathy where we can overcome and leap out of our own historical situation and identify ourselves with the intentions of the authors of texts or the intentions of the historical actors that we are studying. There was a "latent Cartesianism" in this tradition and an acceptance of the basic dichotomy between what is objective and subjective.[6] But it is just this dichotomy that Gadamer seeks to question and undermine. According to Gadamer, it is only with Heidegger that the full dimensions of understanding were fully realized. Implicit in Heidegger and explicit in Gadamer are two central claims: the ontological primacy of hermeneutics and its universality. We are "thrown" into the world as beings who understand; and understanding itself is not one type of activity of a subject, but may properly be said to underlie all activities.

When Gadamer introduces the concept of play and tells us that play is "the clue to ontological explanation" (*TM*, p. 91; *WM*, p. 97), he is seeking to show us that there is a more primordial mode of being for understanding our being in the world—an alternative to the Cartesian persuasion which rivets our attention on the subjective attitudes toward what is presumably objective. "Play has its own essence which is independent of the consciousness of those who play." "The players are not subjects of play; instead play merely reaches presentation through the players" (*TM*, p. 92; *WM*, p. 98). Play has its own rhythm, its own buoyancy, its distinctive to-and-fro movement. This mode of being of play is what Gadamer takes to be characteristic of our relation with works of art, texts, and indeed anything that is handed down to us. Gadamer introduces the concept of play in order to highlight the subtle dialectical and dialogical relation that exists between the interpreter and what he seeks to interpret. We misconceive this relation if we think that we are merely subjects or spectators standing over and against what is objective and what exists *an sich*. We participate in the works of art, texts, and tradition that we encounter, and it is only through understanding that their meaning and truth is realized. The aim of hermeneutical understanding is to open ourselves to what texts and tradition "say to us," to open ourselves to their meaning and the claim to truth that they make upon us.[7] But what Gadamer stresses, building on Heidegger, is that we do *not* do this by forgetting or seeking to bracket our own historicity, our own forestructures, prejudgments, and prejudices. Here we touch upon one of the most controversial features of Gadamer's philosophic hermeneutics, viz., his *apologia* for prejudice against the Enlightenment's "prejudice against prejudice" (*TM*, p. 240; *WM*, p. 255). As Gadamer tells us:

> It is not so much our judgments as it is our prejudices that constitute our being. This is a provocative formulation, for I am us-

ing it to restore to its rightful place as a positive concept of prejudice that was driven out of our linguistic usage by the French and English Enlightenment. . . . Prejudices are not necessarily unjustified and erroneous, so that they inevitably distort the truth. In fact, the historicity of our existence entails that prejudices, in the literal sense of the word, constitute the initial directedness of our whole ability to experience. Prejudices are biases of our openness to the world. They are simply the conditions whereby we experience something — whereby what we encounter says something to us.[8]

Gadamer does want to make the all-important distinction between "blind prejudices" which are unjustified and those "justified prejudices that are productive of knowledge" — what we might call "enabling prejudices." This does not diminish the thrust of his claim that *both* sorts of prejudice are constitutive of what we are. But then how do we distinguish between these types of prejudice or prejudgment? One answer is clearly ruled out. We cannot do this by a solitary or monological act of pure self-reflection where we bracket or suspend judgment about *all* of our prejudices. This is what is ontologically impossible — for what we *are*, and what is revelatory of our human finitude, is that prejudices are constitutive of our being. Indeed the answer that Gadamer gives to the question of how we make this distinction between blind and enabling prejudices is the very one that Descartes rejected from serious consideration. It is only through the dialogical encounter with what is handed down to us that we can test and *risk* our prejudices. Unlike Descartes (and Hegel), Gadamer sees this as a constant open task, not one that can ever achieve finality or closure. For Gadamer then, there is a threefold temporal character to prejudices. They are themselves inherited from tradition and shape what we are, whether we are aware of this or not. It is because our prejudices themselves have their source in the very tradition that we seek to understand that we can account for our *affinity* with, our belonging to, (*Zugehörigkeit*) tradition. While inherited from tradition they are constitutive of what we are *now*. But there is also a projective or anticipatory aspect of our prejudices and prejudgments, a dimension highlighted by Heidegger's own emphasis on fore-structures, i.e., on fore-having, fore-sight, and fore-conceptions.[9] It is through the hermeneutical circle of understanding that we call upon these forestructures which enable us to understand, and at the same time discriminate critically between blind and enabling prejudices.

We can begin to see where Gadamer is leading us and why the problem of application is so important for him. On the one hand, Gadamer tells us that hermeneutic understanding is always tempered to the "thing itself" that we are trying to understand. We seek nothing less than to understand the *same* text or the same piece of tradition. But the *meaning* of what we seek to understand is not self-contained, it does not exist *an sich*. The meaning of a text or of tradition is only realized through the happening (*pathos*) of understanding. But such understanding is only possible because of the prejudices and prejudgments that are constitutive of what we are—our own historicity. This is why Gadamer tells us that to understand is always to understand *differently*. There is a play, a to-and-fro movement that occurs in all understanding in which both what we seek to understand and our prejudices are dynamically involved with each other. Unlike those who think that such appropriation or application to our hermeneutical situation reveals a distortion or a deficiency which is to be overcome, it is the positive enabling roles of prejudgments and prejudices that become thematic for philosophical hermeneutics.

It is in this context that the problem of application becomes so central for Gadamer. It is here that we can see why Aristotle's analysis of *phronesis* is so important to him. For *phronesis* is a form of reasoning and knowledge that involves a distinctive mediation between the universal and the particular. This mediation is not accomplished by any appeal to technical rules or Method (in the Cartesian sense), or by the subsumption of a pre-given determinate universal to a particular case. What Gadamer emphasizes about *phronesis* is that it is a form of reasoning, yielding a type of "ethical know-how" in which both what is universal and what is particular are *co-determined*. Furthermore, *phronesis* involves a "peculiar interlacing of being and knowledge, determination through one's own becoming."[10] It is not to be identified with or confused with the type of "objective knowledge" that is detached from one's own being and becoming. Just as *phronesis* determines what the *phronimos* becomes, Gadamer wants to make a similar claim for all authentic understanding, i.e., that it is not detached from the interpreter, but constitutive of his or her *praxis*. Understanding for Gadamer is a form of *phronesis*.

We gain a subtler comprehension of what this means by noting the contrasts that Gadamer highlights when he explores the ways in which Aristotle distinguishes *phronesis* from the other "intellectual virtues," especially from *episteme* and *techne*. *Episteme*, scientific knowledge, is knowledge of what is universal, of what exists "of necessity" and takes the form of the scientific demonstration. The subject matter, the form, the *telos*, the way in which *episteme* is learned and taught, differ from *phronesis*, the form of reasoning appropriate to *praxis*, where there is always a mediation between the universal and the particular which involves a deliberation and choice. But it is not primarily the contrast between *episteme* and *phronesis* that Gadamer takes to be instructive for hermeneutics, but rather the careful ways in which Aristotle distinguishes *techne* (technical know-how) from *phronesis* (ethical know-how). And here Gadamer stresses three contrasts. 1) *Techne*, or "a technique is learned and can be forgotten; we can lose a skill. But ethical 'reason' can neither be learned nor forgotten. . . . By contrast, the subject of ethical reason, of *phronesis*, man always finds himself in an 'acting situation' and he is always obliged to use ethical knowledge and apply it according to the exigencies of his concrete situation."[11] 2) There is a different conceptual relation between means and ends in *techne* and *phronesis*. The end of ethical know-how, unlike a technique, is not a "particular thing or product" but rather "*complete* ethical rectitude of a life time."[12] Even more important, while technical activity does not require that the means which allow it to arrive at an end be weighed anew on each occasion, this is what is required in ethical know-how. In ethical know-how there can be no prior knowledge of the right means by which we realize the end. For the end itself is only concretely specified in deliberating about the means appropriate to *this* particular situation.[13] 3) *Phronesis*, unlike *techne*, is a distinctive type of "knowledge-for-the-sake-of-oneself." This is indicated when Aristotle considers the variants of *phronesis*, especially *synesis* (understanding). "It appears in the fact of concern, not about myself, but about the other person. Thus it is a mode of moral judgment. . . . The question here, then, is not of a general kind of knowledge, but of its specification at a particular moment. This knowledge also is not in any sense technical knowledge or the application of such. . . . The person with understanding does not know and judge as one who stands apart and unaffected; but rather, as one united by a specific bond with the other, he thinks with the other and undergoes the situation with him" (*TM*, p. 288; *WM*, p. 306).

What does this analysis of *phronesis* and the ways in which it differs from both *episteme* and *techne* have to do with the problems of hermeneutics? The analogy that Gadamer draws, the reason why he thinks it is a "model of the problems of hermeneutics," is that just as application is not a subsequent or occasional part of *phronesis* where we relate some pre-given determinate universal to a particular situation, this is true for *all* understanding. And just as with *phronesis* there is always a mediation between the universal and the particular in which both are codetermined and become integral to the very being of the *phronimos*, this is what Gadamer claims is characteristic of all authentic understanding.

> The interpreter dealing with a traditional text seeks to apply it to himself. But this does not mean that the text is given for him as something universal, that he understands it as such and only afterwards uses it for particular applications. Rather, the interpreter seeks no more than to understand this universal thing, the text; i.e., to understand what this piece of tradition says, what constitutes the meaning and the importance of the text. In order to understand that, he must not seek to disregard himself and his particular hermeneutical situation. He must relate the text to this situation, if he wants to understand at all (*TM*, p. 289; *WM*, p. 307).

What is striking about this passage is that is applies perfectly to the way in which Gadamer himself understands, interprets, and appropriates Aristotle's text. This is what I meant earlier when I said that Aristotle's analysis of *phronesis* is not only a model of the problems of hermeneutics but that Gadamer's interpretation of Aristotle is itself a model or exemplar of what is meant by hermeneutical understanding. In the above passage, Gadamer tells us that if we are to understand what a text or a piece of tradition says then we must not seek to disregard ourselves and our hermeneutical situation. This is characteristic of the way in which Gadamer approaches Aristotle. For what Gadamer takes to be basic for *our* hermeneutical situation is that we are confronted with a world in which there has been a "domination of technology based on science," that there is a "false idolatry of the expert," "a scientific mystification of the modern society of specialization," and a dangerous "inner longing in our society to find in science a substitute for lost orientations."[14] It is this problematic that orients

Gadamer's questioning of Aristotle's text, for Gadamer's central claim is that there has been a forgetfulness and deformation of what *praxis* really is.

Indeed it is through the dialogical encounter with Aristotle's text that we risk and test our own deeply entrenched prejudices which blind us from grasping the autonomy and integrity of *phronesis*. This does not mean that we approach Aristotle without any prejudices and pre-judgments. What enables us to understand Aristotle and appropriate the "truth" of what he says is that we ourselves have been shaped by this effective history. It is not a nostalgic return to Aristotle that Gadamer is advocating, but rather an appropriation of Aristotle's own insights to our concrete situation. Gadamer's interpretation of Aristotle illustrates what he means by the fusion of horizons. We are, of course, questioning Aristotle's text from our own historical horizon. But we distort the very idea of a horizon if we think that it is self-contained, that we are prisoners enclosed within it. "The historical movement of human life consists in the fact that it is never utterly bound to any one standpoint, and hence can never have a truly closed horizon" (*TM*, p. 271; *WM*, p. 288). We come to understand what Aristotle is saying and at the same time come to a deeper understanding of our own situation when we are sensitive to Aristotle's own confrontation with the "professional lawmakers whose function at that time corresponded to the role of the expert in modern scientific society."[15] By appropriating the "truth" of what Aristotle says, especially the way in which he distinguishes practical reason from theoretical and technical reason, we thereby enlarge our own horizon. It is this fusion of horizons that enables us to risk and test our own prejudices. For the dialogical encounter with Aristotle allows us to see how the contemporary understanding of *praxis* has become deformed. We can learn from Aristotle what "practice" really is, why it is not to be identified with the "application of science to technical tasks." Gadamer realizes that in modern society *techne* itself has been transformed, but this only highlights the importance of what we can learn from Aristotle about *praxis* and *phronesis*. He tells us:

> In a scientific culture such as ours the fields of *techne* and art are much more expanded. Thus the fields of mastering means to pre-given ends have been rendered even more monological and controllable. The crucial change is that practical wisdom can no

longer be promoted by personal contact and the mutual exchange of views among the citizens. Not only has craftmanship been replaced by industrial work; many forms of our daily life are technologically organized so that they no longer require personal decision. In modern technological society public opinion itself has in a new and really decisive way become the object of very complicated techniques—and this, I think, is the main problem facing our civilization.[16]

The temporal distance between ourselves and Aristotle is not a negative barrier to understanding, but rather positive and productive for understanding. By opening ourselves to what this "piece of tradition" says and to the claim to truth that it makes upon us, we bring to life new meanings of the text. "Understanding must be conceived as part of the process of the coming into being of meaning . . . " (*TM*, p. 147; *WM*, p. 157). And this understanding, like *phronesis*, is a form of moral-practical knowledge which becomes constitutive of what we are in the process of becoming. What Gadamer seeks to show is that authentic hermeneutical understanding truly humanizes us; it becomes integrated in our very being just as *phronesis* itself shapes the being of the *phronimos*.

This emphasis on the moment of appropriation in hermeneutical understanding enables us to see why Gadamer thinks that the *Geisteswissenschaften*—when authentically practiced—are moral-practical disciplines. As hermeneutical disciplines, they are not concerned with amassing "theoretical" knowledge of what is strange and alien. Rather they involve the type of appropriation characteristic of *phronesis*. The type of knowledge and truth that they yield is practical knowledge and truth that shapes our *praxis*. This also helps to clarify why the "chief task" of philosophical hermeneutics is to "correct the peculiar falsehood of modern consciousness" and "to defend practical and political reason against the domination of technology based on science." It is in this sense that "hermeneutic philosophy is the heir of the older tradition of practical philosophy."[17]

This fusion of hermeneutics and *praxis* through the appropriation of *phronesis* has much broader ramifications. For in a number of different contexts we can discern how a variety of thinkers have been led to a reinterpretation or appreciation of the tradition of practical philosophy in order to come to a critical understanding of modern society. It is an underlying theme in the work of Hannah Arendt and Jürgen Habermas, both of whom share Gadamer's concern sharply to distinguish the technical from the practical. The attempt to clarify and restore the integrity of practical reasoning surfaces in such recent critical appraisals as Richard Rorty's *Philosophy and the Mirror of Nature*, Alasdair MacIntyre's *After Virtue*, and Hilary Putnam's *Meaning and the Moral Sciences*. Differences among these thinkers are as important as the common themes that run through their work. But I do think we are witnessing a new turn in the conversation of philosophy and in the understanding of human rationality where there is a recovery and appropriation of the type of practical reasoning, knowledge, and wisdom that is characteristic of *phronesis*.

I have indicated that Gadamer's appropriation of this tradition of practical philosophy is not without problems and tensions. If we take Gadamer seriously, and press his own claims, then they lead us beyond philosophical hermeneutics. Before I begin my immanent critique, it is important to remember that in *Truth and Method*, Gadamer's primary concern is with the understanding and interpretation of works of art, texts, and tradition, with "what is handed down to us." Ethics and politics are not in the foreground of his investigations. Even his discussion of Aristotle is introduced only insofar as it helps to illuminate the hermeneutical phenomenon. But it is also clear that if we pay close attention to Gadamer's writings before and after the publication of *Truth and Method*, there has been an underlying and pervasive concern with ethics and politics—especially with what we can learn from Greek philosophy. In his writings since the publication of *Truth and Method*, Gadamer has returned again and again to the dialectical interplay of hermeneutics and *praxis*. I emphasize this because when we enlarge our horizon and consider the implications of what he is saying for a contemporary understanding of ethics and politics, then a number of difficulties come into sharp relief.

Let me begin with a consideration of the meaning of *truth* for Gadamer, then move to his conception of *criticism*. This will allow us to take a closer look at some of the difficulties with his understanding of *phronesis*. Finally we can turn to Gadamer's reflections on dialogue and its implications for politics. Truth is not only basic for the entire project of philosophical hermeneutics, but it turns out to be one of the most elusive concepts in Gadamer. After all, the primary intention of *Truth and Method* is to defend and elucidate the legitimacy of speaking of the truth of works of art, texts, and tradition. Gadamer tells us that it was not his intention to play off Method against Truth, but rather to show that there is a "different type of knowledge and truth" which is not exhausted by achievements of scientific method and which is only available to us through hermeneutical understanding.[18] This appeal to truth—a truth that transcends our own historical horizon—is absolutely essential in order to distinguish philosophical hermeneutics from a historicist form of relativism. Gadamer concludes *Truth and Method* with strong claims about this distinctive type of truth.

> Thus there is undoubtedly no understanding that is free of all prejudices, however much the will of our knowledge must be directed towards escaping their thrall. It has emerged throughout our investigation that the certainty that is imparted by the use of scientific methods does not suffice to guarantee truth. This is so especially of the human sciences, but this does not mean a diminution of their scientific quality, but on the contrary, a justification of the claim to special humane significance that they have always made. The fact that in the knowing involved in them the knower's own being is involved marks, certainly, the limitation of "method," but not that of science. Rather, what the tool of method does not achieve must—and effectively can—be achieved by a discipline of questioning and research, a discipline that guarantees truth [*die Wahrheit verbürgt*]. (*TM*, p. 447; *WM*, p. 465)

But what precisely does "truth" mean here? And what does it mean to say that there is a discipline of questioning and research that "guarantees truth"? It is much easier to say what "truth" does not mean than to give a positive account. It might seem curious (although I do not think it is accidental) that in a work entitled *Truth and Method*, the topic of truth never becomes fully thematic and is discussed only briefly toward the very end of the book.[19] It is clear, however, that like Hegel and Heidegger, Gadamer criticizes the notion of truth as correspondence, as *adequatio intellectus et rei*, at least in regard to the distinctive type of truth that is achieved through hermeneutical understanding. What Gadamer means by "truth" is a blending of motifs that have resonances in Hegel and Heidegger. For like Hegel, Gadamer seeks to show that there is a truth that is revealed in the process of experience (*Erfahrung*) and which emerges in the dialogical encounter with the very tradition that has shaped us. Even the above passage echoes the typical Hegelian movement from *Gewissheit* (certainty) to *Wahrheit* (truth). And like Heidegger, Gadamer also seeks to recover the notion of *alethia* as disclosedness (*Erschlossenheit*) and unconcealment (*Unverborgenheit*). There is even a parallel between Heidegger's claim that *Dasein* is "equally in truth and in untruth" and Gadamer's claim that prejudices (both true and untrue prejudices) are constitutive of our being. But Gadamer also distances himself from both Hegel and Heidegger. He categorically rejects what Hegel himself took to be the ground for his conception of truth, viz., that "truth is the whole" which is finally revealed in *Wissenschaft*, the absolute knowledge that completes and overcomes experience.[20] Gadamer also stands in an uneasy relation with Heidegger, for he knows all too well where Heidegger's meditation on *alethia* can lead us. He writes: "When science expands into a total technocracy and this brings on the 'cosmic night' of the 'forgetfulness of being,' the nihilism that Nietzsche prophesied, then may one look at the last fading light of the sun that is set in the evening sky, instead of turning around to look for the first shimmer of its return?" And with explicit reference to Heidegger, he tells us "what man needs is not only a persistent asking of ultimate questions, but the sense of what is feasible, what is possible, what is correct, here and now" (*TM*, xxv; *WM*, xxv). But even if we play out the similarities and differences with Hegel and Heidegger, the precise meaning of truth for Gadamer still eludes us. What is even more problematic and revealing is that if we closely examine the way in which Gadamer appeals to "truth," he is employing a concept of truth that he never fully makes explicit. His typical phrasing is to speak of the "claim to truth" (*Anspruch auf Wahrheit*) that works of art, texts, and tradition make upon us. Gadamer never says (and it would certainly distort his meaning) that something is true simply because it is handed down to us. What he is always doing is seeking to appropriate critically what is handed down to us. This is just as evident in his claims about the tradition of practical philosophy as it is in his criticism of the "Enlightenment's prejudice against prejudice." When Gadamer, for example, says, "When Aristotle, in the sixth book of the *Nicomachean Ethics*, distinguishes the manner of 'practical' knowledge . . . from theoretical and technical knowledge, he expresses, in my opinion, one of the greatest truths by which the Greeks throw light upon the 'scientific' mystification of modern society of specialization,"[21] he is not telling us that this is one of the greatest truths simply because it is what Aristo-tle's text says. Rather it is true because Gadamer thinks we can now give convincing arguments to show why it is true. The force is not simply on what tradition says to us, or even on the "claim to truth" that it makes upon us, but on the validation of such claims by critical argu-ments. Gadamer has warned us against reifying tradition and think-ing that it is something simply given.[22] Furthermore tradition is not a seamless whole. There are conflicting traditions making *conflicting* claims of truth upon us. If we take our own historicity seriously, then the challenge that always confronts us is to give the best possible reasons and arguments that are appropriate to our hermeneutical situation in order to validate claims to truth. Gadamer himself makes this point forcefully in his friendly quarrel with Leo Strauss. Commenting on a theme that Gadamer shares with Strauss — the importance of the con-cept of friendship in Aristotle's ethics for recognizing the limitations of modern ethics — he asks: "Does this insight emerge because we 'read' the classics with an eye that is trained by historical science, reconstruct-ing their meaning, as it were, and then considering it possible, trusting that they are right? Or do we see truth in them, because we are think-ing ourselves as we try to understand them, i.e., because what they say seems true to us when we consider the corresponding modern theories that are invoked?" (*TM*, p. 485; *WM*, p. 507). There is no ambiguity in how Gadamer answers his own question. But then this casts the entire question of truth in a very different light. For when it comes to the validation of claims to truth and the correct interpreta-tions of texts, then the essential issue concerns reasons and arguments which are, of course, fallible, and are anticipatory in the sense that they can be challenged and criticized by future argumentation. In ef-fect, I am suggesting that what Gadamer himself is appealing to is a concept of truth which comes down to what can be argumentatively validated by the community of interpreters who open themselves to what tradition says to us. This does not mean that there is some tran-scendental or ahistorical perspective from which we can evaluate com-peting claims to truth. We judge and evaluate such claims by the stan-dards and practices that have been hammered out in the course of history. If I am right in pursuing this line of thought which is implicit in Gadamer then it is extraordinarily misleading — and betrays his own best insights — to say that there is any discipline that "guarantees truth." Rather we can seek only to justify claims to truth by giving the strongest arguments that we can to show why something is true—and this is in fact what Gadamer himself does.

The point that I am making about the concept of truth that is implicit in Gadamer is closely related to the allied concept of criticism. Gadamer tells us, "It is a grave misunderstanding to assume that emphasis on the essential factor of tradition which enters into all understanding implies an uncritical acceptance of tradition and socio-political convervatism. . . . In truth the confrontation of our historic tradition is always a critical challenge of this tradition. . . . Every experience is such a confrontation."[23] But even if we acknowledge what he is saying here and appreciate that this is characteristic of the way in which Gadamer always approaches tradition, there is a problem that Gadamer does not squarely confront. Implicitly or explicitly all criticism appeals to some principles, standards, or criteria. Gadamer is extremely incisive in exposing the fallacy of thinking that such principles, standards or criteria can be removed from our own historicity, and in showing that there is an essential openness and indeterminacy about them. But even if we grant him everything he wants to say about human finitude rooted in historicity, this does not lessen the burden of the question of what is and what ought to be the basis for the critical evaluation of the problems of modernity. One can be extraordinarily sympathetic with Gadamer's critique of objectivism, foundationalism, the search for some Archimedean point that somehow stands outside of our historical situation. But if we take the theme of application or appropriation seriously, and speak about *our* hermeneutical situation, then we must still address the question of what is the basis for our critical judgments. When Gadamer tells us that "the concept of '*praxis*' which was developed in the last two centuries is an awful deformation of what practice really is" or when he speaks of "the peculiar falsehood of modern consciousness: the idolatry of scientific method and the anonymous authority of the sciences,"[24] he is himself appealing to critical standards and norms of what practice really is, and what is truly a human life—standards and norms that demand rational justification and argumentation. It is not *sufficient* to give a justification that directs us to tradition. What is required is a form of argumentation that seeks to *warrant* what is valid in this tradition.

Characteristically, when questions are raised about the validity of standards and norms that are to serve as the basis for criticism, Gadamer tells us that they too are handed down to us and need to be recovered from tradition. But this response is not adequate. Consider again what Gadamer highlights in his appropriation of *phronesis*—the distinctive type of mediation of the universal and the particular. Let us focus on the *universal* element that is mediated in *phronesis*. Gadamer's meaning is illustrated by his interpretation of the role of natural law in Aristotle. In the realm of *praxis*, natural law is not to be thought of as a law that is eternal, immutable, and fully determinate. He tells us, "For according to Aristotle, the idea of an immutable natural law applies only to the divine world, and he declares that with us humans natural law is in the last analysis just as inconstant as positive law."[25] While natural law is not to be reduced to or confused with positive law, it requires interpretation and specification in concrete particular situations of *praxis*. Finding justice in a concrete situation demands perfecting law with equity (*epieikeia*): "It follows, then, according to Aristotle that the idea of natural law serves only a critical function. Nothing in the idea authorizes us to use it dogmatically by attributing the inviolability of natural law to particular and concrete juridical contents."[26] The claim that Gadamer makes about Aristotle's understanding of natural law (the *universal* element) which is essentially open to interpretation and is only concretely specified when related and mediated in a concrete ethical situation is paradigmatic for the application of all ethical principles and norms. But what Aristotle stresses and Gadamer realizes is that what is required for the exercise of *phronesis*, and what keeps it from degenerating into the mere cleverness of the *deinos*, is the existence of such a *nomos* in the polis or community. Given a community in which there is a living shared acceptance of ethical principles and norms, then *phronesis* as the mediation of such universals in concrete particular situations makes sense. But what has become so problematic for us today, what is characteristic of our hermeneutical situation, is that there is so much confusion and uncertainty (some might even say chaos) about what are the norms of the "universals" which ought to govern our practical lives. What Gadamer himself realizes—but I do not think he squarely faces the issues that it raises—is that we are living in a time when the very conditions required for exercise of *phronesis*—the shared acceptance and stability of universal principles and laws—are themselves breaking down. Furthermore, Gadamer does not adequately clarify the type of discourse that is appropriate when questions about the validity of basic norms (or universals) are raised. When pressed on these questions, Gadamer deals with a different issue. He typically stresses that such universals are inherited from tradition, that they are essentially open, that they require the type of mediation in which their meaning is specified in the application to concrete practical situations. But this does not clarify the issue of what are the norms that are to serve as the universals which are to be mediated and codetermined in particular situations. Nor does it clarify how we are to evaluate a situation in which we are forced to question the validity of such norms. If we follow out the logic of Gadamer's own line of thought, if we are really concerned with "the sense of what is feasible, what is possible, what is correct, here and now," then this demands that we turn our attention to the question of how can we nurture and foster the types of community required for the exercise of *phronesis*. Indeed, there is a paradox that stands at the center of Gadamer's thinking about *praxis*. For on the one hand, he acutely analyzes the deformation of *praxis* in the contemporary world, and shows how the main problem facing our civilization is one in which the very possibility for the exercise of *phronesis* is undermined, and yet on the other hand he seems to suggest that, regardless of the type of community in which we live, *phronesis* is always a real possibility. Just as Aristotle saw the continuity and movement from ethics to politics, one would think that this is a movement necessitated by Gadamer's own appropriation of *phronesis*. But Gadamer stops short of facing the issues of what is to be done when the *polis* or community itself is "corrupt"—when there is a breakdown of its *nomos* and of a rational discourse about the norms that ought to govern our practical lives.[27]

In defense of Gadamer, one can see why he stops short of confronting the practical issues of our hermeneutical situation. We can read his philosophical hermeneutics as a profound meditation on the meaning of human finitude, as a constant warning against the excesses of what he calls "planning reason," a caution that philosophy must give up the idea of an "infinite intellect." Like Heidegger, there is a deep skepticism about the human will and the belief that we can *make* or engineer such communities in which there are living shared universal principles. The claim of his philosophical hermeneutics are at once bold and extremely modest. They are bold insofar as hermeneutics has the task of defending practical and political reason against the various attacks and deformations of it in the contemporary world. But hermeneutic philosophy—or any form of philosophy—cannot *solve* the problems of society or politics. It is dangerous to submit to the temptation of playing the prophet. This is the way to dogmatism. But even if one accepts Gadamer's cautions about prophesy and dogmatism, still there is a practical task that confronts us and to which Gadamer's own investigations lead—seeking to nurture the type of dialogical communities in which *phronesis* becomes a living reality.

The major point of this immanent critique of philosophical hermeneutics—that it leads us to practical tasks which take us beyond hermeneutics—can be approached from a different perspective. Thus far we have been concentrating on Gadamer's appropriation of the "truth" in Aristotle's understanding of *praxis* and *phronesis*, but a full scale analysis of Gadamer's philosophical hermeneutics would require seeing how it represents a blending and appropriation of both Aristotelian and Platonic themes. Here I want to discuss briefly the most important theme that Gadamer appropriates from Plato—the centrality of dialogue and conversation.

A conversation or a dialogue, Gadamer tells us, "is a process of two people understanding each other. Thus it is characteristic of every true conversation that each opens himself to the other person, truly accepts his point of view as worthy of consideration and gets inside the other to such an extent that he understands not a particular individual, but what he says. The thing that has to be grasped is the objective rightness or otherwise of his opinion, so that they can agree with each other on the subject" (*TM*, p. 347; *WM*, p. 363). When Gadamer introduces the concept of play as the clue to ontological explanation, this has its full realization in his understanding of dialogue and conversation.

> Now I contend that the basic constitution of the game, to be filled with its spirit—the spirit of buoyancy, freedom and the joy of success—and to fulfill him who is playing, is structurally related to the constitution of the dialogue in which language is a reality. When one enters into a dialogue with another person and then is carried further by the dialogue, it is no longer the will of the individual person, holding itself back or exposing itself, that is determinative. Rather, the law of the subject matter is at issue in the dialogue and elicits statement and counterstatement and in the end plays them into each other.[28]

Dialogue itself is fundamental for grasping what is distinctive about hermeneutical understanding. Gadamer is, of course, aware of the disanalogies between the dialogue that we have with texts and tradition and that which occurs with other persons. "Texts are 'permanently fixed expressions of life' which have to be understood, and that means that one partner in the hermeneutical conversation, the text, is expressed only through the other partner, the interpreter" (*TM*, p. 349; *WM*, 365).[29] Nevertheless the conversation, questioning, and dialogue with texts and tradition is like a living conversation or dialogue "in that it is the common object that unites the partners, the text and the interpreter" (*TM*, p. 349; *WM*, p. 365). The conversation or dialogue that he takes to be the quintessence of hermeneutical understanding always evokes the memory of a living conversation or dialogue between persons. But consider what he stresses in his analysis of dialogue and conversation — it is the mutuality, the respect required, the genuine seeking to understand what the other is saying, the openness to test and evaluate our own opinions through such an encounter. And in Gadamer's distinctive understanding of practical philosophy he blends this concept of dialogue which he finds illustrated in the Platonic Dialogues with his understanding of *phronesis*. But here too there are strong practical and political implications that Gadamer fails to pursue. For Gadamer can be read as showing us that what we truly are, what is most characteristic of our humanity is that we are dialogical or conversational beings. According to Gadamer's reading of the history of philosophy, this is the idea that he finds at the very beginning of Western philosophy and which in our time again is the most central lesson of the philosophic tradition.

But if we are really to appropriate this central idea to our historical situation, then it points us toward important practical and political tasks. It would be a gross distortion to imagine that we might conceive of the entire political realm organized on the principle of dialogue or conversation, considering the fragile conditions that are required for genuine dialogue and conversation. Nevertheless, if we think out what is required for such dialogue based on mutual understanding, respect, a willingness to listen and test one's opinions and prejudices, a mutual seeking of the objective rightness of what is said, then this provides us a powerful regulative ideal that can orient our practical and political lives. If the quintessence of what we are is to be dialogical — and this is not just the privilege of the *few* — then whatever the limitations of the practical realization of this ideal, it nevertheless can and should give practical orientation to our lives. We must ask what is it that blocks and distorts such dialogue, and what is to be done, "what is feasible, what is possible, what is correct, here and now" to make such genuine dialogue a living reality.[30]

Let me conclude by underscoring the main point of my critique of Gadamer's philosophical hermeneutics. I do think that one of his profoundest insights has been the linkage (or fusion) of hermeneutics and *praxis*, and his claim that all understanding involves appropriation to our own concrete historical situation. But if we pursue the logic of his own argument, if we probe what he means by truth and criticism, or the common ethical and political principles required for the virtue of *phronesis*, or the type of *polis* or community that it demands, or the implications of what he has to say about dialogue or conversation, then the thrust of his reflections is to lead us beyond philosophical hermeneutics. They lead us — with a deepened understanding of human finitude — to the genuinely practical task of concretely realizing in our historical situation what he has so nobly defended as being central to our humanity.

NOTES

1. See Gadamer's discussion of application in the section entitled, "The Rediscovery of the Fundamental Hermeneutic Problem," *Truth and Method* (New York: Seabury Press, 1975), pp. 274ff. The expression "application" (*Anwendung*) is used to translate the corresponding Latin term. This translation can be misleading. For example, when we speak of "applied physics" or "applied mathematics" we normally want to distinguish between the pure or theoretical disciplines and their applications. We do not think of the applications as integral or internally related to the corresponding pure disciplines. We can call this the "technical" sense of application. But, as we shall see, for Gadamer this is *not* what is distinctive about application as it pertains to understanding. Such application is integral to all understanding. The English expression "appropriation" better conveys what Gadamer means — especially when we think of appropriation as transforming and becoming constitutive of the individual who understands.

Unless otherwise noted, all page references in the text are to *Truth and Method*. I have also given references to the German text, *Wahrheit und Methode*, 4, *Auflage* (Tübingen: J. C. B. Mohr [Paul Siebeck], 1975).

2. Gadamer also discusses the Hermeneutical Problem and Aristotle's *Ethics* in "The Problem of Historical Consciousness," which is reprinted in *Interpretative Social Science: A Reader*, ed. P. Rabinow and W. M. Sullivan

(Berkeley: University of California Press, 1979), pp. 135 ff.

3. "Hermeneutics and Social Science," *Cultural Hermeneutics* 2 (1975): 316.

4. See the essay "Hermeneutics and Historicism," included in *Truth and Method*, p. 489. See also "Heidegger and Marburg Theology," *Philosophical Hermeneutics*, ed. D. E. Linge (Berkeley: University of California Press, 1976), p. 201.

5. Cf. "The Problem of Historical Consciousness" where Gadamer says, "it is useless to restrict the elucidation of the nature of the human sciences to a purely methodological question: it is a question not simply of defining a specific method, but rather, of recognizing an entirely different notion of knowledge and truth" (p. 113).

6. There is a parallel between Wittgenstein's critique of the attempt to reduce understanding to "psychological processes" in *The Philosophical Investigations*, and Gadamer's critique of this type of psychological reductionism in the context of hermeneutics. Both stress the essential linguistic character of understanding. See Gadamer's discussion of Wittgenstein in his essay, "The Phenomenological Tradition," *Philosophical Hermeneutics*, pp. 173ff.

7. Gadamer tells us, "The best definition for hermeneutics is: to let what is alienated by the character of the written word or by the character of being distantiated by cultural or historical distances speak again. This is hermeneutics: to let what seems to be far and alienated speak again" ("Practical Philosophy as a Model of the Human Sciences," *Research in Phenomenology* 9: 83).

8. "The Universality of the Hermeneutical Problem," *Philosophical Hermeneutics*, p. 9. See also the analysis of prejudices in *Truth and Method*, pp. 235ff.; *WM*, pp. 250ff. The German word which is translated as "prejudice" is *Vorurteil*. This can be translated as "prejudgment" in order to avoid the exclusively pejorative meaning that "prejudice" conveys in English. Gadamer's main point is to emphasize that *pre*-judices or *pre*-judgments are *pre*-conditions for all understanding. But for Gadamer, *both* negative or unfounded prejudices and positive or justified prejudices are constitutive of our being. He tells us, "This recognition that all understanding inevitably involves some prejudice gives the hermeneutical problem its real thrust" (*TM*, p. 239; *WM*, p. 254).

9. Gadamer cites Heidegger's description of the hermeneutical circle from *Being and Time* which stresses the anticipatory dimension of all forestructures. See *TM*, pp. 235ff.; *WM*, pp. 250ff. See also "The Problem of Historical Consciousness," pp. 148ff.

10. "The Problem of Historical Consciousness," p. 107.

11. Ibid., p. 140.

12. Ibid.

13. According to Gadamer, *phronesis* involves a knowledge of both ends and means. See his discussion of this point in "The Problem of Historical Consciousness," p. 143; and *Truth and Method*, pp. 286ff.; *WM*, pp. 304 ff.

14. See "Hermeneutics and Social Science."

15. Ibid., p. 312.

16. Ibid., p. 313.

17. Ibid., p. 316.

18. There is a problem that arises in Gadamer's frequent appeals to a "different kind of knowledge and truth." Gadamer never provides a detailed analysis of the type of knowledge and truth that is appropriate to the natural sciences. Consequently, it is never quite clear what is *common* to these *different* kinds of knowledge and truth. Furthermore, there are conflicting tendencies in what he does say. At times, Gadamer suggests that these two types of truth are compatible as long as we are aware of the limits and proper domain of scientific method. But there is also a strain in Gadamer's thinking that suggests that Method is never sufficient to achieve and guarantee truth. Although Gadamer, in some of the papers that he has published since *Truth and Method*, acknowledges the recovery of the hermeneutical dimension of the natural sciences, he does not fully appreciate the extent to which the very idea of Method (as an adequate way of characterizing the natural sciences) has been called into question by developments in the post-empiricist philosophy of science. The issue here is not denying that there are important differences between the *Naturwissenschaften* and the *Geisteswissenschaften*, but rather questioning whether the contrast between Method and Truth is helpful in illuminating these differences. For a discussion of the hermeneutical dimensions of the natural sciences, see Mary Hesse, "In Defence of Objectivity," *Revolutions & Reconstructions in the Philosophy of Science* (Brighton, Sussex: Harvester Press, 1980).

19. For a discussion of the concept of truth, see also "Wahrheit in den Geisteswissenschaften," and "Was ist Wahrheit?" *Kleine Schriften*, vol. 1 (Tübingen: J. C. B. Mohr [Paul Siebeck], 1967).

20. Concerning Hegel, Gadamer writes:

For Hegel, it is necessary, of course, that the movement of consciousness, experience should lead to a self-knowledge that no longer has anything different or alien to itself. For him the perfection of experience is "science," the certainty of itself in knowledge. Hence his criterion of experience is that of self-knowledge. That is why the dialectic of experience must end with the overcoming of all experience, which is attained in absolute knowledge, i.e., in the complete identity of consciousness and object. We can now understand why Hegel's application to history, insofar as he saw it as part of the absolute self-consciousness of philosophy, does not do justice to the hermeneutical consciousness. The nature of experience is conceived in terms of that which goes beyond it; for experience itself can never be science. It is the absolute antithesis to knowledge and to that kind of instruction that follows from general theoretical or technical knowledge. The truth of experience always contains an orientation towards new experience. . . . . The dialectic of experience has its own fulfillment not in definitive knowledge, but in that openness to experience that is encouraged by experience itself.(*TM*, p. 318; *WM*, p. 337).

21. "The Problem of Historical Consciousness," p. 107. Gadamer typically links truth (*Wahrheit*) with the thing (*die Sache*) itself. He tells us, "I repeat again what I have often insisted upon: every hermeneutical understanding begins and ends with the 'thing itself' " ("The Problem of Historical Consciousness," p. 159). In appealing to the thing itself, Gadamer does *not* mean Kant's *Ding-an-sich*. Rather he *plays* on the associations of what is suggested by Aristotle in the *Ethics* when he tells us that the appropriate form of knowledge and reasoning is conditioned by the subject matter that it treats; the way in which Hegel in the *Phenomenology of Spirit* is always directing us to *die Sache* in order to reveal the dialectical movement of consciousness (*Bewusstsein*): the significance of the call for the "return to the things themselves" in Husserl; and the way in which this demand is radically transformed in Heidegger's "hermeneutics of facticity." But this appeal to *die Sache* is not sufficient to clarify the concept (*Begriff*) of truth. For the question can always be asked, when do we have a *true* understanding of the thing (*die Sache*) itself? Gadamer implicitly recognizes that this is always a proper question when he emphasizes that our anticipatory interpretations "may not conform to what the thing is" (The Problem of Historical Consciousness," p. 149). The crucial point as it pertains to truth is that however prominent the thing itself may be in testing our prejudices, a *true* although not a final understanding of the thing itself must be *warranted by the appropriate forms of argumentation* which are intended to show that we have properly grasped what the thing itself says.

22. See Gadamer's discussion of the concept of tradition in *Truth and Method*, pp. 245 ff.; *WM*, pp. 261 ff. It is instructive to compare Gadamer's understanding of tradition with that of Alasdair MacIntyre when he says,

A tradition then not only embodies the narrative of an argument, but is only to be recovered by an argumentative retelling of that narrative which will itself be in conflict with other argumentative retellings. Every tradition therefore is always in danger of lapsing into incoherence and when a tradition does so lapse it sometimes can only be recovered by a revolutionary reconstitution. ("Epistemological Crises, Dramatic Narrative and the Philosophy of Science," *The Monist* 60 [1977]: 461)

23. "The Problem of Historical Consciousness," p. 108.
24. "Hermeneutics and Social Science," pp. 312, 316.
25. "The Problem of Historical Consciousness," p. 141.
26. Ibid., p. 142.
27. Gadamer approaches this problem of corruption indirectly. This
can be seen in his perceptive interpretations of Plato's *Dialogues*, especially
the *Republic*. For the central "political" problem that Plato confronts is the
corruption of the polis. Gadamer says the following about the *Republic*:

> Thus the exposition of this ideal state in the *Republic* serves in educating
> the political human being, but the *Republic* is not meant as a manual
> on educational methods and materials, and it does not point out the
> goal of the educational process to the educator. In the background of
> this work on the state is a real educational state, the community of Plato's
> academy. The *Rebublic* exemplifies the purpose of the academy. This
> community of students applying themselves rigorously to mathematics
> and dialectic is no apolitical society of scholars. Instead, the work done
> here is intended to lead to the result which remained unattainable for
> the current sophistic paideia, with its encyclopedic instruction and ar-
> bitrary moralistic reformulations of the educational content of ancient
> poetry. It is intended to lead to a new discovery of justice in one's own
> soul and thus to *the shaping of the political human being. This* educa-
> tion, however, the actual education to participation in the state, is
> anything but a total manipulation of the soul, a rigorous leading of
> it to a predetermined goal. Instead, precisely in extending its question-
> ing behind the supposedly valid traditional moral ideas, it is in itself
> the new experience of justice. Thus this education is not authoritative
> instruction based on an ideal organization at all: rather it lives from
> questioning alone. ("Plato and the Poets," *Dialogue and Dialectic* [New
> Haven, Conn.: Yale University Press, 1980], p. 52. See also "Plato's
> Educational State" in *Dialogue and Dialectic*.)

The "moral" that can be drawn from this for *our* hermeneutical situation is
that the *political* task of the philosopher is to help revive that deep sense
of questioning which can lead to a discovery "of justice in one's own soul
and thus to *the shaping of the political human being.*" My quarrel with
Gadamer is not to suggest that he is wrong about this; on the contrary, I
think he is essentially right. But rather, I want to emphasize the Hegelian
point that the "discovery of justice in one's own soul" is only the *beginning*
of "the shaping of the political human being." This discovery is in danger
of becoming merely "abstract" and "false" unless one confronts the concrete
practical tasks of shaping or reshaping one's actual community in order to
cultivate genuine dialogue among participants.

28. "Man and Language," *Philosophical Hermeneutics*, p. 66.

29. Gadamer's acknowledgment of the difference between a living dialogue where the other person can literally answer questions, and the hermeneutical dialogue where "the text is expressed only through the other partner, the interpreter" opens a Pandora's box of problems for philosophical hermeneutics. It is fundamental for Gadamer's understanding of philosophical hermeneutics that although we always understand and interpret *differently*, nevertheless we are interpreting the *same* text, the same "universal thing." "To understand a text always means to apply it to ourselves and to know that, even if it must always be understood in different ways, it is still the same text presenting itself to us in these different ways" (*TM*, p. 359; *WM*, p. 375). But if the interpreter must not only open himself or herself to what the text "says to us" and the "claim to truth" that it makes upon us, but is also the linguistic medium for answering for the text, then this raises questions concerning what sense if any, we can speak of the *same* text, the same "universal thing." For it is not the text *an sich* that answers the interpreter, but only the text as understood, and all understanding is conditioned by our prejudices and prejudgments. This is a point that was already pressed by Nietzsche and which has become so central for post-structuralist thinking. And as Nietzsche showed, this can lead to a questioning of the very idea of truth, and the "claim to truth" that texts and tradition make upon us. This also raises problems in an ethical and political context concerning what sense, if any, we can speak of the *same* universal principles, laws, or norms that are mediated by *phronesis*.

30. Many critics (and defenders) of Gadamer stress the conservative implications of his philosophical hermeneutics. Certainly, Gadamer seeks to *conserve* the "truth" that speaks to us through tradition, although he strongly denies that the emphasis on the essential factor of tradition in all understanding implies an uncritical acceptance of tradition or a "socio-political conservatism." But what has been neglected is the *latent* radical strain implicit in Gadamer's understanding of hermeneutics as a practical philosophy. This is reflected in his emphasis in recent years on freedom and solidarity that embraces *all of humanity*. He tells us " . . . for there is no higher principle of reason than that of freedom. Thus the opinion of Hegel and thus our own opinion as well. No higher principle is thinkable than that of the freedom of all, and we understand actual history from the perspective of this principle; as the ever-to-be-renewed and the never-ending struggle for this freedom" (*Reason in the Age of Science* [Cambridge, Mass.: M.I.T. Press, 1982], p. 9). And in a passage that echoes the Frankfurt School's radical interpretation of Hegel, Gadamer writes: "The principle that all are free never again can be shaken. But does this mean that on account of this, history has come to an end? Are all human beings actually free? Has not history since then been

a matter of just this, that the historical conduct of man has to translate the principle of freedom into reality? Obviously this points to the unending march of world history into the openness of its future tasks and gives no becalming assurance that everything is already in order" (ibid., p. 37).

Concerning the principle of solidarity, Gadamer tells us ". . . genuine solidarity, authentic community, should be realized" (ibid., p. 80). In summarizing his answer to the question, "What is practice?" he writes: "practice is conducting oneself and acting in solidarity. Solidarity, however, is the decisive condition and basis of all social reason. There is a saying of Heraclitus, the 'weeping' philosopher: The *logos* is common to all, but people behave as if each had a private reason. Does this have to remain this way?" (ibid., p. 87).